THE DESERT GENERALS

THE DESERT GENERALS is a major work of recent history. It gives extraordinarily real and intimate pictures of five men under the strain of command in battle—Generals O'Connor, Cunningham, Ritchie, Auchinleck and Montgomery. It is also the first-ever complete account of the Western Desert Campaign of 1940–43. During three years of research, the author interviewed almost every Senior Desert Officer, with the exception of Field-Marshal Montgomery of whom he is severely critical. The manuscript has been read for accuracy by no less than seven of these generals, including Field-Marshal Sir Claude Auchinleck.

First comes Sir Richard O'Connor, who won the fantastic victories over the Italians in 1940. Then Sir Alan Cunningham and Sir Neil Ritchie, commanders in turn of the newly formed Eighth Army, both fine men but lacking in the dynamism needed for success, both relieved of their command by the C-in-C, Auchinleck.

Taking over the Army himself at a moment of crisis, 'the Auk' brilliantly handled the retreat to El Alamein and there fought and won in July 1942, the battle which the author of this book, Correlli Barnett, considers the true turning point of the Desert War. Field-Marshal Montgomery has told his own story, but there is another side to it, set down here with startling perception.

'This is a brilliant picture of the North Africa campaign from start to finish—vividly written and intensely interesting. Even when his conclusions are debatable they cannot be lightly discounted'—Liddell Hart.

THE DESERT
GENERALS

CORRELLI BARNETT

PAN BOOKS LTD : LONDON

First published 1960 by William Kimber & Co. Ltd.
This edition published 1962 by Pan Books Ltd.,
8 Headfort Place, London, S.W.1

Printed in Great Britain by
Cox and Wyman Ltd., London, Reading and Fakenham

AUTHOR'S PREFACE

The theme of this book is the struggle of individual will against circumstance. The subject matter is human character. In these five uncommon men during the desert campaigns, as in the condensed action of a tragedy, were displayed nobility, frailty, resolution, loyalty, indecision, vanity, fear, simplicity, selfishness, greatness and littleness. The creation of literary portraits of living men is both easier and more difficult than with the dead. Some things that are known cannot be written; other things will not be known until death has opened all private records. Yet to meet and talk with the subjects of the portraiture and with their friends and colleagues is to gain vivid and detailed impressions that no correspondence of the dead, however copious, can yield. The shaping of these various impressions into accurate pictures is a complex process. They have to be balanced against one another, against the author's own judgment of the main subjects, and against his own impression of each witness.

Apart from human character, the desert campaign has other fascinations. There is the pleasure of seeking out the truth; there is the excitement of watching two men fight a battle, possibly the most complete human activity, since generalship involves all the intellectual, physical and moral power in a man. Historically, the desert campaign constitutes the last act of the British Empire as a great independent, and united, power. It ironically epitomizes the suicide of the old Europe: today neither German, Italian nor Briton controls the Middle East for which they fought so bitterly. Again the desert campaign reveals clearly the twentieth-century national characters and talents of Germany and Britain—and confounds accepted images. The methods of thinking, organizing and fighting of each side also adumbrate their industrial and commercial methods in the post-war era.

Yet above all, the desert campaign of 1940–43 is an addition to the great epics. It is the story, set in the wasteland, of how the men of ten nations strove for victory amid the mechanical tumult of a kind of battle never seen before, and likely never to be seen again.

CORRELLI BARNETT

For
My Mother and Father

ACKNOWLEDGMENTS

The author wishes to express his very deep gratitude to the following officers for their kindness in giving unpublished information and comment without which this book could not have been written:

Field-Marshal Lord Harding, GCB, CBE, DSO, MC

Field-Marshal Sir Claude Auchinleck, GCB, GCIE, CSI, DSO, OBE, LLD

General Lord Norrie, GCMG, GCVO, DSO, MC

General Sir Richard O'Connor, GCB, DSO, MC

General Sir Alan Cunningham, GCMG, KCB, DSO, MC

General Sir Frank Messervy, KCSI, KBE, CB, DSO

General Sir Alfred Godwin-Austen, KCSI, CB, OBE, MC

Lieutenant-General Sir Oliver Leese, KCB, CBE, DSO

Lieutenant-General Sir Arthur Smith, KCB, KBE, DSO, MC

Lieutenant-General Sir Alexander Galloway, KBE, CB, DSO, MC

Lieutenant-General T. W. Corbett, CB, MC

Major-General W. H. Ramsden, CB, CBE, DSO

Major-General Sir Francis de Guingand, KBE, CB, DSO

Major-General Sir Michael Creagh, KBE, MC

Major-General J. M. L. Renton, CB, DSO, OBE, JP, DL

Major-General A. H. Gatehouse, DSO, MC

Major-General E. Dorman O'Gowan (Dorman-Smith), MC

Brigadier J. A. Caunter, CBE, MC

Brigadier J. T. Williams

Colonel R. N. Bruce, TD

The author also wishes to thank the following, who were kind enough to read all or parts of the manuscript and make valuable criticisms and comments: Field-Marshal Sir Claude Auchinleck, General Lord Norrie, Lieutenant-General Sir Arthur Smith, Sir Compton Mackenzie, Major-General Sir Michael Creagh, Major-General A. H. Gatehouse, Major-General E. Dorman O'Gowan, Brigadier Desmond Young, Captain B. H. Liddell Hart, D. A. Barnett, Esq and Lionel Brooks, Esq.

The author is indebted to the following publishers and authors for permission to quote from books in their copyright:

Sifton Praed and Co.: *Against Great Odds* by Brigadier C. N. Barclay. Cassell and Co.: *The Second World War* by Winston S. Churchill; *Panzer Battles* by Major-General F. W. von Mellenthin; and *Jan Christian Smuts* by J. C. Smuts. Oxford University Press: *The Sidi Rezegh Battles* and *Crisis in the Desert* by J. A. I. Agar-Hamilton and L. C. F. Turner; *Infantry Brigadier* by Major-General Sir Howard Kippenberger; and *The Battle for Egypt* by J. L. Scoullar. William Collins: *The Turn of the Tide* by Sir A. Bryant; *The Rommel Papers* edited by B. H. Liddell Hart; *The Phantom Major* by Virginia Cowles; *Memoirs* by Field-Marshal Lord Montgomery; *A Full Life* by General Sir Brian Horrocks; and *Rommel* by Desmond Young. Hamish Hamilton: *Montgomery* by Alan Moorehead. The Hutchinson Group: *El Alamein to the Sangro* by Field-Marshal Lord Montgomery; and *The Business of War* by Major-General Sir John Kennedy. Her Majesty's Stationery Office: *The Mediterranean and Middle East* by Major-General I. S. O. Playfair, Vols I-III; *Despatch* by Field-Marshal Lord Alexander of Tunis; and *Despatch* by Field-Marshal Sir Claude Auchinleck. George Harrap and Co.: *Three Against Rommel* by Alexander Clifford. Heffer and Co.: *The Seventh and Three Enemies* by G. M. O. Davy. Heinemann and Co.: *Journey Among Warriors* by Eve Curie. Hodder and Stoughton: *Operation Victory* by Major-General Sir Francis de Guingand. Chatto and Windus: *Eastern Epic* by Sir Compton Mackenzie. André Deutsch: *Nine Rivers from Jordan* by Denis Johnston. Weidenfeld and Nicholson: *Memoirs* by Mussolini. Pavot et Cie: *Rommel et L'Afrika-Korps* by H. G. von Esebeck. Nelson: *7th Battalion The Argyll and Sutherland Highlanders* by Ian C. Cameron. The British Broadcasting Corporation: scripts of television performances by Field-Marshal Lord Montgomery. Carroll and Nicholson: *Down Ramps* by Lampton Burn. Clowes: *History of the Royal Dragoons* by Julian Pitt-Rivers. Queen's Printer, Ottawa: *The Canadian Army* by C. P. Stacey.

Finally, the author wishes to record his immense debt to his wife for reading and criticizing the draft narrative, and for bearing with him during his two and a half years of mental absence in the Western Desert.

CONTENTS

ILLUSTRATIONS
IN PHOTOGRAVURE
(between pages 168 and 169)

SKETCH MAPS IN THE TEXT

THE FORGOTTEN VICTOR

General Sir Richard O'Connor, GCB, DSO, MC

> I do not think a braver gentleman,
> More active-valiant or more valiant-young,
> More daring or more bold, is now alive
> To grace this latter age with noble deeds.
>
> SHAKESPEARE: First part of *Henry IV*, v, 1.

CHAPTER ONE

WHEN Richard O'Connor took the field in a year of disastrous defeat his spectacular victories exhilarated his countrymen and astonished the enemy. Yet they have won fame not for himself but for others. The campaign which cost Mussolini an army of 200,000 men and an imperial province within half a year of his declaration of war is remembered as 'Wavell's offensive'. Even in that guise its lustre is now dimmed by the later victories of the war, although none of them displayed an equal genius. O'Connor deserves better remembrance.

In Jerusalem, on June 7th, 1940, Major-General R. N. O'Connor, who was then commanding the southern district of Palestine, received a signal ordering him to report immediately to Lieutenant-General H. M. Wilson, General Officer Commanding British Troops in Egypt. The signal gave no reason. O'Connor flew from Jerusalem to Cairo, and during the journey had time to speculate not merely on his personal future but on the significance of the latest news from France. The second phase of that battle had begun on June 5th with a violent German attack on he left flank of what the Press and radio so foolishly dubbed 'The Weygand Line'. Already the line of the lower Somme had gone and a deep German penetration had reached Rouen; another force was on the Aisne. It seemed at best doubtful whether the disorganized French could now hold with sixty divisions a front longer than that which they had failed to hold in Flanders with a hundred.

If the French were beaten out of the war, it would reverse the balance of military power both in North Africa and the Levant; for the French were at present the senior partner in the defence against an Italian aggression that might come at any moment; British forces throughout the theatre numbered 50,000 against 500,000 Italians.

In Cairo next day, O'Connor had an interview with Wilson. The two men made a sharp contrast. 'Jumbo' Wilson was big and cumbersome, with a majestic paunch under which was strapped his pistol belt; O'Connor sat poised on the edge of his seat like a bird about to take wing, a small, self-effacing man with the shy and gentle air of a scholar. Wilson told him that he was to go up to Mersa Matruh, the railhead in the Western Desert, and take command of the Western Desert Force, with the task of protecting Egypt from Italian attack. This news O'Connor received with 'surprise, and of course pride.'[1] So poor was the information about the future of the French and about the intentions of the Italians, and so rudimentary was the British Middle Eastern organization, that Wilson could give little in the way of a directive. "My recollection," O'Connor said later, "is that I was given very sketchy instructions as to policy"—which had its advantages—"I did not object really, as I don't mind being left on my own." The phrasing was characteristic of his diffidence and understatement.

Later than day he drove over Kasr-el-Nil bridge, through Gezira and along the tram route to the Pyramids, and then right on to the desert road—the 'barrel track'—to Alamein and Matruh. He arrived at his headquarters hot and dusty, and tired by the long journey over a road little smoother than the sleepers of a railway. His headquarters lay at Maaten Baggush, east of Matruh, in the dunes on the seaward side of the Matruh–Alexandria road. On the other side of this road was the head-quarters airfield of the Western Desert Air Force. O'Connor found his new headquarters simple after the sophistication of Jerusalem, but comfortable enough. The headquarters offices were well dug-in beneath sandhills, and bomb-proofed. A one-storey concrete building housed the senior officers' mess; everyone slept in tents. There were two charming bays for swimming.

That evening in the mess those of his officers who were not old friends and colleagues had an opportunity of forming an opinion of their new commander. He was as small and neat as a bird. He had a fine head with an aggressive rake to it. The high, broad brow suggested great intellect; his eyes, large and deep with slightly hooded lids, powers of imagination. Command showed in the straight nose and mouth and thrusting jaw. O'Connor's voice was light and clear, with a ghost of a lisp; his manner of conversing quiet and diffident. There was little here of the façade of greatness, yet no one could talk a quarter of an

[1] In order not to encumber the text, full source references are given at the end of the book.

22

hour with him without being aware of unusual qualities of character and personality.

In the thoughts of O'Connor and his officers, the question of Italy, and the 300,000 men across the Libyan frontier, hung like an army's dust-cloud. A signal from Cairo two days later told them that Mussolini had answered the question by declaring war on Britain and France as from one am on June 11th, 1940. This news had a significance in Mersa Matruh far more immediate than in London or Paris or Cairo. For O'Connor himself it meant that he had entered the special loneliness of command of an army in the field—a small, ill-equipped army facing another ten times as great and of unknown fighting quality. The headquarters officers watched O'Connor; what would he do?

*　　　*　　　*

The desert war of 1940–43 is unique in history; it was fought like a polo game on an empty arena. With one exception, there were no roads, but as virtually the whole of the arena was good going, at least for tanks, movement was almost as free as that of a fleet. Apart from a few inhabited places along the coast there were neither towns nor villages to provide shelter or obstacles. There was almost no civilian population to get in the way of the battle. The desert campaign was therefore war in its purest form. Yet, equally, there was in this dusty arena no food and little water; all had to be imported. Supply was the major limit to free movement.

The desert of the battles is a large arena; its northern limit stretches along the Mediterranean from the salt-white dunes of Alamein, past the bald escarpments to Derna, a distance of nearly four hundred miles. Inland its limits lie at the oases of Jarabub and Siwa, a hundred and fifty miles from the coast and on the edges of the great Sand Sea, a scorching waste where only Bedouin or British can live and move. To the newcomer the desert was featureless, coverless and trackless; to the veteran, the slight swell of its rock-ocean provided useful tactical features, while maps and compasses enabled him to navigate more surely than in Britain by signposting. Ancient cisterns and ruined tombs constituted features round which major battles raged.

There is one dominating natural feature: the five-hundred-foot escarpment, facing north to the coastal plain, that leads down from the limestone plateau which is the arena of the desert battles. It is like the wall of a terrace that is broken by only a few flights of steps. It is everywhere a barrier to wheeled vehicles and in most places even to tanks. The gaps that are passable by *all* vehicles became therefore immensely important —Fuka, Halfaya and Sidi Rezegh.

As scenery the desert of the battles has little to offer; a sandy, rocky plateau patched with scrub, dun-coloured—monotony made concrete. Yet it has its beauties: the beauties of silence and solitude; dust devils whirling in the morning, and the endless gravel and scrub showing black in the long rays of the setting sun. Near the coast, spring momentarily quickens the barrenness, and bright flowers bloom along the wadis; even after the most searing dead days of summer, there is the sumptuous African night sky, the brilliant moon, and the beauty of silence etched by the tiny sounds of vipers and scorpions as they move amid the sand and rocks.

The desert became a battlefield in the Second World War because it was the western flank of the British defence of the Middle East and the Axis attack from Italian Libya had to pass over it. For the British the Middle East was only just less important to the waging of the war than their own homeland; for it contained round Mosul, in Iraq, and at the head of the Persian Gulf the oilfields without which the Royal Air Force, the Army and the Royal Navy would be paralyzed. The Middle East had other strategic importances; as a support to Turkey, Russia and to action anywhere in the Mediterranean; as a half-way house to India—and Italy. However, the long campaign of 1940–43 was not fought for the Suez Canal (which bore little trans-world traffic at the time, and thus was not a 'life-line'), but for oil.

The Western Desert was only a part of the vast responsibilities of the Commander-in-Chief, Middle East Forces. In 1940 these responsibilities were greater by far than at other times in the war; the allocated forces were of course exiguous. The ability of the commanding general had to supply the difference, and did; for the C-in-C, M. E. in 1940 was one of the very greatest of British soldiers of any age, and certainly the greatest of the Second World War—Sir Archibald Wavell. O'Connor, Wavell—Britain was lucky that year, as she faced mortal danger almost unarmed through the lethal well-meaningness, gullibility and soft-heartedness of her people and politicians in former years.

Set up in June, 1939, Wavell's Middle East Command encompassed nine countries and parts of two continents, an area one thousand seven hundred miles by two thousand miles. To defend this theatre Wavell had, at the beginning, the unformed equivalent of two divisions, two brigade groups, an armoured division well below strength, sixty-four field guns, and—to make up the weight—a camel corps of 500 men. Wavell's duties were conceived on a grand scale: the government's directive enjoined him firstly to prepare war plans for the entire theatre, including arrangements for reinforcements in the case of emergency, and to share out troops and supplies among the subordinate commands. Secondly, he was to consult with the naval and air commanders-in-chief, and arrange for liaison with the French in Syria and North Africa. And thirdly, there were such things as consultation with His Majesty's ambassadors in Egypt and Iraq, the Governor-General in the Sudan, the High Commissioner for Palestine and Transjordan, the Governors of Cyprus, Aden and British Somaliland, and the Political Agent in the Persian Gulf. Wavell was given a headquarters staff of five officers.

In 1939 there was no trace of the immense military base that Auchinleck was to find well on the way to completion in 1941, and Alexander to find complete in 1942. In the autumn of 1939 Wavell had a survey made of all Egyptian ports, and transport and other facilities with a view to turning Egypt into a base for an army of 300,000 men. This was his own idea; the Cabinet was still talking. When at last in December the politicians ordered him to begin building a base for nine divisions, Wavell's survey was already complete. The most immediate military danger was from Libya, where there was an Italian army of well over 200,000 men (Wavell could not be sure of their strength because the politicians would not allow spying, for fear of upsetting Mussolini). One of Wavell's first acts therefore was to instruct General Wilson, General Officer Commanding British Troops in Egypt, to prepare plans for an invasion of Italian Libya, with particular reference to the novel problem of supply in the desert. Nobody could call Wavell a pessimist.

All through the winter of 1939 Wilson worked to create an army out of the military flotsam that Wavell could spare him, using such desperate expedients as making up the transport strength of the one armoured division by stripping other formations of their trucks. By the late spring of 1940 Wilson had collected together at Mersa Matruh a force composed of 7th Armoured Division, two regiments of the Royal Horse Artillery and a screen of motorized patrols. Matruh was a little white village by a copper-sulphate sea, known before 1936 only to Greek sponge-fishers and the middlemen who handled the export trade from Siwa Oasis. But it was the terminus of the railway and the metalled road from Alexandria and now it became a base and a fortress. In 1942 it was to give its name to Rommel's most astonishing victory.

As the French Army fell back in May and June, 1940, betrayed by a decade of traditionalism, it became more and more clear that Italy was at any moment going to buy a Roman triumph at an Italian price. Along the interminable frontiers of Somaliland, the Sudan and Kenya, Wavell posted his handful of troops. What would the Duke of Aosta, Viceroy of Ethiopia, do with his 200,000 men? Wavell hoped that at least he would not do it at the same time as Balbo in Libya. A commander was wanted for Western Desert Force: and the choice fell on O'Connor, who had a reputation for boldness and unorthodoxy, qualities which Wavell valued highly. Certainly mobility was O'Connor's *leitmotif* as a soldier; his formative military experiences illustrated this. 'I think,' he wrote later, 'commanding a Brigade on the North West Frontier of India was great experience; and later commanding the southern half of Palestine during the Arab rebellion taught me a tremendous lot.'

On the outbreak of the war with Italy Wavell stood on the strategic defensive everywhere; the uncertain future of the French, his ignorance of Italian capabilities and his own great weakness forced him to do so. O'Connor was therefore limited to choosing between the tactical offensive and the tactical defensive. His troops began attacking on the first day of the

26

Italian war by cutting the frontier wire and taking seventy prisoners on Italian imperial soil. While the Italian command was mulling this over, the armoured cars of the Eleventh Hussars, together with some tanks, appeared out of the desert before Forts Capuzzo and Maddalena, white-walled evocations of Beau Geste. After RAF bombers had missed the forts, the Hussars took them with the aid of a few rounds of delayed-action high-explosive shells from the two pounders of the tanks. On June 16th—when in France the Germans had reached Orleans, passed through Paris, and nearly reached the Swiss frontier behind the Maginot Line—an Italian column was rolling along the Bardia road in the sunshine. It included in its ranks General Lastucci, chief engineer of the Tenth Army. With the suddenness of a heart attack, the British were upon it. After a brisk action they withdrew, taking Lastucci and eighty-eight others, and leaving forty wrecked tanks.

Behind this continual skirmishing on Italian desert, O'Connor began to shape his small army. He did not make a calculated or dramatic impact in his first few days, for 'I had not studied the ground . . . I made no changes until I knew a bit more about the situation.' He set out to make good his knowledge on both counts. O'Connor's system of studying ground was much like Wellington's or Rommel's—a personal reconnaissance dangerously far into enemy country, with sudden alarming appearances among his own forward troops.

> One night about three weeks after the first Libyan campaign commenced, while I was commanding all our forward troops beyond the frontier wire,

wrote Brigadier Caunter later,

> it was reported to me by the 11th Hussars that one of their forward patrols had reported that General O'Connor had, in his staff car, come on the armoured car patrol from the west, *ie* from the enemy's direction.

Brigadier Caunter commented:

> I did NOT like this.

At the same time as he studied the ground, O'Connor, in his own words, "took the first opportunity of seeing the local commanders and my small divisional staff." He found the most able and thoroughly professional command and staff that any British Force enjoyed in the war, on a scale small enough to permit personal orders and an easy flexibility. The entire Western Desert Force was of regular long-service troops; the senior officers and staff officers of O'Connor's force were old personal friends. Galloway, Brigadier General Staff to General Wilson, and O'Connor had both been Staff Instructors at the Camberley Staff College; and Beresford-Peirse, 4th Indian Division, had served with Wavell's experimental motorized infantry brigade at Blackdown in 1932. Thorough training was O'Connor's principal concern:

> You can't spend too much time on training. A well-trained unit pays dividends every time in the way it gets things done, and saves itself casualties. The training of formation HQ's is just as important as other training: cf a corps headquarters.

On June 22nd, with the Compiègne Armistice, the French became neutrals: the Italian forces in Libya that had been watching the Tunisian frontier were now free to join the Tenth Army in concentrating for an offensive into Egypt. But the British forward troops continued to skirmish aggressively throughout July, achieving a moral ascendency over the Italian army that had an effect on the coming battle.

O'Connor and his men were, in this novel business of war in a desert, explorers; they found the snags and the solutions to them; they made themselves at home in the wasteland; and those who followed in later campaigns benefited from their experience. Now O'Connor, receiving reports of wear and tear on his vehicles, learned that in the desert mobility costs dear both in terms of replacements of all kinds and in terms of supply; and he was the first desert general, British or German, to try to square the circle of finding enough trucks to feed, and move, the forward operations; the first to learn that victory depended on the three-tonner. He decided at the end of July to withdraw his tanks in order to conserve equipment for a major battle. The frontier was now to be covered by the motorized infantry and guns of 7th Armoured Division Support Group.

This expected major battle would follow the offensive now being methodically organized by Marshal Rodolpho Graziani, who had replaced Balbo—shot down by his own anti-aircraft batteries—as Governor-General and Commander-in-Chief in Libya. Graziani was a ruthless and fervent Fascist who had done well in Abyssinia in 1936, but now, faced with the British, he was in no hurry to advance. Graziani believed strongly in establishing a firm base, and all through August, while Mussolini prodded him and pointed along the road to glory, the Marshal methodically arranged himself. Graziani's idea of a firm base included a motorized brothel. No one could tell the Italians anything about mobile war. Graziani, at this time perhaps shrewder at debate than combat, suggested to Mussolini that his grand offensive should follow the expected German invasion of Britain; the disheartened British in Egypt would then offer only feeble resistance. Unfortunately for Graziani, Operation *Sealion* was postponed and postponed; and the idea began to grow in Rome that the Marshal's appetite for glory was smaller than his military discretion. On September 7th Mussolini gave him a final order to attack within two days, *Sealion* or no *Sealion*. On September 13th, Graziani moved.

After a loud bombardment of the empty British frontier posts, the Italian Tenth Army lumbered into Egypt with four divisions and groups of tanks. As they moved along at twelve miles a day, keeping close together in a noisy Italian crowd, the British hung about their dusty flanks, stinging and disappearing. On the fourth day, Graziani halted at Sidi Barrani, sixty miles into Egypt and still eighty miles from the British army at Matruh. He spread his army into a semicircle of defensive camps and began to build a metalled road up from the frontier, construct water-pipelines and accumulate stores well forward. He also erected a monument alongside the road in Sidi Barrani to commemorate the glorious feat of arms achieved by the Italian army in advancing sixty miles into Egypt. When this firm base was ready, Graziani proposed to move methodically on Mersa Matruh. But he was still in no hurry. He displayed rare instinct—for O'Connor had a model defensive battle ready for him:

> We hoped he would try and advance to the neighbourhood of Matruh, as we had prepared a full-dress counter-stroke with all our armour. We worked this out on the ground, and I was greatly disappointed that he never came far enough to put it into execution.

29

Through October and November 1940 both armies lay apart in preparation. In October the arrival of two tank regiments brought 7th Armoured Division to full strength. Next month 4th Indian Division was also at full strength. Behind Western Desert Force, in reserve between Matruh and Alexandria, were 4th New Zealand Division, consisting of one brigade, and 6th Australian Division. Most important of all accessions of strength were the fifty-seven heavy 'I' tanks of the 7th Royal Tank Regiment. This growing army now brightly reflected the qualities of its commander. It was high-spirited, alert, aggressive and full of dash. Its affection for O'Connor, its loyalty, and its confidence in him were genuine and profound. O'Connor had achieved this ascendancy without any of the advantages of what television calls 'personality'. O'Connor's expositions of his plans were modest and tentative. His plans spoke for him. In contrast to Montgomery he had not been an able lecturer at the Staff College. His public manner was always reserved, low-keyed. Comparing him with Montgomery, General Galloway, a friend of them both, wrote:

> The difference between O'Connor and Montgomery was that O'Connor detested publicity and Monty lived on it—not only lived on it, but began it: and for a very good reason.

But even the unsophisticated are more aware of the genuine quality in their leaders, whether advertised or not, than is sometimes believed in this age of contrived publicity; and O'Connor, as General Galloway put it, 'had the complete confidence of the troops'. For there was a subtle magnetism in this brave and gentle man. Major-General (then Brigadier) Dorman-Smith found 'something boyish about him', a quality of intense life: 'He was always springy and alert, even when still—always alive and vibrant'.

In Cairo, Wavell was about to begin that inspired strategic juggling which by its timing and finesse was to suggest to the Italians that the same British soldiers were defeating them in simultaneous battles a thousand miles apart. The Duke of Aosta in Italian East Africa was to be his principal victim; for although that officer commanded a large and powerful army, it was a wasting one, being quite cut off from Italy. But before Wavell could concentrate his small forces against Aosta, he must deal with Graziani's threat to the Delta. On October 18th, 1940, he ordered Brigadier Dorman-Smith, Commandant of the wartime Middle East Staff College at Haifa, to visit O'Connor, spend a few days with Western Desert Force, and report on the possibility of successfully attacking Graziani in his present position. Dorman-Smith, who had a high reputation as an original military thinker, was an old colleague and friend of Wavell's, having been Brigade Major in his experimental infantry brigade in 1932. He was also an old friend of O'Connor's; they had gone on a walking tour together in the Italian Alps soon after the First World War and had been instructors together at Sandhurst. On October 22nd Dorman-Smith brought back to Wavell the opinion that an early offensive should be a success. Wavell, as usual, said nothing, but simply took out of his drawer a directive that he had just drafted to Wilson and O'Connor ordering them to prepare for attack.

The objects set out in the directive were modest: 'We were simply told,' wrote General O'Connor, 'to carry out a five-days' raid. . . . This in fact started the campaign.' Wavell suggested a plan: attacks on both Italian flanks; direct on the coast road, enveloping in the south. O'Connor and his officers sat down in the underground operations room at Baggush to consider the problem. He did not like Wavell's conception, with its turning movement round the Italian extreme right flank. 'This was the obvious way from the map,' wrote O'Connor, 'but the ground to the south of the enemy positions was quite unsuitable for tanks, so it was not considered.' Equally, he was not keen on splitting his forces as Wavell had suggested; and he considered that the separate advances might be difficult to co-ordinate. A better way must be found.

The Italian Tenth Army now lay in a series of camps echeloned in depth between Maktila, on the coast some fifteen miles east of Sidi Barrani, and the Libyan frontier. There was a forward line of camps stretching from Maktila fifty miles inland to Sofafi, garrisoned by the Group of Libyan Divisions which was estimated to contain three and a half divisions with a powerful tank group, but which in fact had three divisions with the tanks mingled with the infantry. Behind this line of camps, at Sidi Barrani, headquarters of the Libyan Divisions, was a Blackshirt Division and part of another. Farther back still were the 21st and 23rd Corps with five divisions between them. By a peculiar arrangement of the command, Sofafi, the camp on the extreme right flank of the forward line, did not come under the Group of Libyan Divisions, but 21st Corps. The Italian equipment was mixed in quality. The Italian tanks were so thinly armoured that even the British anti-tank rifles could penetrate them; and the heavier models had their guns in fixed casement so that to aim the gun the tank itself had to be trained on the target. However, there was a trickle of a new type with a 47-mm gun and a machine gun mounted in a revolving turret. But the Italian artillery, the best trained and equipped arm of the Italian service, outnumbered the British two to one.

The Italian Air Force also heavily outnumbered the British, and O'Connor had to make his plans in expectation of violent Italian air attacks on British troops in daylight. Genius makes the difficult seem easy; so it was with the British Command and the Battle of Sidi Barrani. Beforehand, however, the Italians appeared formidable enough in numbers and some forms of equipment. No one knew how a Fascist army would fight; the Italians' performance in the Spanish Civil War and Graziani's in Abyssinia suggested that they would be more dangerous than in the First World War. On the British side, it was the first offensive battle since 1918, and they were employing for the first time the untried 'I' tanks. Defeat of O'Connor's small force would have handed Egypt to Mussolini.

The Italian dispositions, which O'Connor considered extremely unsound, were curiously similar to those of Eighth Army at Gazala in the spring of 1942—a fortified and fixed forward 'line' in the desert, with a large part of the army pegged in it and at no great distance from the enemy. O'Connor, in contrast, had held his troops in loose mobile groupings well back from Graziani, protected from an Italian stroke both by distance and by a screen of covering troops. Now, looking at these Italian camps or 'boxes' each out of supporting distance of the others, O'Connor conceived a plan of attack great in imaginative boldness; one which Rommel was to copy twice, each time successfully. He would penetrate the gap between Sofafi and Nibeiwa camps, thus cutting the Italian defences in two, and, while Sofafi was masked, swing north, behind the

Map I. The Battle of Sidi Barrani
December 1940

Italian front. Part of his forces would attack Tummar and Nibeiwa camps from the rear and then Sidi Barrani; part would drive to Buq Buq on the coast, across the Italian communications.

On November 2nd Wavell accepted this plan of battle, but his strategic intention remained a five-days' raid followed by withdrawal to Matruh.

Still wearing the Italian Silver Medal for Valour, awarded to him while fighting alongside the Italian Army in 1918, O'Connor began to plan in detail the victory of Sidi Barrani. But neither his judgment nor his resolution were softened by his continuing affection for his old comrades. He now saw beyond Wavell's directive to total victory. 'I felt that they did not plan for a success,' he put it with characteristic understatement, 'only for mediocre results.' As a planner, he was absorbed and intent: 'he worried to get things right—but never showed his worry,' said Galloway. Round him he had that group of officers who were so close to one another as to give almost the character of a conspiracy. There was what he called 'his race of dwarfs in the desert': himself, John Harding (now Field-Marshal Lord Harding) the Brigadier General Staff, and General Michael Creagh, the Irishman who commanded 7th Armoured Division. General N. M. de la P. Beresford-Peirse, of 4th Indian Division, made up some of the weight: he was an extrovert, plain-spoken, orthodox soldier who chain-smoked Indian cheroots, which he kept in a kind of reticule. 'BP was a very genuine personality,' wrote Dorman-Smith. Brigadier Galloway, Wilson's Brigadier General Staff, who was 'lent' for the planning, was a keen, hard man; restless, quick-tempered, able, and equipped with a caustic sense of humour.

On October 30th, Mussolini invaded Greece; but the Greeks in a victorious counter-stroke established themselves in Italian Albania. This Greek victory, won before O'Connor took the field, was destined to be the ruin of his campaign.

On November 19th an important preliminary operation took place in the desert. O'Connor's strategy for the coming battle depended on the gap between Nibeiwa and Safafi camps being neither garrisoned nor patrolled by the Italians. He therefore pushed forward the Support Group into the gap, where they fought and defeated some Italian battlegroups and established British domination of the area. On November 26th there was a full-scale rehearsal of an attack on a desert camp, planned and carried out by Beresford-Peirse and 4th Indian Division. It was a completely orthodox operation, inspired by the official pamphlet *The Division in Attack*.

After the division reached its assembly area, it waited patiently for two hours in full daylight while supporting artillery registered the enemy defences. Then, following the barrage, the infantry made a frontal assault on foot, in conjunction with the 'I' tanks. Timings had to be exact to ensure that tanks and men arrived on the Italian defences simultaneously. O'Connor held a conference to decide whether in fact this Cambrai-style attack would produce decisive results. The tank men, especially Colonel Gatehouse, second in command of 7th Armoured Brigade and chief tank umpire of the exercise, were sharply against it; so also was Dorman-Smith—sent down by Wavell to witness and comment on the exercise. They criticized the two hours' waiting time during which the entire striking force would be exposed to attack by the much larger Italian air force. They pointed out that in aerial photographs there was what looked like a minefield covering the breastwork of the camp on the front of the rehearsed attack. To succeed against superior numbers on the ground and in the air, Western Desert Force would need in their opinion all the speed and surprise that mechanized warfare made possible. Victory lay, therefore, in the unorthodox. O'Connor, though not himself a tank officer, agreed. Close re-examination of air photographs of Nibeiwa camp revealed that all vehicle tracks led into the north-west corner of the camp. This suggested absence of mines. The final and daring plan was now evolved.

The artillery would not wait to register; from the east, it would bombard the whole area of the Italian camp of Nibeiwa with the aim of causing panic and confusion rather than material destruction. Simultaneously the 'I' tanks and infantry would attack from the west, the Italian rear. The infantry would follow the tanks in their trucks and only leave their trucks for the close assault on the north-west corner of Nibeiwa. Since the British attacking force would lie in the middle of the Italian army, it would run less risk of air attack than in an advance from the east. The plan involved an approach march through the enemy's defence zone and a startline in its rear; a daring and imaginative manoeuvre that broke every rule of staff college orthodoxy. It has few rivals in the history of war.

In preparing the operation O'Connor had to contend with a shortage of every kind of equipment, but especially of that specialized equipment which enabled later armies to move economically in the desert. There were no tank-transporters and no tank-towing vehicles. Tanks moved always under their own power, shortening the lives of tracks and engines. If they were stopped in action by slight damage, they could not be immediately recovered for repair. There was the question of nourishing an approach march of a considerable distance, and a battle at the end of it, in the face of a transport famine; and of transporting the troops themselves. O'Connor solved the problem by establishing magazines of petrol, food, water, and ammunition for a five-day battle in the open desert between the British and Italian armies. All transport was first devoted to stocking these magazines; and then, during the battle, to carrying the troops. It was another example of O'Connor's cool nerves and professional skill.

Yet the approach march of sixty miles, followed by a battle, would still throw a great strain on the transport and on the fighting men—too great a strain. O'Connor decided to divide the approach march into two stages. For one day and night his entire army would lie out in the open desert half way from his base towards the Italians.

Of the complete plan for Sidi Barrani, with its litany of risks boldly accepted, and of his state of mind as the moment of action arrived, O'Connor wrote later:

> I can't describe my feelings, other than to say that I was sure it would be successful. It was a sound plan, a bit complicated perhaps, but I had every reason to rely on my commanders, their staff and the troops—all who were in very good heart.

The date of the offensive was fixed for December 9th. On November 28th, Wavell, with the astonishing military intuition that lay behind his continual silence, wrote to Wilson, O'Connor's superior:

> The difficulties, administrative and tactical, of a deep advance are fully realized. It is, however, possible that an opportunity

may offer for converting the enemy's defeat into an outstanding victory . . . I do wish to make certain that if a big opportunity occurs we are prepared morally, mentally and administratively to use it to the fullest.

On December 5th, Wavell issued his formal orders to Western Desert Force for Operation *Compass*. Next day O'Connor gave his own final orders. A year of difficult and ingenious preparation and six months of training and planning had brought O'Connor's small force to a peak of professional skill and fighting dash that was never again reached by the British in the desert. The army began to gather; the routine of camp was over.

O'Connor had two divisions. Fourth Indian Infantry Division, with the fifty-seven 'I' tanks, formed the close assault force; 7th Armoured Division provided the *corps de chasse*. There was also a heterogeneous group, called 'Selby Force' after its brigadier. The entire command numbered 36,000 men.

On the night of December 7th the long wait was over. The convoys rolled away through the darkness of no-man's-land, the lurching trucks full of soldiers wrapped thickly against the cold. The army had gone. O'Connor waited in the concrete ops room at Maaten Baggush as the hours of daylight on the 8th crept slowly past, wondering if his men would be discovered by Italian air or land reconnaissance as they lay out in the desert. It was a bright, cold day, with clear visibility.

During the night of December 8th/9th, 1940, the full moon, huge and white, and sharply delineated as a saucer, served for the first time as a lamp to light men into a desert battle. Beyond the shapes of trucks and tanks the desert stretched away silver, black and empty. It was bitterly cold. At last engines were started up, and the trucks and tanks lumbered off towards the rear of an army more than twice as large as the attacking force. In the doomed camp of Nibeiwa, the Italians were restless, as if they sensed the danger of which they knew nothing. Their flares flamed against the stars, but they illuminated nothing but an infinity of sand and scrub. Shots crashed out against the silence. Then the Italians quietened down.

In Baggush O'Connor waited. It was too late for doubts now. Happily, he did not know—for Wavell had deliberately not told him—that in five days' time, whatever the state of the battle, he must relinquish half his command. For Wavell wanted 4th Indian Division for an attack on Eritrea.

CHAPTER TWO

WHEN IT was full daylight on December 9th, 1940, a haze was seen lying along the desert. In the Italian camps the normal diurnal routine began. And then came the sound that no Italian or German and few Americans expected ever to be heard again—the opening salvo of a British offensive. It was the 4/7th Rajput Regiment firing on Nibeiwa from the east. Meanwhile the main assault force of infantry and 'I' tanks (of the Royal Tank Regiment) passed south of the camp, turned north in its rear, and, after the artillery bombardment by 4th Indian Division had stopped, struck without delay at the un-mined north-west corner of the camp. The Italians only realized that a formidable attack was upon their rear when they heard the growing roar of the 'I' tanks' engines. Twenty Italian medium tanks were caught outside the camp perimeter, warm-ing their engines and quite helpless. The 'I' tanks shot these into ruin in passing, and ploughed on into the camp. Only now did the Italians begin to move, swarming madly out of tents and slit trenches.

Some immediately surrendered. Yet the Italian Army as a whole fought well. Seeing the heavily armoured 'I' tanks for the first time, they attacked them with grenades and machine guns. The Italian gunners fought until all were killed or wounded. General Maletti, the camp commander, was shot down while firing a machine gun in his pyjamas from the mouth of his dugout. But by half past eight in the morning it was over. Two thousand men and thirty-five medium tanks had been captured for the loss of only fifty-six officers and men. The attack rolled on to the Tummar camps farther north.

O'Connor was soon up with his forward troops.

I remained in my headquarters until I got some information in, and then went off and saw the commanders, bringing a small staff with me. I always found this method paid me well. I left my Brigadier General Staff at my headquarters if I was out, and he knew my plans, and could prepare the administrative side.

This method of command was usual in the German panzer forces; an innovation in the British army, adopted later by Montgomery.

The commanders now saw O'Connor for the first time in the role of a leader on the battlefield. The quietness, the deep thought, had given way to bristling energy and crisp decision. At the end of the campaign a senior Australian officer said to one of O'Connor's staff officers: "Do you know what we call your general? The little terrier—because he never lets go."

His tactical headquarters, so small as to have only one office truck, was established at the junction of the Enba-Sidi-Barrani tracks. From here he ranged the battlefield in his staff car, the wound-up spring that kept the battle swiftly rolling.

As the morning wore on the sky became overcast and a sandstorm began to get up slowly. By half past one the 'I' tanks and 4th Indian Division were ready to attack Tummar West. The sand was blowing hard now and very dense. It infiltrated into eyes, noses, mouths, engines and gun-mechanisms. The field artillery fired into the whirling cloud, and the remaining twenty-two runners of the 'I' tanks lumbered into the camp via the fatal north-west corner. By twenty past four the British were finished with Tummar West and were attacking Tummar East.

*   *   *

O'Connor drove out to the headquarters of 7th Armoured Division to see Brigadier 'Blood' Caunter, commanding the division in the place of Creagh, who had gone into hospital two days earlier with an abscess on his tongue. He ordered Caunter to push patrols beyond Sofafi on the 10th to prevent the Italians escaping. Then he swung round and drove north to see Beresford-Peirse. He reached 4th Indian Division outside Tummar East just as the one Italian counter-attack of the day was smashed by British gunfire. However, this attack saved Tummar East for a few hours; the camp did not fall until early next morning. There was a conference on the sand between O'Connor, head cocked, body taut and springy, and Beresford-Peirse, solid, red-faced, cheroot-smoking: Sidi Barrani must be taken next day. Fourth Indian Division with the eight 'I' tanks that remained runners would therefore push on during the night and be ready to attack at first light.

As all the reports came in that evening, it became clear that only Selby Force had failed to gain a resounding success. In darkness and bad going, it allowed the Italians to escape from Maktila. On the other hand, Caunter had pushed his light tanks across the coast road between Sidi Barrani and Buq Buq. O'Connor ordered him to send a brigade to destroy an enemy tank group believed by British Intelligence to be at Azzaziya. But in fact, as Caunter wrote later: 'They were NOT there.'

The second day at Sidi Barrani was far more loose and opportunist than the first. Beresford-Peirse started on Sidi Barrani in a dawn dust storm; it fell at 4.40 pm. Once again the 'I' tanks of the 7th Royal Tank Regiment proved decisive. Seventh Armoured Division found no Italian tanks, but rolled farther west across the Italian rear. Selby had a bad day east of Sidi Barrani in a frontal assault against prepared defences. Yet, though the troops were beginning to tire, there was no slackening in speed and pressure; O'Connor's method of fighting a battle remained, in Caunter's words, 'offensive action wherever possible'. He motored down to Caunter on the evening of December 10th and told him 'that pursuit was the next step'. Caunter replied that he 'had already ordered 7th Armoured Brigade to move in a westerly direction for forty miles an hour before dawn and then strike northwards to the coast road. The brigade was to attack any Italians found with the utmost violence'.

During the night 4th Indian Division closed on the two Italian divisions encircled near Sidi Barrani. Early next morning O'Connor proposed to join Beresford-Peirse for the *coup de grâce*. Before he left his headquarters he read a signal telling him that he was to lose 4th Indian Division that day. With the conduct of a pursuit and the relinquishment of half his command on his mind, he watched Italian resistance melt. The remaining camps of Sofafi-Rabia and Khur-Samalus had been evacuated during the previous night.

On the night of December 11th, 1940, Western Desert Force camped on the field. For the first time men gazed on the scene of a desert victory: trucks and tanks abandoned or burnt, dumps of food and uniforms, guns, rifles, shells, cartridges, grenades, and, blowing in the wind, all the paper without which a twentieth-century organization cannot live. All this sad litter resembled the aftermath of a novel kind of race meeting. Towards Matruh the Italians were marching, dirty, tired and dejected, in dense untidy columns: pawns on their way off the board.

O'Connor had more than carried out Wavell's directive. This was not a successful raid; it was a major victory. In three days' fighting O'Connor had ended the Italian threat to Egypt, smashed two Italian corps, taken 38,000 prisoners, including four generals, 73 tanks and 237 guns. It was achieved at the cost of 624 British Commonwealth casualties, killed, wounded and missing.

O'Connor took victory quietly, without demonstration, without memorable historical asides. There was the question of 4th Indian Division. There was above all the question of whether Western Desert Force, about to be halved in size, should now fall back on Matruh according to the original intention. This was the safest thing to do. The magazines, stocked only for a five-day battle, were partly exhausted; it was difficult to see how both to replenish them *and* move the army with available trucks. The remaining Italian forces were very strong in numbers, many of them fresh formations. To advance farther would be to abandon a firm base, to lose 'balance'.

That night O'Connor told his subordinate commanders that 4th Indian Division would be leaving his command; at the same time he issued fresh orders. In Brigadier Caunter's words: "He told me that he was determined to pursue the enemy with the forces he had left to him—7th Armoured Division, which I was commanding, and Selby's infantry brigade."

The five-day raid had begun to flower into a great campaign.

* * *

On the morrow of the battle of Sidi Barrani, O'Connor was hard after the retreating Italians—with 4th Armoured Brigade along the top of the escarpment, 7th Armoured Brigade on the

41

coast road. Just across the Libyan frontier was the fortress of Bardia: a tiny harbour and town surrounded by modern perimeter defences, and connected with Tobruk and Benghazi by the metalled Via Balbia. In conjunction with the fortress of Tobruk, Bardia had been designed and built as the principal defence of Libya from the east. Upon this refuge the Italian Army now retreated, fighting hard at Sollum and Capuzzo against 7th Armoured Brigade. But O'Connor was already moving faster round their desert flank. He wished to reach the Via Balbia between Tobruk and Bardia before the Italians; trap them against the coast and destroy them. Swinging north for the first time across the dreary plateau of Libya, over which the war was to oscillate for two more years, 4th Armoured Brigade crossed the Trigh Capuzzo track—which lies fifteen miles south of the Via Balbia—and dashed for the coast. During the morning of December 14th men of the 11th Hussars stopped their vehicles and looked at the narrow strip of macadam that before their arrival had linked the remnants of the Tenth Army with Italy. Beside it telegraph poles marched from horizon to horizon, and, until the British cut them, the wires sang in the desert silence. Trapped, the Italians fell back into the shelter of Bardia. By December 16th the fortress was closely invested.

For O'Connor there was now the unglorious hard work and worry of organizing supply between his base at Mersa Matruh and his besieging forces round Bardia: a brain-heating business of estimated minimum consumptions, capacity of available transport, distances, speeds, mechanical wear and tear. But when all had been juggled, the basic fact remained that there was a transport famine. Wavell had now given O'Connor the understrength 6th Australian Division for the assault on Bardia; a fruit perhaps of O'Connor's daring in continuing the pursuit. As elements of it began to arrive on December 18th in the place of the departed Indians, O'Connor also had to reorganize his command.

With the lull in the fighting O'Connor and his men had time to digest Churchill's telegram of congratulation to Wavell on the victory of Sidi Barrani:

The Army of the Nile [a propaganda name for Western Desert Force] has rendered glorious service to the Empire and

42

to our cause and rewards are already being reaped by us in every quarter . . . Pray convey my congratulations to Longmore upon his magnificent handling of the Royal Air Force and fine co-operation with the Army . . .

The telegram thus included everything appropriate except O'Connor's name.

*   *   *

In Western Desert Force there was now a spirit of exuberance and professional self-confidence never afterwards matched by the British in the desert. It was the springtime of war. And the Army but reflected O'Connor; eager to press on, hating pauses however necessary. His was not the kind of leadership that makes of war a game of clergyman's chess; he believed in hustling the enemy, in keeping him in constant movement, in dazzling him by speed and surprise. O'Connor even tried to hustle 45,000 Italians and 400 guns out of the fortress of Bardia by gunfire and a noisy demonstration by the Support Group of 7th Armoured Division. But Bardia was not to be hustled; the garrison was inspired by a message to their commander from the Duce:

> I have given you a difficult task, but one well suited to your courage and experience as an old and intrepid soldier—the task of defending Bardia to the last.

The garrison commander, General 'Electric Whiskers' Bergonzoli, had replied:

> I am aware of the honour and I have today repeated to my troops your message—simple and unequivocal. In Bardia we are and here we stay.

It was all splendidly Roman; and Bergonzoli, considering the strength of his position, probably thought his boast could be made good. Round the little town of Bardia and its harbour, nestling in a valley in the escarpment like a treeless white Mevagissey, was an eighteen-mile belt of modern defences. Behind a steep anti-tank ditch twelve feet wide by four feet deep, a dense barbed-wire entanglement and minefields were two lines of mutually supporting steel and concrete bunkers, about eight hundred yards apart. On the south side of the perimeter, facing Egypt, there was a second, or switchline, defence.

To hold this barrier Bergonzoli had his 45,000 men and 400 guns. To attack it, O'Connor had to operate a hundred and fifty miles from his railhead with a total force smaller than Bergonzoli's and a close assault force only a third of the garrison's strength. But he was briskly confident:

> I knew I should be delayed by at least a fortnight or three weeks by (the) move of 4th Indian Division. But with the 6th Australian Division, I thought we should take Bardia all right, although of course it would require quite different tactics.

Supply was the only thing that really worried him; it absorbed much of his time, and the arrangements adopted testify to his originality and resourcefulness. Magazines like those established for Sidi Barrani were now opened along two lines from his base to Bardia, one inland and the other along the coast. There was the familiar problem of stocking these and dealing with troop movements; he partly solved it by swiftly organizing captured Italian trucks into new supply units. A windfall of heavy trucks arrived from Palestine. Heavy wear and tear on the poorly surfaced coast road and potholed desert tracks sharpened the problem. By the end of December there was forty per cent wastage in the vehicle establishment of Western Desert Force.

On January 1st, 1941, Western Desert Force was re-named 13th Corps. At the same time the anomalous chain of command, by which General Wilson and HQ, British Troops in Egypt, had been interposed between O'Connor and Wavell, was altered so that O'Connor came directly under the C-in-C's orders. This lightened O'Connor's mind. As he wrote later:

> I don't think HQ BTE were really necessary, except at the start and in the early stages. I sometimes received orders from both headquarters, which led temporarily to difficulties.

Three weeks after the victory of Sidi Barrani O'Connor felt himself ready to attack Bardia. Seventh Armoured Division (reduced by wear and tear to 70 cruisers and 120 light tanks) he reserved for pursuit; he did not consider strong fixed defences a proper object for armour. With his capacity always to see and plan a move ahead, he had already given 7th Armoured

Division its orders for the pursuit; a single code word on the fall of Bardia would set it in motion. For the assault on the fortress O'Connor employed the 6th Australian Division, 120 guns and 23 'I' tanks, all that could be got working in the face of a desperate shortage of spare parts. The Australians were seriously short of all kinds of equipment; there were only two instead of three artillery regiments, of which one was equipped with 1914–18 guns; the anti-tank company had eleven instead of twenty-seven two-pounder anti-tank guns.

As at Sidi Barrani the break-in was planned round the 'I'

Map 2. Attack on Bardia

tanks of 7th Royal Tank Regiment, but with significant differences that illustrate O'Connor's freshness of approach to each of his battles. He told Mackay, General Officer Commanding 6th Australian Division, who was to command the assault, that the tactical problem lay in passing the 'I' tanks safely through the powerful anti-tank defences. In contrast to the tactics at Nibeiwa, the infantry would have to go first in order to drive a bridgehead beyond the anti-tank ditch and minefields, bridge the ditch and clear lanes through the mines for the passage of the tanks. His mind already on the pursuit, O'Connor told Mackay to have a brigade ready on the third day of the battle to co-operate with 7th Armoured Division in a drive on Tobruk.

45

O'Connor placed his stroke where the enemy least expected it—on the centre of the western face of the perimeter. Once inside the fortress, tanks and infantry were to fan out to take the southern switchline in the rear.

All through the night of January 2nd/3rd, 1941, tanks with their exhaust baffles removed were kept roaring up and down outside Bardia to delude the Italians over the size of the attacking force. Soon after one o'clock in the morning of January 3rd, the Australian infantry moved forward to their assembly areas. It was a night of pitch darkness and biting cold. The men were loaded like Arab donkeys: woollen underwear and jerseys, battledress, leather jerkins and overcoats, gas masks, a hundred and fifty rounds of ammunition, grenades and three days' iron rations. At five-thirty a bombardment by every gun O'Connor could muster—as he had promised Mackay—opened the battle. To the fitful light of gun flashes the troops moved over the desert towards Bardia, ready to deal with the barbed-wire with Bangalore torpedoes and captured Italian wire-cutters. By the last hour of darkness, the first Italian prisoners began to come out of the bunkers. By half past six, in the grey first light, the Australians had cleared two lanes for the 'I' tanks. The infantry and tanks drove together into the heart of the fortress. There was now what Montgomery would have termed a 'dog-fight', the Italians fighting well and counter-attacking. But by eight o'clock the Australians had reached their first objectives and taken 8000 prisoners. Meanwhile diversionary attacks had been made at either end of the perimeter.

There was now a pause in the attack, while the fleet laid a barrage and the air force bombed Italian airfields. At 11.30 am the second phase opened with a brigade assault east of the Capuzzo road. Staff work here was not good; confusion slowed up progress. Yet by the end of that day the switchline had been turned by the Australians. In the middle of next morning, an Australian brigade led by six tanks attacked in two columns towards Bardia town and the Tobruk road. This assault split the garrison in two; and the fortress of Bardia fell with the resonance and suddenness of a great tree. The water supply—with a production of four hundred tons a day—and the harbour fell undamaged to the Australians, who took luncheon off Italian champagne. The Italians were still fighting sporadically in the north and south of the Bardia perimeter, but O'Connor was already driving westward to Tobruk. On January 5th the battle was over. While 7th Armoured Division raced via El Adem to cut off Tobruk, the magnitude of the new victory became apparent. The Italians had lost over 40,000 men, killed, wounded and captured, 400 guns, 13 medium and 115 light tanks and 706 trucks—an especial windfall to O'Connor.

For Wavell, O'Connor's successes raised an unexpected strategic problem. The Commander-in-Chief had to hold a balance between his various campaigns; the development of the 'five-day raid' into a six weeks' crescendo of victory threatened that balance. How far should Wavell allow himself to be pulled by O'Connor's success? Eight Italian divisions had been destroyed, 70,000 prisoners and a major fortress taken. But in Cyrenaica there still remained an Italian army of nearly 80,000 men and 900 guns. In Tripolitania there were another 90,000, with 500 guns. In view of the sharpening difficulties of supply and transport in 13th Corps and the wear and tear on the precious tanks, there was a strong case for resting content with a six weeks' raid. But O'Connor had already surrounded Tobruk; and Tobruk would be a valuable supply port. And so Wavell was drawn in behind O'Connor's advance. He gave his approval to the extension of the campaign to the capture of Tobruk.

But now O'Connor's victories were causing far-reaching reactions—reactions which were to determine the course of the war in the Middle East and Mediterranean for two years. On January 11th, 1941, a week after Bardia fell, Hitler made up his mind to send German ground forces to Libya. Shortly afterwards it was decided that this force of tanks, armoured cars and artillery—to be known as the 5th Light Division—would begin their move on February 15th. Thus unless O'Connor could destroy the Italian army in Libya in the next month and occupy the whole province, the British would be faced with a German invasion of North Africa. From January 11th, 1941, O'Connor and his troops, though they did not know it, were fighting in borrowed time.

A far more immediate danger, one quite well known in Cairo, lay in the high strategy of the war cabinet in London. The Prime Minister was fascinated and deeply moved by the Greek resistance to the Italians. All through the winter of 1940–41, as the savage fighting went on in the Epirus, the British had sent what help they could. Air Squadrons were diverted from support of O'Connor to support of the Greeks. However, at this time the cabinet and the C-in-Cs, Middle East, had agreed that so far as land forces were concerned the desert came first. But on November 4th, 1940, the Feuhrer had begun to stick his fingers into the Greek affair by ordering a study of ways and means of helping the Italians from Rumania, which Germany already controlled. At this stage, London opinion had been unanimous that Turkey was more important than Greece; and that if Turkey were attacked, *Compass*—the attack on Sidi Barrani—should be abandoned and O'Connor's forces sent to help her. Wavell, with the strategic insight of genius, wrote back that he considered he would have time for *Compass* before the Germans moved in the Balkans. Next day, Hitler told Ciano that German intervention in Greece via Bulgaria could not take place earlier than March 1941.

So far Churchill and his advisers had regarded Greece as second to the desert. Even after Sidi Barrani the Prime Minister wrote to Wavell:

Neither of these [action in the Sudan or the Dodecanese] ought to detract from the supreme task of inflicting further defeats upon the main Italian Army.

But as evidence of German preparations in Rumania grew, the threat to Greece began to make the Prime Minister's mind wobble. Two days after the fall of Bardia, he wrote to the Chiefs of Staff:

Although perhaps by luck and daring we may collect comparatively easily most delectable prizes on the Libyan shore, the massive importance of . . . keeping the Greek front in being must weigh hourly with us.

At this time it was only a thought set down in a minute; it was to grow until it dominated the Prime Minister's obstinate mind, was made fact against all initial advice by his formidable will; it led to two immediate military disasters; and prolonged the war in Africa by two years.

Four days later Churchill made up his mind that after

Tobruk had fallen, Greece must take priority over the Desert; he would offer the Greek Government everything we could spare; that is, the troops of 13th Corps. Wavell with his cool sense of reality asked the Chiefs of Staff to consider whether the German preparations in Rumania were designed to bluff us into taking the heat off Graziani. Wavell added a judgment that events proved exactly right. He said that if the German preparations in Rumania were genuine, *nothing* we could send the Greeks could avert defeat anyway. But by now the Prime Minister was convinced of the need and possibility of building a new Balkan front against German expansion. The Greek question was settled. He replied peremptorily to Wavell through the Chiefs of Staff:

> We expect and require prompt and active compliance with our decisions for which we bear full responsibility.

But luckily for O'Connor, the Prime Minister's offer of aid was rebuffed by the Greek Government—for the time being. O'Connor could march on; but after Bardia his campaign lay under a suspended death sentence.

Meanwhile, O'Connor was briskly preparing another victory. By January 7th, 1941, three days after the fall of Bardia, Tobruk was closely invested. By January 15th, British Intelligence was able to give O'Connor the Italian garrison's order of battle. Under the command of General Petassi Manella, 22nd Corps, there were believed to be 32,000 men, 220 guns, and 45 light and 20 medium tanks. O'Connor thought there were Italian divisions in Derna and Benghazi, and an armoured force under General Babini at Mechili. Two hundred miles from Mersa Matruh, supplied by the Via Balbia and the Trigh Capuzzo track, O'Connor was at the limit of his communications; ingenuity and improvisation could do no more. The possession of the port of Tobruk was essential to a deeper advance.

Tobruk, which was to make so many headlines in the next two years, now faced its first siege. Despite the great fame it was to acquire, Tobruk was not much of a place. There was a small harbour, a scattering of white buildings rather like a transit camp on the flat, naked, sloping ground of the coastal plain. An hotel, a restaurant and a few shops made it an urban centre. It was treeless except for some battered palms in the main square. The narrow ribbon of the Via Balbia suspended it from the hazy horizons of east and west. Round Tobruk, over the barren hinterland, ran thirty-eight miles of perimeter defences similar to those of Bardia: an anti-tank ditch—which was incomplete—dense barbed-wire, a double row of concrete bunkers each with its own ditch and wire, minefields. Tobruk seemed an easier proposition than Bardia: troops were fewer, the perimeter longer and the defences sparser.

At his headquarters at Gambut, amid continued sandstorms, O'Connor planned his assault. There was the temptation to use

Map 3. Attack on Tobruk

the armoured division as a self-contained battering ram. But O'Connor would not risk it against fixed defences; he considered it should be conserved for pursuit and mobile battle. Nevertheless he was more than usually in a hurry. He had news of fresh Italian forces landing at Tripoli; in a short time, if he allowed it, there might be four new Italian divisions and a tank group between Derna and the Gulf of Syrte. Most worrying of all was the threat of help to Greece, which had already reduced his air support. He fixed the date of the assault on Tobruk for January 20th. His assault commanders asked for a postponement of twenty-four hours in order to work on the 'I' tanks, now reduced by the desert surface to twelve. O'Connor

50

agreed, but ordered that in the extra time a squadron of Australian mechanized cavalry should be equipped with Italian medium tanks. His tactical employment of 'I' tanks and infantry was to be the same as at Bardia; the selected point of assault, the south-eastern sector chosen by Rommel in June 1942.

Final preparations began on January 18th on a day of dense sandstorm and a wind that bowled petrol cans along the ground. On the 20th there was clear winter sunshine, and after dark the crystalline stars of the African night sky. The troops were in position. Seventh Armoured Division already had its orders to strike for Mechili the moment that Creagh received the code word that Tobruk had fallen.

At five-forty on January 21st, 1941, the assault on Tobruk was opened with O'Connor's customary bombardment by concentrated artillery, and the Australian infantry charged in to the accompaniment of red Very lights, the explosion of Bangalore torpedoes and an Australian voice bellowing:

"Go on, you bastards!"

In some places the Italians were captured before they were aware that an attack was going on. At a quarter to seven that morning the 'I' tanks lumbered through the gap in the perimeter, and infantry and tanks together began to fan out. The Italians fought bitterly all day, launching counter-attacks with tanks; when night came, their artillery was silent and General Petassi Manella was a prisoner. The long horizons of sand and scrub were lit by blazing dumps as the rest of the garrison still fought on. Dawn found them on the verge of surrender. Mackay, Australian commander of the assault, ordered a general advance; and men, tanks and carriers flowed down the naked slope into Tobruk. By early afternoon, 13th Corps was once more counting the booty while 7th Armoured Division rolled away to the west. There were 25,000 prisoners, 208 guns, 23 medium tanks, 200 trucks and enough canned food to have lasted the garrison two months. Though the Italians had tried to wreck the port, damage was so slight that British stores were being unloaded within three days. From O'Connor's point of view the most welcome prize was water distillation plant and wells with a capacity of 40,000 gallons a day.

He had a new base; a base which would make possible the

further spring to the west that had been in his mind long before Tobruk was attacked. For O'Connor was on edge with the desire to get on, to win final victory, before Greece and German intervention broke his run of success. This anxiety bred another—the anxiety over supply and transport that nagged at him continuously. Yet, by his energy and aggression and his gift of leadership he kept the whole rickety, improvised campaign rolling forward on the heels of the demoralized Italians. It took everything he had to give. In his own words:

> There was really no time for any relaxation, other than sleeping, during this short campaign. I was constantly seeing and talking to the formation commanders, staff officers and officers of the services: talking to the fighting troops, or encouraging the administrative services to further efforts.

No one knew that he was suffering all the time from a stomach complaint. Understandably, his manner was deeply serious: 'He seldom smiled,' wrote Brigadier Caunter, 'and I never saw him laugh.' He had always taken his profession seriously. Many years before, General Godwin-Austen had taken over O'Connor's company at Sandhurst. He stayed with him one night and dined in the mess with the company. Afterwards, walking outside the New Building, Godwin-Austen saw a tent with cadets running up and down its sides. He asked O'Connor what the tent was for; O'Connor replied that it was the scorer's tent for the cricket match. At this moment the tent collapsed. Godwin-Austen remarked what a glorious game it was—he'd love to run up and down a tent. But O'Connor seemed far from amused. Later a cadet told Godwin-Austen that O'Connor had been horrified by the spectacle, and had thought it must have deeply shocked the new company commander.

After the fall of Tobruk, O'Connor's campaign entered its last phase, a finale of amazing brilliance in which great risks were daringly accepted, and the allegedly impossible triumphantly overcome. O'Connor was to drive his troops unceasingly, fretting at necessary delays, cannibalizing truck parts, stealing tanks from one unit to make up another; and at last flinging the remnants of his armour across uncharted country on the last few gallons of petrol and the last few miles of life left in the tank tracks. One of the epic marches of history was about to begin.

CHAPTER THREE

O N JANUARY 21st the Chiefs of Staff had informed Wavell that the capture of Benghazi was extremely important. So O'Connor's advance received strategic sanction for yet another stage. It all had been anticipated, if not foreseen, by O'Connor as long ago as the siege of Bardia. Now, with Tobruk behind him, he advanced to destroy the remaining Italian forces in Cyrenaica and to take Benghazi—the Australians along the coast road through Gazala, the armour inland to Mechili.

He had traversed the desert of the battles now from end to end. He stood at the gates of the Jebel Achdar, the Green Mountains, a region of fertile, settled Mediterranean countryside—wide fields of grain, stony hills dotted with grey olive trees and the white cubist farmhouses of Italian settlers. Pretty modern towns with green and pleasant gardens and abundant water lay ahead of the dust-covered army, and at the back of the Jebel Achdar, Benghazi. The coastline swings north round this isolated segment of Italy or Greece, and then sharply south to the blinding sand wastes of the Gulf of Syrte. South of the Jebel Achdar lay half a continent of desert. The Via Balbia followed the coast round the bulge of the Jebel to Syrte; the chord to this arc was supplied by unreconnoitred desert tracks from Mechili through to Beda Fomm; going so bad that the Italians took it to be impassable to an army.

The Jebel Achdar offered better prospects of defence for the Italians than the open desert. Its hills were broken and rugged and offered little scope to armour, and its two gateways were strongly held. On the Italian left, barring the Via Balbia, was Derna, held by one division, a natural position of great strength, for it lay in a gigantic wadi that stretched twelve miles inland with nearly sheer sides up to seven hundred feet high. On the right—or desert—flank at Mechili, centre of desert track-routes south of the Jebel, was a powerful force of infantry, guns and up to seventy tanks under General Babini.

O'Connor decided to smash open these Italian defences and

gain a victory before London opinion, now in favour of taking Benghazi, veered back again to Greece. By January 24th the Australians were feeling their way along the fringe of the Derna defences. They found the Italians well posted in the broken ground and full of fight. At the same time an Italian tank force near Mechili fought a brisk action with 4th Armoured Brigade. Both Italian wings thus seemed quite formidable, especially when British march wastage was considered: 7th Armoured Division was down to fewer than seventy cruisers. The Italian weakness, which O'Connor noted, lay in that their wings were too far away to help each other. O'Connor therefore decided to destroy Babini at Mechili and sweep on south of the Jebel Achdar to turn deeply the Italians at Derna and Benghazi. On January 25th he ordered Creagh to envelop Babini with the armour and then destroy him with the infantry. He pointed out to Creagh the route northwards by which Babini was most likely to retire, and suggested that if the going there was too rough for tanks, Creagh should use the Support Group. But on the night of the 26th, after the British armour was in position, Babini escaped north-west into the Jebel Achdar. It was O'Connor's first major setback, and he did not take it lightly. General Creagh wrote afterwards: 'O'Connor was very disappointed and annoyed.' Creagh's own explanation of the failure to block Babini's retreat is that 'armour is definitely blind at night and I don't think there was sufficient active patrolling by the infantry of the leading brigade. Hence they withdrew unnoticed until daylight.' Yet it was all for the best: the way was now open for O'Connor's long-meditated drive to the Gulf of Syrte. And a battle at Mechili might not have been an unclouded success. Brigadier Caunter studied the ground at Mechili after the Italian withdrawal, and found that 'our maps did not tell us the topographical faults. The steepness of the slopes on the eastern and southern faces made tank attacks there extremely difficult, if not unsound.'

O'Connor himself also made a tour of the scene of the Italian escape, like, said Dorman-Smith, 'a terrier ratting.'

Although the way was open, O'Connor could not march. Desert and distances were more formidable opponents than Babini. Seventh Armoured Division was down to fifty cruisers and ninety-five light tanks; and there was not enough fuel or ammunition for a long march over bad going as well as a battle. There was no alternative but to sit and wait and fret while a new magazine near Mechili was stocked and two fresh regiments arrived from 2nd Armoured Division, newly landed in Egypt. This would take a fortnight; a time of agony for a man of O'Connor's temperament. Supposing the Italians evacuated Cyrenaica before he could move? Supposing the Commander-in-Chief stopped him or took away his army to send to Greece? While the trucks bumped their slow way from Tobruk to Mechili with the fuel, food and petrol, O'Connor sent the Australians against Derna to delude the Italians that his main attack was coming astride the coast road. Derna fell on January 30th and the Australians pushed on through the green, herb-scented landscape to Giovanni Berta. It would still be ten days before O'Connor would have the essential supplies ready for his great march in the south.

But time was running rapidly out. On February 1st, Marshal Graziani, Governor-General of Libya and Commander-in-Chief, decided to evacuate the remainder of Cyrenaica and concentrate his forces round Syrte for the defence of Tripolitania. General Gariboldi was to relinquish command in Cyrenaica in order to organize this defence, his place being taken from February 3rd by General Tellera. On February 2nd, aerial reconnaissance reports confirmed earlier intimations that, while O'Connor's field magazine was still only half stocked, his prey was slipping away.

In O'Connor's headquarters at Bomba on a bleak estuary littered wih collapsed Italian aircraft there were tense discussions. It was bitterly cold except in the airfield hut where the headquarters staff lived on a balanced diet of parmesan cheese, bully and chianti. O'Connor and Harding, his Brigadier General Staff, had been joined on January 29th by Brigadier Dorman-Smith, sent down by Wavell to prepare a study of the campaign and to witness its end. The facts before them were not encouraging. The armoured reinforcements had not arrived. The existing armoured force was mechanically on its very last legs. Only fifty cruisers remained runners. This was the force which, if O'Connor decided to advance immediately, would have to make a march of a hundred and fifty miles at top speed over desert unreconnoitred but reputed to be very bad going. When—if—the force reached its objective, it would bring to battle a greatly superior and desperate Italian army. There would be just enough fuel for the armoured division to start with full fuel tanks, enough supplies to allow it to carry its own quota of food and ammunition. A convoy of trucks could follow with two days' food, water and petrol, and two refills of ammunition. That was all. There was no hope of further supplies reaching the division before these were exhausted.

During every moment O'Connor spent in deciding what to do the Italians were slipping further away. But the risks spoke only too eloquently. No one could have blamed O'Connor if, with his three victories behind him, he had limited himself like Montgomery to following up the enemy retirement. Instead, a resolve to put everything to hazard swiftly took hold of O'Connor and fired his officers. O'Connor sent Dorman-Smith to Cairo by air with the battle plan in his pocket in order to ask Wavell's permission to advance. The escape of Babini still rankled; he asked Dorman-Smith to "tell the C-in-C how sorry I am the Italians escaped from Mechili. I'm furious about it." Wavell replied to Dorman-Smith:

"Tell General O'Connor not to fret. It is contretemps like those that add interest to that very dull business, war."

Next day Dorman-Smith was back at Bomba with Wavell's permission for an immediate advance to the Gulf of Syrte. Creagh was now there, far from well, with a very sore throat. He had arrived by accident, as he himself describes:

> There was an apparent lull for ten days whilst supplies were being brought forward. It was arranged that I myself and some of my staff should fly to Cairo for a few days' rest. We stayed for the night at O'Connor's Headquarters at Bomba. After breakfast next morning O'Connor told me that it appeared that the Italians were retreating from Cyrenaica and must be caught. We had a conference on the spot and then I returned to 7th Armoured Headquarters to lay on the battle.

O'Connor ordered Creagh to march on February 4th through Solluch to the coast road south of Benghazi. Mackay and the Australians were to hustle the Italians through the Jebel Achdar, if necessary by ferrying forward one unit at a time.

At first light on February 4th, 7th Armoured Division, with

fifty cruisers and eighty light tanks, rumbled out of Mechili into the west. The going was as bad as could have been feared —strewn boulders and soft sand. But the division moved with great élan. General Creagh wrote later:

> Off we went across the unknown country in full cry. It was definitely exciting and the Division pushing on and on across the desert was a stimulating sight. Some of this desert was very rough and slowed us up; so I sent a wheeled column ahead which was faster than the tracked tanks. This column was to get on to the coast road and hold up any retreating forces until the main body of the Division could go into action.

Map 4. O'Connor's march to Beda Fomm

In the evening of the 4th, after meeting Wavell at Tmimi, O'Connor followed the armour in his staff car, with Dorman-Smith as a companion. Bouncing and slewing over the terrible

57

ground, they soon left 13th Corps headquarters (also on the move) far behind. O'Connor was determined, in Dorman-Smith's words, 'to follow up 7th Armoured Division in person to ensure that it operated with the utmost energy'. What O'Connor saw during the race with the retreating Italians did not reassure him that he had made the right decision: on all sides there were broken-down British tanks littered along the track. In a rare moment of revelation of his inner anxieties, he was moved to remark to Dorman-Smith:

"My God, do you think it's going to be all right?"

After the first fifty miles 7th Armoured Division struck better going, but also dust so dense that parts of the column became lost and rejoined hours later. At three in the afternoon the 11th Hussars reached Msus, still sixty miles from the coast road. In the evening Brigadier Harding flew up to Creagh's headquarters at Msus. They discussed the news that the Italian retirement was now beginning to move very fast, and decided to send a second force south-west to the coast road via Antelat as well as due west through Solluch as according to O'Connor's orders, in case the Italians passed Solluch before the British armour reached it.

At 7 am Colonel Combe with a vanguard of armoured cars drove away from Msus towards Antelat. Meanwhile air reconnaissance showed that the road south of Benghazi was crammed with Italian transport driving fast southward towards the as yet unclosed trap. O'Connor himself set off early for 7th Armoured Division headquarters in his staff car with an armoured car and another car as escort. He kept control of his racing army by wireless. One of the cars and the armoured car now broke down. O'Connor and Dorman-Smith drove on alone in the remaining car, without contact with the army, in a silence wherein anxieties could multiply. It was a long day: a day in which to wonder if Creagh had managed to close the trap in time, in which at any moment a breakdown might strand O'Connor in the open desert. But that evening his staff car drove up to Wadi Azzin, headquarters of 7th Armoured Division, and, tired and stiff, O'Connor climbed out to hear the news from Creagh. The Italians had dropped container bombs—looking like Thermos flasks—across the track, and O'Connor was greeted by the sound of rifle fire as the Free French blew them up.

Creagh had good news. Combe had entered Antelat at 10.34 that morning, found it deserted and immediately sent armoured cars on to Beda Fomm and Sidi Saleh. By noon these cars, joined by C Battery, Royal Horse Artillery, reached the coast road and blocked it. At half past twelve the first column of Italian trucks appeared from the north. O'Connor's trap had closed with half an hour to spare. The British guns opened fire and the annihilation battle of Beda Fomm had begun. At 3 pm a column of thirty trucks tried to break through Combe's force; they were defeated and captured. At five a huge column appeared and was also captured. Meanwhile 4th Armoured Brigade had been battling over the fearsome ground and had reached Antelat at 4.30 pm. Here Combe radioed to them that the Italians were pouring down the coast road in great strength. Creagh had instantly ordered part of his division to strike them in the flank through Beda Fomm; part to cut them off in the north at Solluch. Creagh's news delighted and relieved O'Connor.

The Armoured Division had been ordered (by me) to reach the coast, which they did splendidly. Farther to the south than I originally intended, but they (Creagh and Harding) were quite right.

The dawn on February 6th, 1941, was grey and miserable with torrential rain sweeping across the coastal plain. By its dismal light the Italians made their first attempt to break through the southern British road block. It failed under the guns of the Royal Horse Artillery. O'Connor and Dorman-Smith now retraced their steps to find the corps headquarters. It lay between Mechili and Msus, out of touch with everything. O'Connor drove on to Msus to get some food and that night slept in the car without rugs. Early on the 7th, he drove back again to Antelat and Headquarters, 7th Armoured Division. As Dorman-Smith writes: 'O'Connor's energy was tremendous, unsurpassed even by Rommel's.'

Meanwhile the desperate Italians strove to escape. They were caught in a flat but hummocky plain between Beda Fomm and the sea along fourteen miles of road. Low north-to-south ridges gave cover to the British armour. All day on the 6th the Italians strove to knock Combe's force and the 2nd Royal Tank

59

Regiment off their road to Tripoli. The 2nd Royal Tanks had nineteen cruisers and seven light tanks. The Italians were a *mélange* of trucks and tanks and guns, although they sometimes managed to unscramble an organized force that tried to find a way through the scattered British cordon. By midday forty Italian medium tanks had been knocked out. Yet the Italians still possessed at least fifty, against the fifteen remaining British cruisers. The only British reserve of tanks—eleven all told—lay at Antelat paralysed by want of fuel. Across the confused battle the winter rain squalls drove unceasingly. All through the afternoon the weary British pounded away at attack after attack by the desperate Italians. At last some thirty Italian tanks burst through 2nd Royal Tanks and headed south towards Combe's force, who were instantly warned. The Italians arrived after dark, but were received with vigour by Combe. Only four Italian tanks and lorries got through.

First light on February 7th found O'Connor and Dorman-Smith driving up to 7th Armoured Division Headquarters at Antelat after their cold and cramped night in the car. They breakfasted off a cold sausage each. Meanwhile the Italians were making their last violent and desperate attempt to break out. A column of trucks led by thirty tanks drove through the forward companies of the Rifle Brigade, and for a moment it seemed that the Italians were clear. Then permission was given for the British artillery to fire on them while mixed up with the Rifle Brigade. The last Italian tank was knocked out just before it reached the officers' mess-tent. It was the end of the Italian Tenth Army. Fourth Armoured Brigade rounded up another surrendering mob; the Australians, hustled by O'Connor, drove into the Italian rear, and by nine o'clock on the morning of February 7th, 1941, O'Connor had completed that rare military achievement: a victory of total annihilation.

The news of the Italian surrender reached O'Connor at Creagh's headquarters. He turned to Dorman-Smith and said:

"We'd better send a message to Archie. What shall we say?"

Dorman-Smith suggested that Wavell would appreciate a hunting metaphor: 'Fox killed in the open . . .'

The full message was radioed to Cairo in clear for Mussolini's benefit. Then O'Connor said to Dorman-Smith:

"Let's go forward to see how things are."

60

As they drove towards the sea over the hummocky ground, herds of antelope moved in front of them, parting to let them through. They saw some bustards. The smell of the sea came strongly in through the open window of the car. Dorman-Smith asked O'Connor what it felt like to be a completely successful commander. O'Connor was silent for a moment, his calm, reflective eyes on the moving gazelle. Then he answered:

"I would never consider a commander completely successful until he had restored the situation after a serious defeat and a long retreat."

Dorman-Smith was to recall this modest and wise reply eighteen months later when he accompanied Sir Claude Auchinleck on his flight up to Maaten Baggush, O'Connor's old headquarters, to take over command of the wreckage of Eighth Army, which had retreated two hundred and sixty miles with the loss of 80,000 men.

Now the scene of victory opened before them: the sea, the plain, the débris of an army. Along fifteen miles of road and ground this débris was piled and littered in spectacular confusion. There were hundreds of trucks either shattered by gunfire, abandoned or on their sides, derelict tanks in the dark green of the Italian army lying where they had been caught as they tried to squirm out of the trap. Field guns, sitting abandoned in a litter of ammunition cases, pointed at nothing. The plain was strewn with small arms as thickly as seaweed on a beach. And then there was the office paper blowing about the battlefield or caught in the camel thorn.

'One of the most amusing sights,' in General Creagh's words, 'was a busload of Italian ladies sitting in the middle of a battlefield powdering their noses and brewing some tea'. They were protected by a lone priest in a soutane; 'a highly inappropriate figure,' as Dorman-Smith put it.

For the last time the booty of a victory was counted: 20,000 prisoners, 112 medium tanks, 216 guns and 1500 wheeled vehicles. The commander of the 10th Army, General Tellera, had been killed, and General 'Electric Whiskers' Bergonzoli captured.

The British army, exhilarated by victory, was holding a vast celebration. O'Connor and Dorman-Smith drove down to the headquarters of Rifle Brigade and saw the knocked-out

Italian tank by the mess-tent, looking like, in Dorman-Smith's words, 'a collapsed elephant'. A party was in progress; it went on all day, with relays of guests for food and drink at outside trestle tables, resembling, said Colonel (later General) Renton, 'badly organized catering at a point-to-point'. O'Connor sipped a victory drink in his birdlike way, but his mind was already on the next advance, for which the captured Italian transport would be essential. He was worried that the Australians might seize all they could find, and he ordered Gott of the Support Group to go and halt their advance from the north. There was also the prisoners' food and welfare to organize. Later he drove to Solluch where Italian senior officer prisoners were confined to two large empty villas, guarded by vinous Free French. O'Connor pushed his way through the throng of disconsolate Italians, and asked in Italian for the senior general, who appeared in a splendid uniform, complete with spurs. O'Connor, in contrast, wore his usual campaign rig—corduroy trousers, leather jerkin, a tartan scarf and a general's red-banded cap. To the Italian general O'Connor said:

"I'm sorry you are so uncomfortable. We haven't had time to make proper arrangements."

The Italian replied politely: "Thank you very much. We do realize you came here in a very great hurry."

It was O'Connor's hope that his victory of Beda Fomm would win the approval of Wavell and of London for a further advance into Tripolitania. Each of his previous victories had sucked in behind it strategic permission to march another stage; surely now even the Prime Minister would prefer to invest in success in Libya, rather than in certain failure in Greece. But speed was essential. O'Connor therefore sent Dorman-Smith to see General Wilson, who, having just been appointed Military Governor of Cyrenaica, was once more his immediate superior. Dorman-Smith found Wilson in Barce, a town full of armed but docile Italians. Wilson was in favour of asking Wavell's permission for a further advance; they drafted a message, but there were no signals in the town. So Dorman-Smith drove to Tobruk, there sent Wilson's signal to Wavell, and then drove on to Cairo, arriving at 4 am on February 12th. At 10 am he entered the map room of the Commander-in-Chief, Middle East. To his dismay he saw that all the desert maps had gone, replaced by maps of Greece. Wavell swept an arm sardonically at the new maps.

"You see, Eric," he said, "I'm starting my spring campaign."

* * *

On January 29th, 1941, Metaxas, the Greek Prime Minister—or, rather, Dictator—who had spurned Churchill's offer of armed assistance, died. His successor, alarmed by the German concentration piling up in Bulgaria, was now induced by Churchill to ask the British Government what help they could furnish, should the Germans invade Greece. No appeal for aid against Germany ever failed to touch the heart of the Prime Minister. For emotion was the drug that equally stimulated his tremendous primeval force, and sometimes distorted his judgment. Therefore Churchill added this rider to his telegram congratulating Wavell on O'Connor's victory at Beda Fomm:

> We are delighted that you have got this prize [Benghazi] three weeks ahead of expectation, but this does not alter, indeed it rather confirms, our previous directive, namely that your major effort must now be to aid Greece and/or Turkey. This rules out any serious effort against Tripoli . . . You should therefore make yourself secure in Benghazi and concentrate all available forces in the Delta in preparation for a move to Europe . . . Therefore it would seem that we should try to get in a position to offer the Greeks the transfer to Greece of the fighting portion of the Army which has hitherto defended Egypt [that is O'Connor's 13th Corps].

The Prime Minister's advisers had done their best to induce him to look objectively at the strategic implications of intervention in Greece. As long ago as December 13th, 1940, General Kennedy, Director of Military Operations at the War Office, had written in a minute:

> Though the defence of Salonika is important, it would be dangerous to attempt it with less than twenty divisions, which cannot now be made available.

On February 11th, 1941, General Dill, the Chief of the Imperial General Staff, told Churchill that all troops in the Middle East were fully occupied and none was available for Greece. Churchill replied: "What you need out there is a Court Martial and a firing squad . . ." This was four days after Beda

Fomm. On February 16th, a general staff minute drawn up by Kennedy stated:

> Nothing we can do can make the Greek business a sound military proposition . . . In the Middle East we must not throw away our power of offensive action by adopting an unsound strategy in Greece . . .

But Churchill was now determined to attempt a Balkan front. Intervention in Greece became a fact: O'Connor's advance was stopped and his magnificent army disbanded. The results of this attempt to succour the Greeks were to be just as predicted by the Prime Minister's advisers. The Greek army collapsed swiftly: the British expeditionary force reached its allotted line only to retreat immediately to its ships. We lost precious equipment, some warships, and had an army thrown into complete disorganization. We neither helped the Greeks nor embarrassed the Germans. Field Marshal Lord Alanbrooke summed it up:

> I have, however, always considered from the very start that our participation in the operation in Greece was a definite strategic blunder. Our hands were more than full at the time in the Middle East, and Greece could only result in the most dangerous disposal of force.

Churchill was unrepentant:

> If Hitler had been able, with hardly any fighting, to bring Greece to her knees and the whole of the Balkans into her system . . . might he not have had terms with the Soviets upon the conquest and partition of these vast regions and postponed his ultimate, inevitable quarrel with them to a later part of his programme? Or, as is more likely, would he not have been able to attack Russia in greater strength at an earlier date?

In fact, the timing of the German attack on Russia was not affected at all by the British expeditionary force to Greece, but seriously upset by the unconnected event of the sudden change of régime in Yugoslavia, which changed peaceful occupation into desperate war.

The Greek question was a major crisis in grand strategy; by his decision to intervene, the Prime Minister showed for the first time in the war that although he was a Churchill, he was

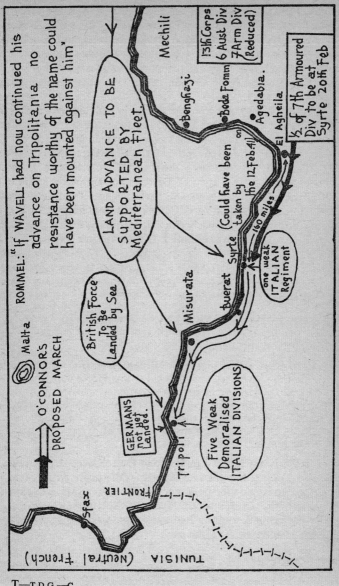

ROMMEL: "If WAVELL had now continued his advance on Tripolitania no resistance worthy of the name could have been mounted against him"

O'CONNOR'S PROPOSED MARCH

Malta

British Force To Be Landed by Sea

LAND ADVANCE TO BE SUPPORTED BY Mediterranean Fleet.

Mechili

Benghazi

Beda Fomm

Agedabia.

13th Corps
6 Aust Div
7 Arm Div
(Reduced)

½ of 7th Armoured Div to be at Syrte 20th Feb

El Agheila.

Syrte (Could have been taken by the 12 Feb.41)

150 miles

one weak ITALIAN Regiment

Buerat

Misurata

GERMANS not yet Landed.

Tripoli

Five Weak Demoralised ITALIAN DIVISIONS

FRONTIER

Sfax

TUNISIA (Neutral French)

Map 5. O'Connor's Plan for Ending North African Campaign
February 1941

T—T.D.G.—C

not a Marlborough. Instead of his ancestor's cold and long-sighted sagacity, he displayed emotional impulse; sometimes generous, sometimes ruthless, always overwhelming. Greece was the first occasion in the war that these impulses had worked disastrously. It was a mistake the more disastrous because of the alternative objective of Tripoli, which O'Connor believed he could attain.

He proposed to take Syrte immediately with armoured cars, artillery and the Support Group. On February 20th, backed by the entire available Middle East air strength and the Royal Navy, as well as by all the military and supply resources of the Middle East, an armoured striking force—made up from cruiser tanks of 7th Armoured Division and the newly arrived 2nd Armoured Division—would have advanced from Syrte on Tripoli. At the same time O'Connor had in mind that an in-fantry brigade might have been landed from the sea at Tripoli. Speed of execution was essential. O'Connor later stated:

> In my opinion the operation would not only have been possible, but would have had every chance of success provided all three Services gave their maximum support and were not deflected by other commitments.

When Wavell received Wilson's signal on February 10th, 1941, he immediately telegraphed London in the vain hope of winning a last-minute stay of execution.

> The extent of Italian defeat at Benghazi seems to me to make it possible that TRIPOLI might yield to small force if dispatched without delay. I . . . hesitate to advance farther in view of the Balkan situation. But you may think the capture of Tripoli might have favourable effect on attitude of French North Africa . . . I will make plans for capture of Syrte which must be the next step. Please cable your views . . .

On the 13th Churchill replied that Greece ruled out Tripoli (see page 63). After the war Wavell loyally made an excellent case (as he would) for pronouncing a further advance beyond our strength, Greek intervention or no. But Rommel himself, who arrived in Tripoli on February 12th, five days after Beda Fomm, agreed with O'Connor:

> On February 8th leading troops of the British army occupied El Agheila . . . Graziani's army had virtually ceased to exist.

All that remained of it were a few lorry columns and hordes of unarmed soldiers in full flight to the west. If Wavell (*sic*) had now continued his advance into Tripolitania no resistance worthy of the name could be mounted against him.

Thus the Greek episode lengthened the campaign in North Africa by two years—a campaign that sucked in the major ground efforts of the British Commonwealth, and left the Far East almost undefended against the Japanese.

On February 13th, 1941, the day following Lieutenant-General Rommel's arrival in Africa, O'Connor learned after six days of silence and anxiety that his campaign was dead. This was a moment of great anguish—a moment when so many men would have given way to bitterness and recrimination as they totalled up the prizes of which they (and their country) had been robbed, as they bleakly considered the nature of the Greek adventure.

The temptation was there to advance without orders, present the *fait accompli* of a victory, and force the Cabinet into support. There have been generals who, when convinced they are right, have not balked at covert disobedience. It was repugnant both to O'Connor's character and his sense of public duty. Suppressing his deep feelings in the matter, he obeyed with outward composure. Even after the war O'Connor refused to proclaim that he had been right. On the contrary: 'Suffice to say,' he wrote, 'that I was sorry for our own selfish reasons that the Greek campaign had been decided on.'

He had therefore to rest content with the ten-weeks' campaign in which he had advanced over five hundred miles, destroyed an Italian army of ten divisions, taken 130,000 prisoners, 400 tanks, 1290 guns, and two major fortresses, all for the cost of 476 killed, 1225 wounded and 43 missing. It was a model campaign, opening with a set-piece battle of great originality and faultless execution, continuing with a relentless pursuit with improvised supply services, and ending with a daring strategic march and a battle of annihilation. Sidi Barrani, Bardia, Tobruk and Beda Fomm—their brilliance sparkles against the darkest setting of the war; hardly rivalled, never surpassed.

* * *

Now, on the morrow of Beda Fomm, the apparatus of O'Connor's victories, and their effects, vanished with the suddenness and completeness of a phantom at first light. It is a sad story, quickly told. Thirteenth Corps was disbanded and a static area command was set up—Cyrenaica Command. The personnel of 7th Armoured Division were scattered through Egypt on miscellaneous duties, thus destroying a well-knit and experienced team. O'Connor, still with stomach trouble, became General Officer Commanding, British Troops in Egypt. Standing on the defensive under General Neame, Cyrenaica Command, was an Australian Brigade Group and one of the armoured brigades of the green 2nd Armoured Division, partly armed with captured Italian tanks. Wavell saw no danger in this: British intelligence considered that the newly-arrived Rommel and his fledgeling Italo-German force could not be ready to advance before May, or at the very earliest, mid-April. This, by normal standards, was a sound estimate, for Hitler had in fact ordered Rommel only to prepare plans by April 20th for the reconquest of Cyrenaica, and not to move beyond Agedabia before the arrival of 15th Panzer Division. But Rommel, like O'Connor, was a man who considered the enemy's sound estimate of the possible as the main ingredient of his own success. He attacked on March 31st, 1941. He came on cautiously at first; then he found there was nothing very coherent or dangerous in front of him and began to hustle. Pushed about by Rommel in a hurry, the inexperienced Neame, his static command and his raw troops fell into confusion. Rommel drove forward in three columns: along the coast road through Benghazi, along O'Connor's route of Msus-Mechili, and farther south on Mechili-Derna. As the news reached Wavell, he sent O'Connor back to Libya to advise Neame. O'Connor arrived on April 3rd, On the 6th, in a car with Neame, he lost his way in the dark and ran into a German detachment behind our forces. Both were captured. This tragic accident robbed the British of the greatest of all their desert generals and inflicted on the eager, ardent little commander the gnawing frustration of the prison camp. The most fascinating of desert encounters—O'Connor versus Rommel—would never take place.

PART TWO

THE BLUNT BATTLEAXE

An Interlude

THE BLUNT BATTLEAXE

THE UNIQUE opportunity of winning final victory in North Africa had gone. The Prime Minister was to spend eighteen months attempting to retrieve it by egging on his commanders-in-chief in the Middle East to premature desert offensives. The cool reaction of Wavell and later Auchinleck to these demands lost both generals their reputations with him; to Churchill their closely reasoned replies proclaimed tiredness and defeatism. Nevertheless, they did, at the risk of their reputations, generally resist the Prime Minister's desire for premature battle—except in one case, Operation *Battleaxe*, in June 1941.

On April 6th, 1941, with O'Connor and Neame captured, the British forces in what had so recently been the quiet backwater of Cyrenaica were now headless as well as disjointed. Benghazi and the Jebel Achdar had fallen; Tobruk formed a precarious rock amid the rising German tide. On April 9th Wavell decided that the best way of checking Rommel's progress towards Egypt was to hold Tobruk. He ordered his temporary Director of Military Operations, Brigadier Dorman-Smith, to fly to headquarters, Cyrenaica Command, believed to be now in Tobruk, to hand over this order. On April 10th Dorman-Smith flew up in a Lysander. Tobruk was totally obscured by a dust storm but the pilot made a perfect landing, although he could not even see the airfield buildings. Dorman-Smith saw Brigadier John Harding and General Morshead (1st Australian Division) and handed over Wavell's written order. Both, it seemed to Dorman-Smith, were quite unconcerned and well in control of the situation. That afternoon Dorman-Smith, on his way back to Cairo, passed low over what looked like Afrika Korps troops on the Bardia road near to and east of Tobruk. It is therefore possible that there was no alternative but to hold out in the fortress. On April 13th and 14th Rommel, who perfectly well appreciated the effects on his advance of a major fortress on his lines of communication, tried to storm Tobruk and was beaten off by Morshead's Australians. He failed again on April 16th and 17th. Meanwhile his troops drove on towards Egypt;

the frontier was reached on April 28th, and Sollum, at the base of the escarpment, and Fort Capuzzo were captured. From April 30th to May 4th, 1941, Rommel made a carefully prepared assault on Tobruk, and again was beaten off. The Axis forces on the frontier, running out of fuel, could advance no farther, and the desert war was in equilibrium. The lull was broken only by an abortive British attack, well-named *Brevity*, under General 'Strafer' Gott, in the middle of May.

This quiet in Cyrenaica was very badly needed by Sir Archibald Wavell, the speed and intensity of whose strategic juggling was now working to a climax. On April 29th we had been thrown out of Greece with a loss of a fifth of our expeditionary force. On May 5th a pro-German revolution broke out in Iraq under Rashid Ali, who seized control of most of the country. On May 20th the Germans attacked Crete in the greatest airborne operation of the war. Meanwhile German infiltration into Vichy-French Syria had apparently become so dangerous—though post-war research shows it to have been exaggerated—that it had been decided to invade that country, and Wavell was deep in planning how so to do with smaller forces than the Vichy French. The invasion of Syria began on June 8th.

It was while Wavell was coping with this welter of lost battles and new dangers that Churchill pressed him to attack Rommel in the desert. Before the Greek adventure was even over, the Prime Minister's supreme object had become 'a victory in the Western Desert to destroy Rommel's army. . . . This would at least save our situation in Egypt from the wreck.' The telegrams began to flow. On May 12th he asked Wavell for the date when the 300 assorted tanks sent round the Cape, and only just arriving in Egypt, would be used in battle. He told Wavell that 'Our first object must be to gain a decisive military success in the Western Desert.' On the same day however Wavell telegraphed to the CIGS that it would be at least June 7th before an attacking force could be cobbled together, and 'I think it right to inform you that the measure of success which will attend this operation is in my opinion doubtful.' His reasons for doubt lay in the mechanical unreliability of British cruiser tanks, the vulnerability of the 'I' tanks to German anti-tank guns and a calculated inferiority of numbers. Three days later Wavell put off *Battleaxe* until June 15th, 1941. At home Churchill displayed, in his wife's words, 'terrible anxiety and even anger' at the delays.

Battleaxe began on June 15th, 1941. The operation had been planned by General Beresford-Peirse, commander 13th Corps, and Brigadier Harding—both of whom had been with General O'Connor at Sidi Barrani. The force included 25,000 men and about 180 mixed cruisers and 'I' tanks. Creagh commanded 7th Armoured Division, General Frank Messervy 4th Indian Division. Seventh Armoured Division was not the thoroughly-trained, highly-experienced and well-run-in machine of O'Con-

Map 6. Battleaxe
Phase A

nor's campaign; it had been stripped of its equipment when it was withdrawn from Cyrenaica and re-equipped piecemeal and in haste. Its personnel had been completely dispersed, and then reassembled. In General Creagh's words: 'The position in the Division as a whole showed a serious shortage of MT, a lack of trained personnel in the "I" Brigade and some disorganization in the matter of spares.' There were two armoured brigades in the division: 7th, equipped with A15 cruiser tanks straight off the ships—which were capable of twenty-six mph; and 4th, equipped with 'I' tanks borrowed from army tank battalions, which could only manage eight mph.

In planning the attack, little was known of enemy dispositions, partly owing to a shortage of cameras for air reconnaissance, British intelligence thought there were about seventy German tanks on the frontier supporting the powerful German fixed defences round the Halfaya Pass up the escarpment; and the rest of the German and Italian armour (130 tanks) eighty miles away at Tobruk. Creagh thought that the Germans on the frontier were much stronger—two complete regiments. This matter was important, for the whole British plan depended on a temporary local British superiority in the forward area leading to a German defeat in detail.

Beresford-Peirse, as his mock-attack on a desert camp before Sidi Barrani had shown, was completely orthodox and unimaginative. He had never commanded armour. The final plan for *Battleaxe* consisted of a frontal approach to the well-sited German frontier defences, with the main body of the armour and part of the infantry swinging left-handed towards Capuzzo. Halfaya Pass—according to Rommel 'the crucial position in this battle'—where the coast road climbed from the sea to the top of the escarpment, was to be assaulted frontally by two separate forces, one on the escarpment and one below. When the Axis defences had been carried by this infantry and 'I' tank attack, and 7th Armoured Division had defeated the forward German armour, the success was to have been exploited, in conjunction with the Tobruk garrison, as far as the line Derna-Mechili. The plan of *Battleaxe*, in its directness of approach and in its general disposition, resembles Montgomery's plan at El Agheila in December 1942. But the essential ingredients of success in frontal assault—overwhelming artillery and air support and superiority of numbers—were completely lacking in June 1941. The fearsome haste with which the operation had been prepared dimmed what little hope the equipment, the commander and the battle plan provided. It was only on May 29th that Creagh had received the operation instruction; the date of attack was given as not later than June 10th. It was put back to June 15th because Creagh pointed out the unreadiness of his division. As regards the chances of success, Creagh wrote later:

An answer was difficult since it depended on which side could reinforce the quicker—though we could concentrate on undoubted initial superiority, the Germans could reinforce with their second Armoured Division from Tobruk, only eighty miles distant, while as far as I knew we had no means of re-inforcement at all.

All was thus set for defeat. As if to emphasize the unprepared, amateurish quality of the whole enterprise, some of the new tanks had to calibrate their guns on the way to the startline. The frontal attack on the Halfaya Pass on June 15th broke down completely. The 22nd Guards Brigade and the 4th Armoured Brigade ('I' tanks) took Capuzzo but were stopped west of Sollum. The 4th Armoured Brigade ran into serious

Map 7. Battleaxe
Phase B

trouble. Beresford-Peirse had ordered the tanks to 'rally forward'—that is to leaguer in front of the infantry and guns. Brigadier (now General) Gatehouse, of 4th Armoured Brigade, thinking that the Corps Commander, out of his ignorance of tank warfare, had confused the well-understood tank order to 'forward rally'—leaguer *behind* the infantry and guns, ready to support them, but protected while essential repairs were made—questioned this order, which would expose the tanks to enemy gunfire or capture while immobile. Beresford-Peirse, in the sudden flaring anger of the man in command caught out in ignorance, had replied:

"You have your orders, Gatehouse—carry them out!"

75

In the course of *Battleaxe*, Gatehouse lost 99 out of 104 tanks—many of them only slightly damaged, but, because of Beresford-Peirse's order, irrecoverable.

It had been intended that when the infantry had taken the Halfaya defences, 4th Armoured Brigade should abandon its role of infantry co-operation and rejoin Creagh for the armoured battle. Creagh planned, in his own words, 'to lead the German tanks on to the "I" tanks (of 4th Armoured Brigade) situated in a hull-down position. But the plan never materialized as the "I" brigade could not be released from their role of infantry support.' On the second day of the battle, renewed frontal attack of Halfaya failed, owing, according to General Messervy, to the first appearance of the 88-mm gun in an anti-tank role, with the consequent surprise. Yet its use in this role had been noted in the War Office during the Spanish Civil War. Fourth Armoured Brigade therefore remained caught up in the infantry battle. The Germans had now had plenty of time to react: a large force of tanks forced Creagh's remaining armoured brigade and the support group back from Sidi Omar. On June 17th Rommel, all his armour up, attacked the left flank of 4th Armoured Brigade, while another force, in a manoeuvre typical of Rommel, felt more deeply for the British rear. The British command was in a real dilemma: Creagh could not effectively counter-attack unless Messervy released 4th Armoured Brigade, and this Messervy could not do without exposing his own flank. This day Wavell came up from Cairo to see how the battle was going, visited Beresford-Peirse, who was well behind the front and out of touch, and concluded that success depended on Creagh's tanks. He therefore flew out to 7th Armoured Division headquarters. Meanwhile, Messervy, who considered that his entire infantry division was seriously threatened by Rommel's operations against his flank and rear after Creagh's withdrawal the night before, ordered a retirement on his own responsibility. The armour had to conform. It was the ignominious end of *Battleaxe*'s swing; and far from being cleaved to the marrow, Rommel was hardly dented.

But in fact the battle was already lost on the first day when 13th Corps had failed to gain an immediate and decisive success over the portion of the Axis forces posted round Halfaya. In all respects *Battleaxe* is the reverse of Sidi Barrani; it deserves attention as an example of what happens to an army when there is no great commander to animate its limbs and supply its brain; when mediocre minds plod narrowly along a precedent. Yet all its shortcomings—in equipment, skill, training, leadership, strategy and tactics—are really traceable to one cause: the hurriedness of preparation.

Churchill was bitterly disappointed with the failure. But he did not see that *Battleaxe* had been hopelessly premature; and therefore its lesson was forever lost on him. By an amazing injustice, however, the failure of *Battleaxe* caused the Prime Minister to decide to relieve Wavell of his command. He blamed the collapse of O'Connor's conquests not on himself for his decision over Greece, but on Wavell. And so on June 21st, 1941, he telegraphed Wavell that he was to be relieved by Sir Claude Auchinleck, Commander-in-Chief in India.

There was no valid case for relieving Wavell. In his two years in the Middle East he had built a base and a command structure from nothing. He had conquered the whole of Italian East Africa, had captured 200,000 prisoners, including the Duke of Aosta, Viceroy of Ethiopia. Under his strategic aegis, O'Connor had taken Cyrenaica and another 200,000 prisoners. Between February and June 1941 he had conducted six major campaigns, never less than three at a time, and in May five at a time. No other British soldier of the day had the strategic grasp, the sagacity, the cool nerves and the immense powers of leadership to do all these things and steer a course free of total disaster. Certainly Wavell's career had been latterly clouded by defeat— Greece, Cyrenaica, Crete. Yet Greece and Cyrenaica, the most serious of the three, were the Prime Minister's responsibility.

Dismissal of Wavell, in fact if not in intention, made him a scapegoat for Churchill's own mistakes. Now the Commander-in-Chief was going, Churchill could recognize that he had asked too much of him, and could ease the responsibilities of his successor:

> It was only after the disasters had occurred in Cyrenaica, in Crete, and in the Desert that I realized how overloaded and under-sustained General Wavell's organization was. Wavell tried his best; but the handling machine at his disposal was too weak to enable him to cope with the vast mass of business which four of five simultaneous campaigns imposed upon him.

As first fruits of the Prime Minister's belated recognition, Oliver Lyttelton was appointed Minister of State in the Middle East to shoulder the political responsibilities, and General Haining was made Intendant-General to look after rearward administration and supply.

Auchinleck arrived in the Middle East on July 2nd and formally assumed the command on the 5th. Though Churchill alleged that Wavell was tired, Auchinleck did not receive this impression:

> Wavell showed no signs of tiredness at all. He was always the same. I think he was first class; in spite of his silences, he made a tremendous impact on the troops. I have a very great admiration for him . . . but he was given impossible tasks.

Sir Claude Auchinleck was an able and strong-minded officer always ready to attempt the bold and novel course. In northern Norway in June 1940, for example, after allied evacuation had been ordered, he had attacked and taken Narvik in order to deceive the Germans into thinking that the Allies meant to stay. The deception was successful; not a man was lost during the subsequent evacuation, although the Germans had command of the air. However, Auchinleck brought to his new post two shortcomings that were not his fault: he was an Indian soldier and he knew little about armoured warfare. The Indian Army and the British Army, though they served together in India, formed two professional worlds separated by mutual pride. The British service looked down on the Indians—'frontier soldiers'—and the Indians resented this because in their view India had the men and the space for proper training and preparation for war, while Britain had neither. Whatever the justice of these attitudes, the result was that Auchinleck, late professional head of the Indian service, knew very few of the officers of the British service and was not aware of the comparative reputations of its rising men. He was therefore handicapped in making a sound choice of subordinates from the British service. In his practical ignorance of armour, however, Auchinleck was joined by every senior officer of both the British and Indian armies.

Settling in amid the peacetime luxury of Cairo—Egypt was not at war—Auchinleck received, rather like Macbeth from the witches, a sombre warning from the Chief of the Imperial General Staff, General Dill, about Cabinet pressure for premature battle. It was Auchinleck's first acquaintance with that special anxiety which dwarfed all the other mammoth anxieties of the Middle East Command. Auchinleck was not as diplomatic a man as Wavell; his instinct was to oppose the Prime Minister's interference bluntly and resolutely. The battle between them was soon under way. Before Auchinleck had even formally taken up his command Churchill was asking him about a renewed offensive in the Western Desert. Auchinleck replied that there should certainly be another offensive—but with adequate forces, which he put at two, possibly three armoured divisions and a motor division, and after adequate time for thorough training. He decided that he could not be properly prepared for at least three months. But Churchill continued to question him about this and even about his placing of a certain division in Cyprus. Auchinleck determined to stop this interference at once. He told the Prime Minister apropos the Cyprus division:

> If you wish I can send you detailed reasons which actuated me and which appeared to me incontestable. I hope you will leave me complete discretion concerning dispositions of this kind.

He was equally austere on the topic of an early offensive:

> To launch an offensive with the inadequate means at present at our disposal is not, in my opinion, a justifiable operation of war . . . To gain results risks must be run, and I am ready to run them if they are reasonably justifiable.

Churchill did not like this and asked Auchinleck to come to England for consultation. In London, Auchinleck refused to budge from his decision not to launch an offensive—which was code-named *Crusader*—earlier than November 1st. Of Auchinleck's visit Churchill observed later: 'He [Auchinleck] certainly shook my military advisers with all the detailed argument he produced. *I was myself unconvinced*' (Author's italics). Auchinleck returned to Cairo resolved never to expose himself again to the ruthless personal pressure employed by the Prime Minister to get his way in default of rational exposition. Thus within a month Churchill was already dissatisfied with his new broom; like those in *The Sorcerer's Apprentice* it had a life of its own instead of passively obeying the Prime Ministerial directions. Auchinleck took back to Cairo agreement on November 1st, 1941, as D-Day for *Crusader*. He also took back concurrence with another crucial decision of his: General Alan Cunningham to command the battle, rather than General Wilson, who, being associated by the Prime Minister with O'Connor's successes, had been London's preference. It was the beginning of a tragedy.

PART THREE

THE PRICE OF DUTY

General Sir Alan Cunningham, GCMG, KCB, DSO, MC

O God of battles! steel my soldiers' hearts;
Possess them not with fear: take from them now
The sense of reckoning, if th' opposed numbers
Pluck their hearts from them!

SHAKESPEARE, *Henry V*, iv, I.

CHAPTER ONE

IN THE summer of 1941 General Alan Cunningham enjoyed far greater fame than O'Connor. On February 10th, 1941, he had advanced from Kenya into Italian Somaliland with four infantry brigade groups and fought a battle on the 22nd against six brigades of Italians and some local levies at Jelib, north of the Juba river. In Cunningham's words, 'The Italians in front of me broke'. In the next three days he covered two hundred miles to capture Mogadishu, capital of Italian Somaliland. There was still nothing in front of him. He decided to march the seven hundred and forty miles to Jijiga in Abyssinia, thus threatening the rear of the Italian forces opposing our invasion of Eritrea. Wavell consented, and after a halt of only three days Cunningham set out on March 17th. March 26th brought him to Harrar and March 29th to Diredawa. On April 6th Cunningham entered Addis Ababa, capital of Abyssinia. In eight weeks he seemed to have marched half across Africa; his speed and dash delighted the British public. His success was taken as complementary to O'Connor's victories in Libya. But whereas O'Connor had had only a few brief mentions by Press and Prime Minister, Cunningham now became well known.

Sir Claude Auchinleck, the new Commander-in-Chief in the Middle East, had also been deeply struck by this performance. He decided to appoint him to command the new army forming in the desert—Eighth Army.

> I asked for Cunningham [he wrote later] as I was impressed by his rapid and vigorous command in Abyssinia and his obvious leaning towards swift mobile action. I wanted to get away from the idea, which seemed to be prevalent, of clinging to the coastal strip, and to move freely and widely against the enemy's flank and communications.

In July 1941 Cunningham had rounded off his astonishing successes in East Africa by placing Haile Selassie, Lion of Judah and King of Kings, on that throne from which the Italians had driven him in 1936. Then he flew to Nairobi, where he received Auchinleck's letter of appointment. It marked his great professional opportunity; the letter made him, as he said later, 'extremely proud and hopeful'. Cunningham travelled by air down the Nile valley to Cairo, saw Auchinleck, a stern and formidable figure, and joined his as yet unformed army. He was now in the centre of the British Commonwealth's war. He commanded the only British land forces in contact with the enemy, and the best equipped. He enjoyed the support of both a strong air force under the command of Air Vice-Marshal Coningham, and of the Mediterranean Fleet, under the command of his own elder brother, Andrew, the great sailor. At his back in Egypt he had the resources of what had now become a great military base—a miniature war economy. As the implications of his new surroundings sank in, the greatness of his opportunity became more clear to him. So did the greatness of his problems and responsibilities:

I arrived in August and was told that there would be an offensive in November. I therefore had two months only in which to form and train an army. Some of the divisions were not there. Apart from 4th Indian Division and 7th Armoured Division, most of the troops were quite untrained. Time was so short. That was my trouble.

He made a good first impression on his new command; his personality lived up to his East African reputation as a commander. As Brigadier (now Major-General) Gatehouse put it, 'Cunningham was a magnificent-looking chap. I thought, this is the man. . . .' Like O'Connor, Cunningham was small, but unlike O'Connor, he gave an immediate impression of energy and decision. He was a handsome man, with a high-coloured, high-nosed face, and flashing blue eyes. He talked easily and well. He was charming, in a jovial way; but he was also, in General Godwin-Austen's words, 'somewhat choleric'—this touchiness of temper was noted—'he would weigh everything you told him, very carefully, and though he might "blow up" at first, would never do so after calm reflection.'

Cunningham never had much opportunity with Eighth Army for calm reflection.

The assembly of forces for *Crusader* were already under way when Cunningham arrived in the Desert. He had therefore the task of leaping into the saddle of a moving horse and taking control of it. It was far from easy for him. In the first place there was the desert itself, which he had never seen before, with its agorophobic vastness, and emptiness and sameness; an arena as naked and overwhelming as a bare stage to a green actor. To a newcomer, it was so much more than a strange kind of topography. It made a deep impression on Cunningham: 'The terrain was so different from that of East Africa, where we had to make use of tracks through bush country—the desert was all the same, and just nothing, with navigation as if you were at sea.' He had only two months in which to get so used to the desert that he could handle an army in its spaces with easy confidence.

Cunningham was also somewhat overwhelmed by the vast scale of military operations in Egypt. 'In East Africa, we had almost nothing at all—everything was improvised.' For supply he had depended on the Royal Navy's kindness in landing small stores along the Somaliland coast. His command had never been larger than four brigades of infantry. In Eighth Army he had two army corps, including three armoured brigades and more than two divisions of infantry. The size and complexity of command and staff organization were equally new to him. He was rather like the successful owner of a village shop suddenly put in charge of a London department store.

He faced a further difficulty. He knew little about armour and had never commanded it. This was true of all British officers of his rank. But whereas O'Connor had had six months of relative quiet in which to learn about it, Cunningham had two at a time of frantic preparation and rapid expansion. He was to control a swiftly moving armoured battle against Germans who had been practising tank warfare in the field since 1936; yet when he first reached the desert he so little understood radio-telephony that he is remembered fumbling helplessly with a radio-telephone, trying to use it like an ordinary telephone. Sureness of command depends on professional knowledge and experience. However great the qualities of leadership in a man, he cannot make use of them unless he is a master of the technical details of his profession—unless he knows his subordinates' jobs at least as well as they. Otherwise his orders, made in partial ignorance, must be given and received with underlying diffidence. In the desert, in command of a large tank army, Cunningham was the green newcomer, the outsider, in the presence of many officers to whom the desert was a familiar thing, a friend; who had seen Western Desert Force grow into Eighth Army; and whose military mind had grown with it. Slight though their knowledge might be, it was yet more than that of their army commander. Thus, though it was no fault of his, Cunningham found himself in a difficult and embarrassing position of learning and at the same time giving orders to his teachers. The result was a weakening of his authority and, personally, an added emotional strain. As General Godwin-Austen, who served under Cunningham both in East Africa and the Desert, wrote later: 'I felt he was not as happy in Egypt . . . he did not dominate conferences as he had in East Africa.'

As Brigadier General Staff, Cunningham had Galloway; and daily association with him could only bring home constantly to Cunningham his own inexperience. Galloway himself was a forceful personality, crisp in speech, impatient, and, like his Army Commander, inclined to short temper. Though he supplied some of the knowledge of desert warfare that Cunningham lacked, he was hardly the man to make Cunningham feel any more easy and comfortable in his headquarters. Yet Cunningham was fortunate in not having to assert himself over a larger number of senior desert veterans; Creagh had gone back to England after *Battleaxe* and Caunter was in India. By the end of October, Morshead too had left the Desert. The general lack in Eighth Army of familiarity both with the desert and with command in tank warfare was sharpened by a tragic loss. The corps commander designate of the armour, Pope, a tank officer with long experience, had been killed with some of his headquarters staff in an air crash, and was replaced by General Willoughby Norrie, a cavalryman who had been commanding 1st Armoured Division in England. The infantry corps was to be commanded by General Godwin-Austen, who, like Cunningham, was fresh from East Africa.

The formation of Eighth Army therefore marked in not altogether a happy sense a fresh start in the history of the British desert forces. To most observers in and out of the army, however, the summer and autumn of 1941 marked a fresh start of the right kind. Trucks, tanks and aircraft were flowing into Egypt in quantities that seemed prodigal to veterans of O'Connor's make-do-and-mend campaign or of the money-starved peacetime army. It was clear that at last British and American war production had caught the Germans up; and that at last the British too were putting in the field a superb modern tank army. Soon a British-made blitzkrieg would revenge on the Germans their easy successes of Norway, France and Greece. A new confidence—more, an elation—seized all ranks as they hastily learned to handle this magnificent and copious new equipment. There was a mood of eagerness and novelty never seen again in the desert, yet different from the earlier professional élan of Western Desert Force. A contemporary piece of public relations copy catches it well:

> Libya is full of our troops. It is grand. Everywhere there are eager faces: convoy commanders sitting up aloft their trucks like sunburned gods—their sun compasses pointing a black sliver of shadow towards the Boche; dispatch riders bumping incredibly through the sandy, rutted tracks; officers in groups, their maps on their knees, listening to their orders; lorried infantry, waiting, waiting, waiting; guns, their dust covers off, marching through the infantry and off to a flank in majestic indifference.

But when Cunningham set up his headquarters in the desert on September 9th, 1941, all these troops and equipment had still to be organized into an army and trained. At the same time Cunningham had to invent a plan for a battle that was scheduled to begin in eleven weeks' time. First came the organization of what was to be Eighth Army, strong in armour. There were no British precedents for the functional combination of tanks, guns and infantry in a panzer army. Instead there was either the orthodox 1914–18 concept of an army's organization which had been official doctrine until 1940, or there was the pre-war theory of thwarted and embittered British armoured experts such as Hobart. The first was plainly inapplicable in the desert, though in the next two years some devoted efforts were made to apply it; the second was strongly urged by British armoured officers in the desert. Before the war, Hobart, finding that the decisive importance of the tank was rejected by the cavalry- and infantry-dominated army, had in his turn rejected all other arms and proclaimed that tanks could and would win battles (and the war) by themselves alone. Tank would kill tank with its gun and then massacre the infantry and artillery. The decision lay therefore in the clash of tank battlefleets. Cunningham's organization of Eighth Army closely reflected these views:

I formed an infantry corps (13th) and an armoured corps (30th) with the idea of using the armour [on its own] as a corps.

Seventh Armoured Division was to consist of three armoured brigades (more than equal to the tank strength of both Rommel's panzer divisions together) and a Support Group of guns and lorried infantry. Thus though 30th Corps did not quite fulfil Hobart's ideal of a striking force composed of nothing but tanks, the tanks and infantry were kept segregated. The infantry corps (1st New Zealand Division, 4th Indian and 1st Guards Brigade) also contained tanks—225 'I' tanks, which, by that departmentalism of the British mind, had been designed only for co-operation with infantry and, though a powerful weapon, had not the speed for a battle of manoeuvre and could not take part in the decisive tank action.

Cunningham did have second thoughts about the separation of infantry corps from tank corps, and therefore the division of the offensive into two battles:

I sometimes wondered if it were the right formation. The alternative would have been mixed groups.

This was in fact the German system.

On September 2nd Auchinleck issued his first directive to Cunningham, on the planning of *Crusader*, by which he was to work out in detail two alternative plans: the first for a wide turning movement through Jalo and Jarabub and the second for a direct blow along the coast, with feints in the centre and on the left. Cunningham did not like the Jalo plan at all; in his view, 'it was hitting at nothing'. Nor did he accept Auchinleck's alternative. During September he worked out his own plan in consultation with Galloway. At midnight on September 26th the Eighth Army was officially born. Two days later Cunningham submitted to the Commander-in-Chief his plan for Eighth Army's first offensive. In its final form it was, in his words, 'entirely mine'. However, there are signs that others, especially Galloway, had an important share in it.

The theory of armoured warfare that dictated Cunningham's organization of the Army, also determined the plan of the offensive. It was based on seeking and winning a decisive tank battle. Tobruk, the relief of which had been in Auchinleck's plans both the object and the occasion of battle, was seen as only incidental. Thirtieth Corps under Willoughby Norrie would swing round the right of the German frontier defences that ran from Bardia through Sollum to Sidi Omar, and occupy the area about Gabr Saleh. Here Rommel was expected to meet Norrie's three armoured brigades with all his armour in the decisive encounter. Meanwhile 13th Corps would envelop the frontier defences, but would remain passive and inactive until the tank battle had been won. Only then, and in conjunction with 30th Corps, would it fight its own battle against the Axis infantry in the frontier defences and round Tobruk.

Cunningham himself saw that in this plan the distance between his tank and his infantry wings could be dangerous if Rommel struck with his armour through the gap on to the left flank of his infantry; it was a possibility that the infantry commanders appreciated very keenly. He therefore compromised the purity of his dispositions by reserving one of the three armoured brigades (4th) as a flank guard to 13th Corps. Eighth Army would thus advance on three divergent axes. However, once it was clear that Rommel was not threatening 13th Corps, 4th Armoured Brigade would be released for the decisive tank battle.

Auchinleck accepted his Army Commander's plan. On October 6th and 21st Cunningham explained his intentions to his corps commanders and heard their views. Norrie was strongly critical of the dispositions. He considered the use of 4th Armoured Brigade as a flank guard to 13th Corps was a dangerous dispersal of effort and intention when a decisive tank battle was being sought. In his view, the presence of 30th Corps itself was a sufficient flank guard. He could not see why Gabr Saleh had been chosen as the objective that our armour was to reach, halt at and await German reaction: it had no military significance to the Germans and there was no reason to suppose our occupation of it would force a decisive action. He suggested that the

British armour should drive straight for Tobruk; Rommel would then be forced to fight us.

Godwin-Austen insisted on specific flank protection. Though infantry divisions were equipped with anti-tank guns and field artillery, the infantry also believed the Hobartian doctrine that only tanks could fight tanks; and throughout the battle there were to be constant local pleas on the infantry's part for armoured escort. Cunningham listened to the arguments of each corps commander, and said that the use of 4th Armoured Brigade as a specific flank guard to 13th Corps would stand. But he emphasized that 'it was a temporary arrangement, until the direction of Rommel's main movement was known'. Cunningham also refused to substitute Tobruk for Gabr Saleh as an objective for 30th Corps: 'Gabr Saleh was chosen because Rommel was bound to pass it, north and south.' Our presence in this central position would force Rommel to concentrate in order to defend either his siege of Tobruk or the frontier defences; or even to split his forces up. Should he divide his command, Cunningham explained, we could divide ours. This was an odd and novel military principle. But the oddest aspect of the *Crusader* plan lay in the vagueness with which the results of it were visualized. We were to advance to Gabr Saleh—and then? Cunningham's answer seemed to hand the attacker's perquisite, the initiative, to the defender. For, he told Norrie and Godwin-Austen, by Rommel's reaction to our approach march 'we should know what he meant to do; by the first evening his intentions would be known, and a decision could be taken'.

Though the corps commanders issued their own orders for this plan on November 8th, and 7th Armoured Division held a war game rehearsal in Norrie's and Cunningham's presence on the 9th, Norrie remained unconvinced. He returned to the old point. The whole elaborate and rigid plan depended on the premise that the Germans would fight at Gabr Saleh. Why? We should drive, rather, straight for Sidi Rezegh, the key to Tobruk. Exposed to Norrie's able reasoning, Cunningham began himself to wonder. Perhaps Rommel would not oblige by fighting at Gabr Saleh. Yet this was the basic premise of the plan. It was far too late now to undo his and Galloway's month of work, invent a new conception and issue fresh orders. The present plan would have to serve; but his faith in it was shaken. He decided therefore 'to travel with Willoughby Norrie for the first few days. We did not know what Rommel's reaction would be.' If Rommel did not react at Gabr Saleh on the first day, he himself would decide whether the tanks should push on farther and in which direction. He was still worried about 13th Corps: 'I thought Rommel would attack the infantry.'

Thus after two months of exhausting work, and of the emotional strain of trying to establish personal ascendancy over more experienced men, in a strange and overaweing environment, Cunningham found himself on the eve of battle with a compromised plan that seemed quite likely to produce no desired results, but instead a wide choice of unpleasant possibilities. It was not a situation conducive to buoyant confidence or calm resolution. It was aggravated for Cunningham by a personal matter. He had always been a very heavy pipe smoker; but he had recently stopped smoking altogether, because he had slight trouble with one of his eyes, said by his occulist to be caused by smoking. But he concealed his anxieties; General Freyberg even thought him overconfident. In his eve-of-battle press conference his voice was hoarse, perhaps with strain, but his talk was resolute enough: "I am going to seek old Rommel out and destroy him and his armour."

Yet despite Cunningham's and Norrie's doubts, the army was throughout its ranks cock-a-hoop with optimism. It was the lavish quantity of new equipment that had convinced them that for the first time they were to meet the German on equal terms. In particular the tank commanders and their men had no doubt that when they had found Rommel's armour they would be able to destroy it. But to those with deeper perceptions and greater knowledge, the picture was not so full of sunshine. The Crusader tanks, for example, that looked so squatly powerful, had come off the ships with nuts and bolts hand-tight. Even when properly assembled they were, in Cunningham's words, 'extremely unsound mechanically'. Above all, this mechanized equipment which seemed so abundant to the uninformed was in truth dangerously scarce.

Auchinleck had told the Prime Minister that he would require for the battle fifty per cent reserves in strength: twenty-five per cent to cover those in workshops, and twenty-five per cent to replace battle casualties. On this requirement, which in view of our tanks' mechanical unreliability was only moderate, Churchill's comment was: 'Generals only enjoy such comforts in heaven.' Auchinleck had hoped to put in the field three armoured divisions; instead there was only 7th Armoured Division with its tank strength augmented to equal one and a half British armoured divisions (a British armoured division at this time contained six battalions of tanks, a German two). One of its three armoured brigades (22nd), which had been expected to arrive in Egypt between September 13th and 20th, actually completed its disembarkation only by October 14th. This forced Auchinleck to postpone D-Day for *Crusader* from November 1st to 15th; but even then this brigade had no more than four weeks in which to train and become desertworthy. It was composed of highly inexperienced territorials. The delay 'vexed' Churchill, who telegraphed to Auchinleck that 'It is impossible to explain to Parliament and the nation how it is our Middle East armies have had to stand for four and a half months without engaging the enemy.' But Auchinleck had to order a further delay of three days as, in his own words, 'the 1st South African Division, which was to play an important part in the initial operations, had not had enough time to train for a mobile role owing to the late arrival of the bulk of its vehicles'. Even with its total postponement of eighteen days, the offensive was a gamble. 'We were working to very close margins as regards equipment and training,' wrote Auchinleck later. 'The same conditions applied to the building up of supplies and the construction of pipelines and railways.' All this was hidden from the rank-and-file of the army and its war correspondents, who could see, but not count, the fresh troops and new equipment. But the Commander-in-Chief was thus far from wild optimism about Cunningham's chances: 'I thought the quality and quantity [of troops and equipment] was just adequate, and gave a reasonable chance of success.'

By the evening of November 15th, the forward concentration of Eighth Army was complete. There was a pause of silence and stillness between the frenzy of preparation and the agony of battle.

Cunningham now had actually with 7th Armoured Division 453 gun-armed cruiser tanks, of which 166 were American

'Honeys' or Stuarts (in 4th Armoured Brigade) and the rest Crusaders. The Stuarts, powered by a Pratt and Whitney radial aero-engine, were reliable, and faster, at 36 mph, than any other tank in Africa. But because of their aviation petrol, they had a tendency to flare up easily. They mounted a 37-mm high-velocity gun that had a slightly better power of penetration than the two-pounders of the Crusaders; their armour was thinner. *Battleaxe* had confirmed British confidence in the solid-shot two-pounder, which formed both their anti-tank artillery and their principal tank-gun. British intelligence calculated German tank strength at 272 tanks, of which 96 were Mark II light tanks and unfit for battle; and Italian strength as 138 gun-armed tanks. This gave Cunningham an apparent superiority for the decisive clash of more than four to three over the combined German and Italian battleworthy armour and more than two to one over the Germans alone. Therefore, in Cunningham's words, 'the armoured commanders were quite confident of themselves and their equipment before battle'.

That a British offensive was impending was well known to Rommel; it placed him in a dilemma, for he himself was preparing a grand assault on Tobruk with both his panzer divisions. It was to take place on or after November 20th, in the new moon. It was tempting to Auchinleck and Cunningham, who were aware of this impending attack, to delay *Crusader* until Rommel was fully embroiled in Tobruk, and then strike him in the back; but, in view of the Prime Minister's impatience, it was impossible. As knowledge of British preparation grew, Rommel decided not to commit 21st Panzer Division against Tobruk, but to place it south of Gambut. Even 15th Panzer was ordered to make its plans so that at twenty-four hours' notice it could break off and join 21st Panzer. As a forward defence against the British, Rommel had prepared the twenty-five-mile line from Bardia to Omar, thickly mined and garrisoned by the Italian Savona division and German anti-tank guns; and far to the south, the Italian Ariete armoured division well dug-in at Bir Gubi, on the flank of a British march towards Tobruk. These dispositions were known to Cunningham.

Throughout the night before the battle there was pelting rain, with thunder and brilliant lightning: nature imitating the art of war. Generals and privates waited for the morning with dry mouths and queasy stomachs. They were all aware of the crucial importance in the war of their offensive; it had been pointed home to them by a message from the Prime Minister:

> For the first time British and Empire troops will meet the Germans with an ample supply of equipment in modern weapons of all kinds [sic]. The battle itself will affect the whole course of the war. Now is the time to strike the hardest blow yet struck for final victory, home and freedom. The Desert Army may add a page to history which will rank with Blenheim and Waterloo. The eyes of all nations are upon you. All our hearts are with you. May God uphold the right!

But for Cunningham this revelation of how much now hung upon the coming battle constituted another tremendous anxiety at a moment when, after an exacting period both emotionally and physically, he was suffering from the first-night nerves common to all soldiers before a battle. The long night of November 17th, 1941 was a time of loneliness and self-awareness, a time to think with heated and beating brain: there were old questions—supposing the Germans did not fight at Gabr Saleh? Supposing Rommel attacked Godwin-Austen's infantry? There was the new realization of responsibility—responsibility for the precious first products of Allied war production, for the lives of hurriedly raised, hurriedly trained soldiers, for the British reputation before the eyes of the world, for bringing back a victory as great as Blenheim. The rain swept over trucks and tanks and bivouacs, beating in squalls against the steel sides of Cunningham's caravan. The thunder reverberated, a constant reminder of battle. In the desert there was no refuge, not even in sleep.

CHAPTER TWO

CUNNINGHAM, it now seems clear, was not fit enough to bear the weight of commanding a major battle. Since February he had been under pressure almost without a pause. This pressure had culminated in ten weeks of overwork and emotional strain. His physical strength, his nerves and his capacity for clear judgment and decision had all suffered. On the eve of *Crusader* he seems to have already reached that stage of mental and physical fatigue when even ordinary tasks and decisions loom immense and daunting to a man. Yet Cunningham would never admit it, not even to himself; his duty lay in leading Eighth Army into battle, as it was his brother's duty to lead the Fleet; he could not go sick on the eve of the action. While the army marched into Libya, therefore, Cunningham fought a private battle against the effects of overstrain.

On the morning of November 18th, 1941, he rose early and, while it was still pitch dark, drove away from his own head-quarters to join Willoughby Norrie. It was an unfortunate journey over ground made miry by the heavy rain: the Army Commander's car got stuck in the mud and Cunningham had to wait while it was pulled clear. He joined Norrie an hour later at Alam Abu Ngeira, thirty miles on the Egyptian side of the frontier wire. Daylight illuminated a depressing waste of gravel and scrub under a low sky of racing storm clouds. At six o'clock Eighth Army began to roll towards the German rear in an enormous column of transport led by the armour. *Crusader* had begun.

For the lower ranks of the army there were plenty of tasks, plenty of orders to give in the course of the long mechanized advance of 100,000 men. For Norrie and Godwin-Austen— above all, for Cunningham—there was nothing to do but look at the unchanging waste, the crawling tanks and the bumping trucks. There was a halt in the middle of the morning while the armoured brigades refuelled. The armoured cars reported a screen of German armoured cars and tanks in front of them covering the Trigh el Abd. The British armour rolled on again and by last light the German cars had withdrawn, leaving Cunningham in possession of his objective of Gabr Saleh and the surrounding desert. The British had apparently achieved complete surprise. At six o'clock in the evening orders for the next day were issued: to make secure the prearranged battle positions and push out strong reconnaissance forces towards Bir Gubi and the Trigh Capuzzo. These colourless orders reflected Cunningham's and Norrie's puzzlement; the entire Eighth Army had marched all day into Rommel's rear without causing noticeable reaction on his part. There had been no hardening resistance, and no local counter-attacks. So far as British information went, there had been no regrouping of the German panzer divisions in preparation for a major counter-stroke.

Though this was only the first day, its events seemed to bear out Norrie's prediction that occupation of Gabr Saleh would not force Rommel to accept battle. The silence and stillness in the German part of the desert induced a sense of unease. The troops were not bothered by such things, however: leaguers of vehicles pointing in every direction peopled the desert with villages, in which men strolled about, cooked on little flaring petrol fires, or even played football amid the camel thorn.

There was a reason for the failure of the Axis forces to regroup to face the British advance. The commander of *Panzergruppe Afrika* still had no idea that a major British offensive was rolling up from the south. His armoured cars had reported a reconnaissance in force, and Rommel was far too interested in his own impending attacks on Tobruk to worry about reconnaissance troops. General Cruewell, commanding the Afrika Korps, pressed him to send a battle group south towards Gabr Saleh: Rommel, irritated and reluctant, agreed, but otherwise reserved his forces for Tobruk.

In the morning, (November 19th) at 30th Corps HQ there was still no news of German reaction upon which Cunningham could base tactical decisions; instead there was an uncanny absence of signs of movement that suggested the stalking wild animal. Norrie seemed finally to have been proved right about Gabr Saleh; and there was nothing else to do but push on deeper into Rommel's rear. Yet with the German armour's situation and intentions a mystery despite air reconnaissance, Cunningham did not feel he could release 4th Armoured Brigade—as he had hoped to do by now—from its special role as left flank guard to 13th Corps. Therefore the further north-westwards advance of 30th Corps was limited to two of its three armoured brigades. But now, as with Hougoumont at Waterloo, a local action was to draw in a disproportionate strength of the attacking forces; a dispersal of armour that wrecked Cunningham's new plan.

About eleven in the morning of November 19th tanks of 22nd Armoured Brigade found Italian tanks near Bir Gubi on the left flank of the British advance. It was known that Bir Gubi was occupied by Ariete Division. Gradually a battle flared up between Ariete and 22nd Armoured Brigade, a battle which moved to Gubi itself, where the Italians were strongly posted with anti-tank guns. General Gott, commanding 7th Armoured Division, seemed to think this action offered an opportunity for the comparatively easy destruction of an Italian

Map 8. The 'Crusader' Battle
Phase A, November 1941

armoured division and the securing of Bir Gubi, on our flank, as a defended locality to be held by 1st South African Division.

With Gott's approval, the whole 22nd Armoured Brigade was now drawn into this action, and away from the northward advance ordered by Cunningham. It was the beginning of a process of disintegration in the control of the British offensive. The first that Norrie and Cunningham heard of the battle at Bir Gubi was in the evening, when news came in that the green territorial troops of 22nd Armoured Brigade, only a month in

Egypt, had charged home on the dug-in Italians as if on a fox, and had been beaten off with the loss of fifty-two tanks. The principal northward advance had thus been made by 7th Armoured Brigade alone, a third of the British strength; this brigade now occupied the Sidi Rezegh area, with Axis forces on every side but the south. By nightfall on November 19th, therefore, one of the British armoured brigades had been defeated with heavy losses, and one was in a dangerously exposed situation far out of supporting distance of the rest of the army. Only 4th Armoured Brigade remained in the old battle positions at Gabr Saleh.

Here it was attacked, just as Cunningham might have hoped, by the battle group that Cruewell had prised out of Rommel. But of course the Germans now encountered only a single brigade instead of three; however, they withdrew eastwards after an indecisive action, 4th Armoured Brigade following them. After forty-eight hours, Cunningham had still not brought the main body of the German armour to battle. Intelligence reports were scanty and gave no real lead. It remained a most uneasy situation, aggravated for Cunningham by his inability to act, and by the long blank hours of waiting at Norrie's headquarters. In his state of health, an immediate general action might have had a better effect than this agonizing dalliance.

By nightfall on November 19th Cunningham desperately wanted Rommel to declare his main direction of attack. Seventh Armoured Division's orders for the 20th (whether ultimately derived from Cunningham, Norrie or the divisional commander himself) therefore reflect a commander groping for a principle of action: 4th Armoured Brigade to return to its original battle positions, still to cover the left flank of 13th Corps and the right of 30th, 7th Armoured Brigade merely to make reconnaissance to the north, 22nd Armoured Brigade not to join 7th until Bir Gubi had been captured by the South Africans, Support Group to join 7th Armoured Brigade.

Rommel however had now in fact begun to react—and exactly as intended in the original *Crusader* plan. Cruewell was ordered to use both panzer divisions 'to destroy the enemy battlegroups in the Bardia–Tobruk–Sidi-Omar area before they can offer any serious threat to Tobruk.'

That night (November 19th/20th) a wireless breakdown in Eighth Army added to the general uncertainty: Cunningham could receive no news from his own headquarters, and could transmit no orders to it. He was like a man already blind who felt himself going deaf and dumb. He decided to fly back to his HQ first thing in the morning.

When he left Norrie he had still not been able to give him free control of 4th Armoured Brigade, his principal reason for travelling with him at all. Galloway greeted Cunningham with a letter setting out what was known at Eighth Army Headquarters: nothing, except that air reconnaissance had seen much German transport heading westwards. Again this obscurity and negativeness instead of the violent armoured shock that the British had visualized and for which they had nerved themselves. Cunningham spent another cold, grey morning in an operations caravan worrying and waiting; for a change it was in his own headquarters at Maddalena and with Galloway's brisk company instead of Norrie's.

Then at last events began to move with unpleasant speed—as Cruewell, with two panzer divisions at his back, carried out Rommel's orders of the previous night. He had problems similar to those of Cunningham; his knowledge of British dispositions was confused and incomplete, and he could not decide which of Cunningham's scattered armoured brigades constituted the main British attack. All morning Cruewell ranged up and down the Trigh Capuzzo looking for British armour that had never been there, until 21st Panzer ran out of fuel. He then analysed his information again and concluded that the British main thrust was aimed at relieving Tobruk. Cruewell could now choose between attacking the British troops nearest Tobruk— 7th Armoured Brigade at Sidi Rezegh—or smashing the forces that covered the hub of the British wheel into Libya and protected its dumps and supply lines.

In the afternoon of the 20th, Cruewell, with 15th Panzer Division, advanced southwards towards 4th Armoured Brigade, which was now in the strength of 123 Stuarts. In the operations caravan at Eighth Army headquarters at Maddalena, Cunningham watched Cruewell move down the battle-map. Here at last, after two and a half days, was German acceptance of battle at Gabr Saleh. But instead of relief, the news caused consternation. There were no longer three armoured brigades grouped there in readiness for a major action, but a single brigade fettered by its obligations to the infantry of 13th Corps. If it were beaten, 13th Corps would be massacred by 15th Panzer Division. Time, of which there had recently seemed such a surplus, now became desperately short.

Cunningham ordered Norrie to send 22nd Armoured Brigade from Bir Gubi east to Gabr Saleh to join 4th Armoured Brigade. It was a belated attempt to rebuild his lost concentration; was it soon enough? From twelve noon until about three in the afternoon, Cunningham lived in suspense. Godwin-Austen, of 13th Corps, suggested that he should support 4th Armoured Brigade with the New Zealand Division and its heavy 'I' tanks. Cunningham turned this down: 30th Corps alone was the instrument of decision. It was an example of the rigidity and departmentalism of the British mind. Cunningham's hopes and worries remained on the race between 15th Panzer and 22nd Armoured Brigade. Cruewell and 15th Panzer got there first. Throughout the late afternoon Gatehouse and his brigade of light Stuarts fought a savage battle against the heavier German armour. Twenty-second Armoured Brigade was now ordered to drive into the German right flank. Not until half past six did part of this brigade get into action; Gatehouse had already been forced away to the south. As night fell the fighting died, with the Germans, as was their custom, camping on the battlefield, and the British, as was theirs, withdrawing from it.

For Cunningham, however, the outcome of November 20th had been immensely heartening. Cruewell had not destroyed the 4th Armoured Brigade, nor made any dangerous advance towards Eighth Army's communications: he was believed to have lost thirty-four tanks. On the other hand, Cunningham now had two of his armoured brigades concentrated near Gabr Saleh. He believed that the decisive tank action had taken place, and that he had won it. After the worry and disappointment of the first two days of the offensive, a wave of success buoyed him up. His orders for November 21st verged on a general chase: 4th and 22nd Armoured Brigades to attack the German armour as soon as possible after first light, and pursue it relentlessly if it withdrew, the Tobruk garrison to break out through El Duda to make a junction with 7th Armoured Brigade at Sidi Rezegh, 5th South African Brigade to advance in support to Sidi Rezegh.

On the German side, the battle was still being conducted by Cruewell, because Rommel was unwilling to admit that his own attack on Tobruk was defunct, and refused to turn his thoughts to the unwelcome reality of a major British offensive. Cruewell suggested that 21st Panzer (now refuelled) should join 15th Panzer by a night march, and that both should move north and west—along the original British axis of advance—to take 7th Armoured Brigade in the rear. This movement exactly dovetailed into Cunningham's intentions for November 21st. Soon after first light both Panzer divisions set off to destroy 7th Armoured Brigade, pursued only distantly by 4th and 22nd Armoured Brigades, who jubilantly reported that the German armour was in full retreat. Norrie reported this tremendous news to Cunningham at a quarter to nine in the morning. Here was a moment of great relief and pleasure. Cunningham had gained his victory after all. He rang up Godwin-Austen of 13th Corps and told him that he could advance if and when he wished. Godwin-Austen immediately ordered the New Zealand Division with 200 'I' tanks to advance along the Trigh Capuzzo towards Sidi Rezegh and Tobruk and the 4th Indian Division to take the fortified Axis positions round Sidi and Libyan Omar. The whole of the Eighth Army was set in motion after the 'beaten' enemy.

In Cairo, by a conspiracy of foolishness between press and public relations, the 'victory' was announced to the world with vulgar flamboyance. Since the beginning of the offensive the Press had destroyed more German tanks than Rommel had ever possessed—three times heavier losses than those of Cunningham. There were stories of 40,000 men being encircled south of Tobruk.

The resolution of the battle into clear terms, and favourable ones, displayed Cunningham as he had been in East Africa: energetic, thrusting and impatient. When he heard from Norrie that 30th Corps could do nothing to help the sortie of the Tobruk garrison until the next day, and that none of the South Africans had yet reached the Sidi Rezegh area, he sharply pointed out the necessity for speed; that if the Tobruk sortie reached Duda, a junction with it 'would appear to involve only a short night march'. Cunningham went further: if a firm junction was not made with the Tobruk garrison he would 'certainly require to see the Corps Commander tomorrow'. He also spurred on his other corps by telling Godwin-Austen's Brigadier General Staff, Harding, that 13th Corps could advance according to their initiative 'and need not refer unnecessarily to the Army Commander. At the same time, the Commander 13th Corps was not to take unnecessary risks.'

Tobruk remained all day his chief anxiety. In the evening he ordered Godwin-Austen to send the New Zealanders westwards as fast as possible.

The illusion of victory became hour by hour more lovely. That night a liaison officer from GHQ arrived at Cunningham's headquarters with news that 170 German tanks had been hit during the day, and that the German armour, in fragments, was running westwards with the British armour striving to cut it off. Four hours later Cunningham read an Eighth Army situation report which said that sixty German tanks were surrounded at Sidi Rezegh.

In fact the major events of the day had been that Rommel had personally stopped the sortie of the Tobruk garrison with a scratch force, and that 7th Armoured Brigade at Sidi Rezegh, attacked by two panzer divisions, had been reduced to twenty-eight tanks.

Next day, November 22nd, 1941, was the fulcrum of a swift transformation scene that substituted disaster for victory. A dispersed, murderous and uncontrolled battle smouldered round Sidi Rezegh all day long, as Rommel (now in active command) and his two panzer divisions strove to clinch the destruction of 7th Armoured Brigade by forcing it and the guns and infantry of the Support Group off the Sidi Rezegh aerodrome. The British clung stubbornly to this naked and flattened piece of desert. It was the sort of battle that suited the national temperament. 'Half-naked, weary, dust-begrimed gunners of all regiments,' said a Royal Artillery account, 'repulsed attack after attack. Shelled, battered from the air, and machine-gunned by infantry, they steadily fought on.' The gunners of the Support Group earned a German tribute: 'The British artillery was the best trained and best commanded element in the British army, and the quality of these gunners was fully proved in the desperate fighting round Sidi Rezegh . . .'

Meanwhile the British Armour was coming up to the rescue. But instead of both 4th and 22nd Armoured Brigades being launched together in a properly conceived attack, they joined the fighting one an hour and a quarter after the other, and with no more coherent purpose than to shoot it out with any German tanks they might see through the smoke and the dust. There was great confusion. Twenty-second Armoured Brigade lost heavily to German anti-tank guns before 4th Armoured Brigade came up. As the light faded, the British were forced backwards to the south, and Sidi Rezegh aerodrome fell to Rommel. According to the Royal Artillery Commemoration Book:

> The final scene was awe-inspiring enough. In the light of burning vehicles and dumps our guns slipped out of action, leaving the field to a relentlessly advancing enemy, who loomed in large, fantastic shapes out of the shadows into the glare of bursting shells.

Only forty-five tanks remained to 22nd Armoured Brigade out of the seventy-nine with which they had begun the action. Gatehouse's 4th Armoured Brigade with a hundred Stuarts was the only large British tank force left. Now, in the bad luck of war, its headquarters was overrun by 15th Panzer Division as it plunged through the confusion and darkness.

In the flaring light of burning tanks, the Germans captured most of the headquarters personnel and the wireless links; they had smashed the brain of the brigade and for twenty-four hours its hundred tanks were out of the battle. The result was to be disastrous. Gatehouse, on his way back from a conference, escaped. None of this was yet known to Cunningham at Eighth Army Headquarters.

Rommel judged that the fighting of November 22nd was a German victory, and that he now held the initiative. With an accuracy that contrasted with the fantasy of British estimates of German tank losses, he calculated that he had destroyed 207 British tanks. He proposed to clinch his success by attacking the remnants of the British armour on November 23rd concentrically.

At Maddalena Cunningham remained cut off from the facts of the forward battle by the delays and inaccuracies of situation reports. In particular he did not know that General Gott (7th Armoured Division), working desperately to sort out the wreckage of the armour, had now decided that 'with present forces, no further advance appeared possible without assistance', and had gone over to the defensive. On the contrary, Cunningham's thoughts were busy on the regrouping of his army for the continued pursuit and destruction of the beaten enemy. At half past six in the morning of November 23rd, he took off in his personal aircraft to visit Godwin-Austen (13th Corps). It was 'a bright, sunny morning. White racing clouds made moving islands of shadow on the desert surface.' He explained to Godwin-Austen his new grouping: 13th Corps now to include the South Africans and the Tobruk garrison and to be responsible for operations to relieve that fortress, 30th Corps to protect the left flank of 13th Corps and the army's communications, and to destroy the enemy's armour.

Cunningham then flew back to Maddalena, having, as he thought, completed his arrangements for the consummation of victory. It was turning colder and showery. Within a few moments of re-entering his headquarters he learned that far from consummating a victory, he was in the midst of a disaster.

Reports of yesterday's defeats had at last reached Eighth Army: Cunningham read for himself that 7th Armoured Brigade, which had begun the battle with 129 tanks, had not a single runner, that 22nd Armoured Brigade (originally 158 tanks) had only thirty, and that nothing was known of 4th Armoured Brigade, whose headquarters had been destroyed. He had in fact lost the decisive armoured battle that was the basis of the *Crusader* plan.

In Cunningham's own words:

the main thing was to destroy Rommel's armour. One entered the battle with that object and then found one hadn't the means. One night the tank state showed forty-four runners.

However, there was in this crisis of November 23rd, 1941, a much more profound meaning than the miscarriage of a particular battle. The unfortunate Cunningham had picked up the bill for twenty years of military decadence.

It is generally true that an army is an extension of society; military disaster is often national decline exposed by the violence of a battle. Examples are Imperial Russia and Austria–Hungary in the First World War, France in the Second. Any army thus reflects in sharp focus the social structure, the state of technological progress and the creative vigour of a society. The opposing armies at Crécy illustrate this general rule. However, the British army in the Second World War is an exception, perhaps the only one in history. Although the army of a twentieth-century social democracy and a first-class industrial power, it was nevertheless spiritually a peasant levy led by the gentry and aristocracy. Its habits of mind and work, its mental and emotional life were those of the social order based on birth and lands that had passed from supremacy in the national life by the end of the nineteenth century. Few poor men of great ability chose the army as a rewarding outlet for their talents—pay for all ranks was less than an income. Purchase had died with Cardwell, but its soul went marching on. Men of great ability did of course make their careers in the army, but because it was a tradition of their caste and because they enjoyed private means. Therefore in a true sense most regular officers of the British Army were amateurs as well as gentlemen. Born into the gentry or the aristocracy, spending their lives in the last sanctuary of privilege in Europe, their mental characteristics and morality were not surprisingly very different from those of the managers, the scientists and technicians of industry. Cleverness, push, ruthlessness, self-interest and ambition were considerably less prized than modesty, good manners, courage, a sense of duty, chivalry and a certain affectation of easy-going non-professionalism. There was therefore in the British professional soldier little identification with the world of twentieth-century technocracy and little sympathy. They rightly judged it sordid and barbarous. But this did not help them prepare for its wars.

Within the army's own structure this nineteenth or even eighteenth-century mentality was reflected by the veneration for the regiment, which had long ceased to be a functional unit on the battlefield, and by the amazing prestige and pre-eminence of the cavalry. The regimental system was of course limited to the infantry and the cavalry. The artillery, engineers, supply and technical services formed single arms of the service in much the same way as cavalry and infantry in the American, Russian and German armies. These branches were, significantly, quite ready for and equal to their task in modern war. Functional reality had by 1941 almost disappeared from the regiment: the Scottish regiments were full of English, West Country regiments salted with Yorkshiremen, the cavalry regiments amalgamated in pairs. To allow training and reinforcement with the scale and flexibility necessary in modern war while retaining the eighteenth-century regiment, elaborate compromises had to be worked out. Yet for the regular British soldier—officer or private—the regiment was a tremendous emotional reality, a focus for all his military pride and loyalty. Memories of ancient battles and the practice of peculiar customs kept alive this heartfelt parochialism. As a result the real organizations of a modern army—the division, the branches of the service, the army itself—were denied the corporate spirit that they so badly needed to give them cohesion.

In this spiritually eighteenth-century army, the cavalry, as the arm of fashion and aristocracy, was the haughty queen. Over its stiff-necked elegance and pride the heroes of the past —Uxbridge, Lucan, Cardigan and Haig—nodded approval; approval of a military code based not on technical competence, but on high birth, an esoteric way of life, and veneration for the horse. To these lancers and dragoons and hussars —each regiment of each species jealously guarding its separatist pride—was to be given the oily, smelly, clanking product of a technical society: the tank. And with it they were to be invited to fight a homogeneous German panzer arm composed of twentieth-century men of all social classes, who were more interested in sprockets than spurs.

The result between 1918 and 1939 of the natural conservatism of the British officer, of the preservation of the regiment and of the pre-eminence of the cavalry, was the stultification of development of an army in Britain as modern in equipment and thought as the Royal Air Force. This stultification was sharpened by the use of the British army in peacetime as an imperial gendarmerie. Development of tanks and of a theory of tank warfare suffered particularly.

After the First World War, few officers thought there would

be another major war; the concept of tank warfare, which by 1918 had progressed as far as deep breakthroughs, seem irrelevant. One or two radical theorists such as Liddell Hart and Fuller proclaimed that the future army should be based on the tank as the decisive weapon and consequently completely mechanized. But this was so costly a conception, and the army was so needed battalion by battalion for police duties in far-flung colonies, that such a revolutionary and comprehensive reorganization seemed out of the question to conservative, easy-going minds. In the late 1920s the army did progress as far as experimenting with a mobile, semi-armoured force on Salisbury Plain, that hearthrug of a manoeuvre ground. Early in 1930 a similar formation was devised for the infantry: 6th (Experimental) Infantry Brigade at Blackdown, with Archibald Wavell as Brigadier and Dorman-Smith as Brigade Major.

Throughout the year 1935, when the German army was in bud and about to bloom, the future of the British army was at hazard. Army and Royal Air Force fought a bitter battle for the limited amount of money allotted for defence, the RAF arguing *au fond* that an army was no longer necessary; the overseas defence of Britain could be entrusted to an Independent Bomber Force with a small fighter component. Far from being reorganized and mechanized, the army, in the view of the RAF, could be reduced to a gendarmerie without tanks or medium artillery. The Air Force, at a time when the Germans were developing the close-support dive-bomber, also refused to develop any specialized army co-operation aircraft, except the stringbag Lysander. While this battle for the army's survival was going on, the army's own radicals, several ranks from the top, were trying to get revolutionary changes past the World War One veterans in high places. Dorman-Smith, whose reputation for original military thinking was extremely high, was now on the staff of a section of the War Office, SD2, that was charged with experimentation and the preparation of the army for modern war; it also prepared the army estimates. SD2 set about producing plans for complete mechanization of the army along the lines of the experimental brigades—for the elimination of the horse, which at that time not only formed the instrument of reconnaissance and of exploitation of breakthroughs, but also pulled guns and transport. But Dorman-Smith and his colleagues balked at destroying the cavalry regiment, although this was the logical consequence of abolishing the horse. Even slavering revolutionaries must have some sense of the possible, and the cavalry was too well protected by its influence in high military and political circles to give the smallest hope that a plan for its destruction would ever mature. There was also the emotional pull, the veneration that ancient regiments exercised even over British military radicals. The problem was solved by sliding easily along a fallacious analogy. A modern armoured corps performed the same function as an antique cavalry corps—reconnaissance, shock action, mobile exploitation. The existing cavalry had been trained in these roles. Therefore it was obvious that the cavalry should be converted to armour; objections would be loud about the loss of the horses, but not so loud as about the loss of the regiments.

There had existed since the First World War the Royal Tank Corps. Although larger than a cavalry regiment (eight battalions instead of one), it was far short of being an arm of the service like the artillery—or the cavalry. It therefore had no influence, and its officers no high seniority in the army. It contained of course all those who really believed in the future of armour, and who understood and loved mechanical things. The alternative in the 1930s to armour-plating the cavalry lay in creating a mass, technical panzer arm, like that of the Wehrmacht and analogous to the Royal Artillery, and based on the nucleus of the Royal Tank Corps. Recruited freely from all classes of an industrial country, mentally free from irrelevant traditions, the Royal Tank Corps had in fact worked out by 1934 the tactics, strategy and mechanical techniques of armoured warfare with revolutionary thoroughness. These were borrowed by Guderian for his panzer arm. The Royal Tank Corps could, like that arm, have become a new mass *corps d'élite* completely of the twentieth century, based on a central system of depots and reinforcements and with the division as a focus of loyalty. In the German army the creation of such a corps was not only possible, it became the instrument of victory; in the British, it had no more chance than universal suffrage in 1815. For two effects of the class structure of the British army were that in fact the cavalry officer did display greater powers of leadership than the tank officer, and also that British soldiers preferred to be commanded by 'gentlemen' than by able men of their own class.

Nevertheless, by 1936 the mechanization of the army and the conversion of the cavalry to armour had been accepted; it was some mercy. The mentality of the army's senior and rising officers could not be similarly converted by decree to suit mobile armoured warfare. The stiff, positional war of the Western Front between 1914 and 1918 was the only modifying influence in a world of polo, the social round, and the close life of the regiment. Though the 1936 Field Service Regulations, written by Wavell, emphasized mechanized mobility, the current Infantry Training Regulations had been written by Montgomery before modernization.

Meanwhile the neglect of the tank and the low seniority in the army of the tank officers, however able, had a pernicious reaction within the Royal Tank Regiment. Like a persecuted minority sect, it became bitterly extremist. Tank men now began to proclaim that the tank alone would decide the battles of the future; infantry and artillery were useless encumbrances to be mopped up by the victors of a tank-to-tank battle. For them—particularly for their plain-spoken and prickly leader, General Hobart—an armoured division consisted entirely of tanks, and the battle was decided by the guns of the tanks.

Thus as the British armoured forces began to take shape, there had been no such fundamental thinking and no such fundamental agreement about their role and organization as Guderian had fostered in Germany; on the contrary there was the uneasy marriage of the 'tank-alone' school of the Royal Tank Corps, and the 'armour-is-cavalry' school of the cavalry. To this want of intellectual preparedness was added want of operational experience owing to the lateness of British re-armament. The Germans tried out and modified their conceptions of armoured warfare in the Spanish Civil War in 1936–39. They attempted their first major mechanized advance in the peaceful march to Vienna in 1938; it was a muddle that taught them much. *Crusader* was the first British operation of this size. The Germans refined their technique in the advance into Czechoslovakia in 1939, and perfected it in the brilliant campaigns of Poland and France.

Meanwhile, in their half-baked British way, the British were still cobbling together with empiricism and pragmatism a panzer arm. Only in 1940 was the Cavalry Division in Palestine converted (with reluctant emotions) to armour; its units fought with O'Connor and in *Crusader*. The War Office, fearful of 'tanks-alone' extremism, gave the command of 7th Armoured Division to Creagh, a cavalryman, instead of Hobart. The holy odour of the horse clung to the British armour. In *Crusader*, the GOC 7th Armoured Division commanded from his 'charger' (a tank or armoured car); supply trucks went to a rendezvous on the order 'Lead horses'. Only much later in the war did the cavalry become armoured in mind as well as fact: and then the class tradition of leadership of the cavalry officer vindicated itself.

O'Connor's victories did not really test the armour; *Battleaxe* was the first encounter with the veteran German panzer troops. *Battleaxe* and the five months that followed offered the British a belated opportunity to think hard and deep about such basic matters as the organization and tactics of an armoured division, and to evolve a coherent theory. The lessons of *Battleaxe* were apparently noted. In a lecture on the battle, General Creagh said: 'When on the defensive his [the German] policy was to draw our tanks on to his guns, and then to counter-attack with tanks.' Middle East Headquarters issued *Notes on Enemy Tactics and Training*, showing that the Germans used mobile artillery as an offensive weapon; that they attacked by pushing forward a mixed force and then fighting defensively on the ground occupied. In September, 1941, a Training Memorandum was issued on the conduct of the next battle; it suggested tactics very like the German. But the officers and men of the British armoured brigades were as generally untouched by these warnings as road-hogs by road safety propaganda. A coherent system of tactics and training was neither evolved nor practised. An exception however lay in 4th Armoured Brigade, trained and led in the German style by Brigadier A. H. Gatehouse—a tank officer. General Gott, General Officer Commanding 7th Armoured Division in *Crusader* (by supreme British inconsequence, a light-infantry-man) himself summed up the state of British theory of armour on the eve of the battle, when he told his men: "This will be a tank commander's battle. No tank-commander will go far wrong if he places his gun within hitting range of an enemy."

The Germans, on the other hand, had spent the five months since *Crusader* adapting their excellent and proven general system of armoured warfare to the particular circumstances of the desert. In their thorough, serious, clever German way, they not only perfected their operational handling and such battlefield services as tank-recovery, they also practised them over and over again on the ground. As a result, in the words of a German staff officer:

> A German panzer division was a highly flexible formation of all arms, which always relied on artillery in attack or defence. In contrast the British regarded the anti-tank gun as a defensive weapon, and they failed to make adequate use of their powerful field artillery, which should have been taught to eliminate our [the German] anti-tank guns.

After the *Crusader* battle was over, Gott wrote in his secret report on the operations of his division:

> The German will not commit himself to tank versus tank battle as such. In every phase of battle he co-ordinates the action of his anti-tank guns, Field Artillery and Infantry with his tanks and he will not be drawn from this policy.

All this could—should—have been foreseen before the battle; before the war.

There was a last adverse factor: the quality of British equipment. Post-war researches have indicated that in guns and armour-plate the British tanks of 1941 were much on a par with the Germans. However, the latest armour-plate on some German tanks could only be pierced by capped two-pounder shot— which the British did not have. And the British-built cruisers, mass-produced straight from the drawing-board, were greatly inferior to the German in mechanical design and reliability. Moreover there is no doubt about German superiority in two crucial things—telescopic sights and anti-tank artillery, in particular the 88-mm gun, though subsequent research has shown that its relative importance was exaggerated in wartime. This magnificent German weapon had been designed as an anti-aircraft gun, but the Germans had found that it was far superior in hitting tanks to their own new 50-mm anti-tank gun, which was arriving just before *Crusader*, and itself more powerful than the two-pounder. The 88-mm was so dangerous that four of them could stop an armoured brigade. General Messervy considered the surprise of their first appearance in *Battleaxe* was a major cause of the failure of that operation. Yet its possible influence on *Crusader* does not seem to have been appreciated or countered. The tragedy however lay in that the British also had a magnificent anti-aircraft gun, the 3.7-inch, no more of a conspicuous target than the 88-mm, and of even greater penetrative power. In November 1941 there were in North Africa more 3.7s than 88s. But the British never used them in an anti-tank role, either in *Crusader* or in later desert battles. It was a depressing example of a streak of conservatism, rigidity and departmentalism in the twentieth-century British mind. The 3.7 was an anti-aircraft gun. It was to be used therefore to shoot at aircraft. The two-pounder was supplied to shoot tanks. And that was that.

When *Crusader* opened, the British thus advanced to battle with an armoured corps trained and organized according to a haphazard set of wrong principles, led by officers who had never commanded armour in battle before, and who were not tank men—Gott, Norrie, Cunningham—and with defective equipment. During the engagements which led up to the crisis of November 23rd, the British phalanxes of tanks had tried to get at the German armour, ensconced amid its lorried infantry and artillery, in a series of 'cavalry' charges (if a cavalry unit) or 'tank *v* tank' (if Royal Tank Regiment) actions. They had been shot to a standstill by the German anti-tank artillery ('I did not myself know,' said Cunningham later, 'that the Germans had rearmed with 50-mm guns. Though it appeared in a Middle East intelligence summary, nobody pointed it out to me') and they had broken down through mechanical weakness.

The cumulative and accelerating effects of twenty years of military decadence were thus on the morning of November 23rd, 1941, presented to the overstrained Cunningham as a situation of immediate and terrible danger. The suddenness and force of the shock overwhelmed him. The facts of the matter allowed only one deduction: we had lost the battle and must break it off. Out of 450 cruiser tanks, Eighth Army had lost already at least 300. In yesterday's battle alone the British losses had been almost sixty. If Rommel pressed home his attack today against our weakened and disorganized forces, we might easily lose another sixty. In two days we might have no cruiser tanks at all—with Godwin-Austen's infantry spread out over Cyrenaica and the Axis Halfaya defences between them and Egypt. And beyond the immediate danger to Eighth Army there was the broader threat to Egypt and the Middle East.

For Cunningham there were other disquieting implications in the morning's news. It was now revealed how little control—or indeed knowledge—was enjoyed by Eighth Army headquarters in regard to the forward operations: and one of the most terrifying of emotions is a sense of impotence in the presence of unfolding disaster, an awareness that events are slipping beyond the limits of one's technique.

Cunningham now sent an 'urgent request' to the Commander-in-Chief, General Auchinleck, to fly up at once to discuss the situation; or, in plain terms, to decide whether the offensive should go on, or whether Eighth Army should regroup for defence. Cunningham's own inclinations were clear to his staff, who were far from agreeing with him. But they were without Cunningham's responsibilities; there was no emotional pressure on them. It is easy to offer cool and resolute counsel about another mans' troubles. Brigadier Galloway, Brigadier General Staff Eighth Army, now went to Norrie's headquarters to acquaint him (and Godwin-Austen who came over specially) with the morning's news of disaster and solicit opinions as to future action.

The meeting began at 12.15 pm. Norrie, fully immersed in battle, was represented by Major R. M. P. Carver. This meeting witnessed the beginning of a movement of morale that was to transform the *Crusader* battle. In this movement, the gentlemen who led the British army displayed those virtues which were as much a part of their social and intellectual order as the shortcomings that had got them into the present mess. They had defied reason in the inter-war years; they defied it now with an instinctive faith that the right thing to do was the most dangerous and difficult. They had been bred to provide leadership; they prized bravery and resolution above any kind of cleverness and expertize; and they were to fight their way out of catastrophe, as had their country in 1940, by treating facts as less real than willpower.

Galloway explained in his blunt, vigorous manner the army's situation and Cunningham's reactions to it. Godwin-Austen, a solid, robust, eighteenth-century kind of general, formed the impression from Galloway that Cunningham was already thinking of breaking off the battle. Galloway asked him his opinion of a retreat into Egypt. Godwin-Austen was horrified. He replied in his renowned foghorn voice:

"I couldn't possibly ask Freyberg and the New Zealand Division to call off their attacks—it is absolutely unthinkable."

Cunningham's state of mind was not altogether a surprise to Godwin-Austen: when they had met earlier in the battle Cunningham had not been happy about his tremendous responsibility in view of the Prime Minister's valedictory telegram and the general focus of interest on *Crusader*. Godwin-Austen had gained the impression too that Cunningham personally did not feel happy or at home in his headquarters.

Galloway returned to Maddalena after the meeting, and Godwin-Austen conferred with his brother corps commander, Norrie on the telephone. It is difficult to resist the impression that Galloway had set out to canvass a solid opinion in favour of going on with the battle. He certainly succeeded. Godwin-Austen found Norrie calm and easy. He assured Godwin-Austen that he could hold on at least for a day. Godwin-Austen then wrote to Freyberg to say:

I heard the question of withdrawal mentioned today, but refuse to consider it while our prospects on the whole are so rosy by comparison with the enemy's, whose mobile German forces are so small . . .

All now depended on the Commander-in-Chief. Some strange events occurred to keep the army in place until he arrived: tents and caravans at Eighth Army headquarters took an astonishing time to be struck, telephone lines were cut so that orders to retire or cease advancing, should they be issued, could not be received. For Cunningham was a spent man: with that determination which Godwin-Austen considered his most outstanding characteristic, he had driven himself beyond the limit.

More tidings of disaster now came in: of the state of 4th Armoured Brigade's disorganization, and of the annihilation of 5th South African Brigade by German armour. In the evening Auchinleck arrived, a tall, big-shouldered man whose austere manner suggested moral strength. The grimness of his visage was accentuated by the jut of his jaw, by the stare of fierce blue eyes. In Galloway's caravan, he heard Cunningham set out the facts of defeat, and draw the logical conclusion that prompt disengagement while some armour remained was the only course that might save the army and Egypt. Auchinleck wrote later:

> Cunningham was obviously worried by the collapse and disintegration of his armoured formations. He had every reason to be so—I should have been in his place. He did not strike me as emotionally disturbed but obviously under great strain—again very naturally—as the battle had not gone according to plan and the change in it had been kaleidoscopic. He said that if we went on as we had been, we might be left without tanks, while the Germans might still have some; in which case, Egypt would be in danger.

Auchinleck had no doubts about the reality of the danger, nor illusions about the possible consequences of either retreat or continued attack. Auchinleck and Cunningham had no large reserves of armour and men to pour into the battle. But Auchinleck, with the intuition that is the mark of a great general, saw —or felt—beyond the facts on the sitreps, the tank-states and the battle-map, beyond the confusion of the disintegrating battle into Rommel's own situation:

> My opinion was different from Cunningham's. I thought Rommel was probably in as bad a shape as we were, especially with Tobruk unvanquished behind him, and I ordered the offensive to continue. I certainly gambled [in fact, by going on, we might have lost all] and Cunningham might very well have been proved to be right and I wrong!

On the evening of November 23rd, 1941, the course of the history of the war in the Middle East, perhaps world history, thus turned on the character of a single man. 'This,' wrote a German staff officer, 'was certainly one of the great decisions of the war: Auchinleck's fighting spirit and shrewd strategic

insight had saved the *Crusader* battle and much else besides.'
The Prime Minister wrote: 'By his personal action Auchinleck
thus saved the battle and proved his outstanding qualities as a
commander in the field.'

Auchinleck's intuition about Rommel's weakness was correct:
on the evening of November 23rd Rommel was down to a hundred tanks, and his army was in wild confusion. 'The wide area

Map 9. The 'Crusader' Battle
Phase B, November 1941

south of Sidi Rezegh,' wrote General Bayerlein, 'had become a
sea of dust, haze and smoke.' When darkness fell, 'hundreds of
burning vehicles, tanks and guns lit up the field'. But Rommel
also was a great general, and he too had sensed intuitively the
mind of the man who faced him distantly across the tumult—
Cunningham, though; not Auchinleck. He now decided to lead
his entire armoured force off the Sidi Rezegh battlefield, and on
to Cunningham's communications with Egypt in the area of the
Omars. By academic military principles this tangential move

116

from the centre of the battle was wildly unsound; psychologic-
ally it was a sure success, for it was in fact the one manoeuvre
that Cunningham feared above all. At ten-thirty in the morning
of November 24th, Rommel left his Ia, Colonel Westphal, in
charge of *Panzergruppe Afrika* headquarters, and led the Afrika
Korps towards Egypt in a column forty miles long. His route
took him in succession through the headquarters of 30th Corps,
7th Armoured Division, 1st South African Division, 7th Support Group and 7th Armoured Brigade, mostly caught basking
in the sunshine of a brilliantly fine and warm day.

Half an hour before Rommel began this rampage, Godwin-
Austen arrived at 30th Corps headquarters to discuss plans with
Norrie. Norrie was twelve miles away with Gott, but they spoke
on the field telephone. Between them it was decided that 13th
Corps should drive with all its strength towards Tobruk and
Sidi Rezegh along the Trigh Capuzzo. Then Godwin-Austen
returned to his corps. Soon afterwards Cunningham arrived by
air at 30th Corps, found Norrie absent, and motored over to see
him. He clearly did not in his own mind believe that Auchinleck's orders were feasible, for he told Norrie, in Norrie's words,
'that things had not gone according to plan and at the back of
my mind I should think how my troops would withdraw back
to where we had started, should such an order be given'.

While this talk was going on, Rommel was storming towards
them on a direct course. First there were reports of his approach,
then shells. Norrie thought that the Army Commander should
leave. He was therefore driven, accelerator to floorboards,
across country to the airstrip amid shell and tracer and a thick-
ening mob of fleeing transport. Cunningham climbed on board
the revving Blenheim, which instantly took off, clearing a three-
tonner by inches.

It was now 11.45 am. What General Norrie christened 'The
Matruh Stakes' had officially started. All the soft transport
of 30th Corps pounded to the east, half a length in front
of Rommel, with at least one officer, caught sponging himself down, driving stark naked. But the fighting troops stayed
put.

When Cunningham after his exciting morning arrived back
at Maddalena, Auchinleck handed him a directive setting out in
detail Auchinleck's reading of the situation and his orders for a

continued battle. His conclusion re-affirmed his decision of the night before:

You will therefore continue to attack the enemy relentlessly using all your resources even to the last tank.

Auchinleck saw firm possession of the Rezegh–Duda ridge by 13th Corps and the Tobruk garrison as the key to the battle.

The Commander-in-Chief, the Army Commander, and Galloway, discussed this directive. To Cunningham, after his morning's excursion, it did not appear entirely reasonable. Auchinleck was disturbed

by what seemed to be excessive anxiety on his part lest the enemy should break through in force to our rear areas and dislocate our vulnerable supply and repair organization east of the frontier. His anxiety undoubtedly grew when the enemy swiftly followed up his recent success by a powerful counterstroke with that very intention.

In the afternoon Cunningham had another exciting flight:

After lunch I went out by plane to Godwin-Austen, and then back to my headquarters at a hundred feet. As we were flying along the [frontier] wire, I looked down and saw a tank battle going on. When I got back to HQ, the staff could hardly believe me. Rommel was in the right direction for my base— water and supplies. This rather shook me. He stopped fifteen miles short—he didn't know the base was there. Four divisions were depending on that water.

Auchinleck was unruffled. Eve Curie, the war correspondent, was taken to see Air Vice-Marshal Coningham in his caravan, and found herself in the presence of another commander,

a strong sun-burned man with light-brown hair and blue eyes, who sat . . . in almost complete silence . . . The silent officer was no other than the Commander-in-Chief in the Middle East, General Sir Claude John Eyre Auchinleck . . . He sipped his drink quietly and listened—or perhaps did *not* listen—to our conversation.

After a while he referred to the question in everybody's mind —Rommel's advance:

He is making a desperate effort, but he will not get very far. That column of tanks simply cannot get supplies. I am sure of this.

Auchinleck was right. The Afrika Corps milled inconclusively about the Omars throughout November 24th and 25th, its units periodically paralyzed through want of fuel, and its men more concerned in foraging for petrol and supplies than carrying out Rommel's orders. The 4th Indian Division, in the Omars, beat off German attacks with heavy losses. Rommel's tremendous counterstroke had guttered out in a military vacuum, for, with Auchinleck at Eighth Army, the psychological principle behind it no longer applied. But a surface panic still agitated Eighth Army. In the morning the Germans were only twenty-eight miles from Maddalena, and it was feared that their armour was heading for Eighth Army headquarters. Until noon the military phenomenon of a 'flap' made HQ hearts flutter. In Auchinleck's words: 'There was a scare that German tanks were moving on 8th Army HQ. This made Cunningham naturally very anxious and insistent to get me, the C-in-C, out of danger and farther to the rear—not himself but me.' Before Auchinleck was hurried into his aircraft, he gave Cunningham a message to him and his army for general publication:

During three days, at your Advanced Headquarters, I have seen and heard enough to convince me, though I did not need convincing, that the determination to beat the enemy of your commanders and troops could NOT be greater, and I have NO doubt whatever that he will be beaten. His position is desperate, and he is trying by lashing out in all directions to distract us from our object, which is to destroy him utterly. We will NOT be distracted and he WILL be destroyed. You have got your teeth into him. Hang on and bite deeper and deeper and hang on until he is finished. Give him NO rest. The general situation in NORTH AFRICA is EXCELLENT. There is only one order: ATTACK AND PURSUE. ALL OUT EVERYONE.

C. Auchinleck.
General C-in-C

Auchinleck flew back to Cairo resolved to relieve Cunningham who, it was plain to all observers, was mentally and physically exhausted with battle-fatigue. It was not an easy decision and one which Auchinleck only implemented after long thought, and discussion with the Minister of State in the Middle East, Oliver Lyttelton (now Lord Chandos).

To remove Cunningham [wrote Auchinleck later] was a very serious step. It might have adversely affected the morale of the Eighth Army very greatly. It would certainly encourage the enemy, who would count the removal as a confession of defeat. It would lower our prestige and morale everywhere, not only in Egypt, because it was a confession of failure. Therefore it was a difficult decision but it did not worry me once I had decided it had to be done—rightly or wrongly.

Meanwhile the scattered troops of 30th Corps south of Sidi Rezegh were making good use of the lull in the battle caused by Rommel's disappearance into the east. The formations began to regain cohesion: 4th and 22nd Armoured Brigade repaired its tanks and scrounged the quiet battlefields for potential runners. Most important perhaps of all was the rest accorded to the men after five days of constant fighting. As the British refreshed themselves, the Germans, behind Rommel, were still at full stretch. November 25th was, however, far from being a day of complete peace round Sidi Rezegh. The 1st South African Brigade was attacked at Taieb el Esem by Ariete and rescued by Gatehouse and 4th Armoured Brigade. Gatehouse led his brigade sitting with tartan rug across his knees in an armchair strapped to the top of a tank.

"What else could I do?" he remarked later. "I had no head-quarters."

The New Zealanders reached Sidi Rezegh. At *Panzergruppe Afrika* headquarters, Colonel Westphal frantically signalled Rommel to come back to the centre of the battle.

In the morning of November 26th, 1941, David Stirling, of the Special Air Service, was asked to see Cunningham, who wished to hear what traffic Stirling had seen on the Gazala–Tobruk road during his recent raid. Stirling was taken to a small tent in the headquarters at Maddalena; Cunningham was sitting at his desk. He questioned Stirling for five minutes. Stirling was 'struck by the strain and fatigue on the general's face'.

In the afternoon General Sir Arthur Smith, Chief of the General Staff, Middle East Command, arrived by air with Major-General Neil Ritchie, lately Deputy Chief of the General Staff, who was to replace Cunningham. Smith handed Cunningham a letter from Auchinleck to the effect that he had most reluctantly decided to relieve him of his command because he had begun to think defensively. However, Cunningham's relief was not announced publicly until December 11th. When Cunningham's personal gear was ready, he and Smith climbed on board the aircraft and flew back to the luxury and peace of the Delta. It was a painful journey for both officers. Smith was moved both to sympathy and admiration for Cunningham. 'He was,' said Smith, 'a grand chap. How sad it was that at this critical time and because of his health he lost grip. He was not himself—he was not Cunningham.' Even now, with the Army's battle fading behind him, Cunningham did not give up his own battle with himself. 'He was absolutely tired,' said Sir Arthur Smith, 'but was fighting against it with tremendous courage. I had great difficulty in persuading him to enter hospital for a check-up.' After Cunningham had been in hospital some days, his doctors found that he was suffering from severe overstrain.

It was now nearly four months since Cunningham had arrived in the desert; he had fought his private battle to the last round.

PART FOUR

THE IMAGE OF A GENERAL

General Sir Neil Ritchie, GBE, KCB, DSO, MC

Be sure yourself and your own reach to know,
How far your genius, taste, and learning go;
Launch not beyond your depth; but be discreet,
And mark that point where sense and dulness meet.

ALEXANDER POPE,
An Essay on Criticism.

CHAPTER ONE

MAJOR-GENERAL Neil M. Ritchie, the Deputy Chief of the General Staff in Cairo in November, 1941, was an officer for whom life had apparently unrolled a red and softly piled carpet. He seemed surely destined for professional success because of his talents and not less because of his connections. He was rich; and he had served as Brigadier General Staff to General Alan Brooke in Second Corps in Flanders in 1939–40. Alan Brooke had found him an able and cool-headed staff officer. Personally Alan Brooke had become 'devoted to Neil'. Later in 1940 Ritchie had been Brigadier General Staff to Auchinleck as GOC Southern Command. To Auchinleck Ritchie was no less impressive than to Brooke. He was vigorous and thorough. His personality and appearance made him the image of a British general. Ritchie was very tall and very big. He was handsome and authoritative; good-humoured in a slightly heavy manner. There was a bovine strength about him. Yet his brain was good. He was liked and trusted. His immediate superior in Cairo, General Sir Arthur Smith, said of him later: 'He was straightforward and absolutely honest. If one could criticize him, he was a little slow—but caution is often better than being too slick.'

To Auchinleck, returning to Cairo on November 25th from Cunningham's headquarters, Ritchie appeared the best possible candidate for the command of Eighth Army. The choice was limited. There was no time for a new Army Commander to fly out from England; Cunningham must be replaced in a matter of hours. Among Middle East generals, Norrie or Godwin-Austen would have been the most obvious choice. Auchinleck rejected it. The present confused battle was being directed more from the two Corps headquarters than from army headquarters. Moving a corps commander would upset the entire command structure; bringing in an army commander from outside would leave Eighth Army's organization undisturbed. The army was morally shaken. It needed a strong, unflustered, self-confident commander. Ritchie seemed therefore on all counts just the man. However, he was only a staff officer; his last command in the field had been of a battalion in France in the First World War. He was junior to both Norrie and Godwin-Austen. For these reasons Auchinleck viewed his appointment as temporary, to last until the present battle crisis was resolved and a permanent army commander could be flown out from England. His want of experience in command Auchinleck intended to supply himself; he wrote afterwards:

> Ritchie was perforce pitchforked into a command at a desperate moment [really desperate], knowing little or nothing of his subordinate commanders or troops and told to retrieve an apparently lost battle. I, therefore, thought it only right to 'hold his hand' and make myself very readily available for consultation at short notice. I had not done this with Cunningham, who had formed and trained the 8th Army and was fully equipped to act on his own. This relationship continued to the end.

Ritchie, when told of the appointment, was ready and eager to go up to Eighth Army. It was a unique, a wonderful opportunity for a junior major-general who four years before had been a major. Self-doubt did not seem to trouble him. He was always, in General Godwin-Austen's words, 'very full of himself and very self-assured—was prepared to occupy any position and quite confident he could do the job'. When Smith and Cunningham flew back to Cairo and left him experiencing for the first time the peculiar loneliness that consists in command of an army, he seemed quite at home. David Stirling, who had seen Cunningham before lunch that day, saw Ritchie in the afternoon and found him genial, smiling and confident. A public relations officer was most impressed: 'huge, handsome man, most extraordinarily smartly turned out and fairly oozing energy and vigour.'

But his appointment had no great moral effect on the army. 'When one heard that he was taking Cunningham's place there was no general reaction,' said General Godwin-Austen later. 'The fact was that neither Cunningham nor Ritchie were generally known to 8th Army.' The events of the battle were equally indifferent to Ritchie's arrival. *Crusader* had reached a stage of confusion and dispersal never before seen in warfare, with British and Axis formations intermingled inextricably from the Omars to El Duda. Effective and realistic control could only be exercised by officers much nearer events than the Army Commander, whose information was late and unreliable, who was new to the battle and who had no reserve. On neither German nor British side was there now a coherent plan; only a purpose, expressed in a hundred vicious engagements. Yet in the forty-eight hours between Auchinleck's departure from Eighth Army headquarters and Ritchie's arrival, the balance had tilted away from the Axis and towards the British. Rommel's own hand had moved the balance by his raid into Egypt, which had given the exhausted and shaken British time to collect themselves.

On the first night of Ritchie's command, Freyberg and the New Zealanders, by Godwin-Austen's order, had passed Sidi Rezegh, captured Belhammed and joined hands with the Tobruk garrison, who had broken out over the El Duda escarpment. On his return to the main battlefield on November 27th, 1941, Rommel therefore found the British once more holding the vital ground from which he had so painfully expelled them on November 24th. On November 28th there was a lull while Rommel considered his prospects. On 29th he struck again at Sidi Rezegh and after two days' fighting won a second tactical victory on this unpleasant stretch of gravel. The New Zealanders, South Africans and the British armour had been driven away to the south and Tobruk isolated once more. 'But the price paid had been too heavy,' wrote a senior German staff officer, 'the *Panzergruppe* had been worn down, and it soon became clear that only one course remained—a general retreat from Cyrenaica.' With characteristic obstinacy and persistence, Rommel refused to recognize this.

Auchinleck had joined Ritchie at Maddalena; he was to remain at his headquarters for ten days. In fact Auchinleck commanded the British battle with Ritchie as his deputy. It was their old relationship of commander-in-chief and staff officer translated to new circumstances. As Churchill put it in the House of Commons,

> behind all this process working out at so many different points and in so many separate combats has been the persisting will-power of the Commander-in-Chief, General Auchinleck. Without that will-power we might very easily have subsided to the defensive . . .

Placed therefore between the authority of the Commander-in-Chief and the seniority of his corps commanders, Ritchie found himself in a situation difficult both militarily and personally. He did his best to cope with it and at the same time seize hold of a kaleidoscopic battle, so different from any of his own experience or of the tradition in which he had been trained as a staff officer. In the words of a German account: 'The situation was now extremely complicated and confused, and both sides were almost at the end of their tether. The conditions were very severe; the troops were fighting in waterless country where the normal water supply had virtually broken down.' Ritchie flew up to see Norrie (30th Corps) and Gott (7th Armoured Division); they were elsewhere, immersed in battle.

When Ritchie did meet Norrie, he made some semi-apologetic, semi-humorous reference to his getting the army command before his senior. On December 2nd, he visited Tobruk, where Godwin-Austen (13th Corps) now had his headquarters. Godwin-Austen found him 'a very confident fellow—thought he was the goods. But universal agreement [about this] was doubtful'. However, the anomalies of Ritchie's character and of his position did not seem important to senior officers of the Eighth Army at this busy time: Auchinleck was directing the battle; Richie's appointment was temporary, and in the meantime he was admirably acting the part of a bluff army commander.

His efforts to interpret and influence the tail-end of somebody else's battle displayed the optimism, perhaps complacency, that dominated his mind and temperament. Blended with Auchinleck's own energy and aggressiveness, it found expression in orders to attack and pursue a supposedly broken enemy. Though a premature and overcoloured estimate of Rommel's weakness, it was in the right spirit, and better by far than a too-sober caution.

The days between December 1st and 4th, 1941, witnessed the passing of the final decision in *Crusader* to the dogged British and their greater reserves of tanks. Rommel in his refusal to admit defeat planned yet another dash to the frontier wire. At the same time Ritchie ordered Norrie to advance through Bir Gubi on El Adem. This attack was repulsed by the Italians in Bir Gubi, but it caused Rommel not only to cancel his own operation but to order the Italians to evacuate their siege lines on the eastern perimeter of Tobruk. Hour by hour, imperceptibly, the battle now quietened down and melted into a German retirement. On December 4th an Italian officer arrived at Rommel's headquarters from Rome with the news that the *Panzergruppe* would get no more bulk supplies until the end of December, when aircraft of the Luftwaffe would be installed in Sicily and able to give air cover over the central Mediterranean sea routes. For Rommel, aware of the prostration of his men and of acute shortages in supplies, and harassed by British mobile 'Jock' columns at El Adem and round his own headquarters, this news was decisive. He began to issue orders for a retirement on Gazala; he feared it might even have to be on El Agheila.

A report that the Germans might be going reached Ritchie, who ordered Norrie to resume the advance to El Adem. But British and Axis troops had now fought themselves out: not all the sanguine and aggressive generals in history could have stirred them into another hard fight. The advance on El Adem simply did not take place. On the night of December 7th/8th, 1941, Rommel began to go. The *Crusader* battle was over, and Eighth Army had won it. In terms of courage and resolution, *Crusader* was the greatest achievement of British Commonwealth soldiers in the desert. 'This battle,' said General Sir Frank Messervy afterwards, 'was an epic of British doggedness and optimism in adversity.'

Yet the adversity that they had met so resolutely need never have existed in view of their quantitative superiority. The British blamed their difficulties on their equipment. This half of the truth enabled them to ignore the other half—that except in courage they themselves had been found wanting. They had failed intellectually over the theory of modern war, and they had failed operationally in the techniques of mobile organization and command. Nevertheless in muddling through to victory, the Eighth Army had inflicted damage on the *Panzergruppe* almost as severe as in Second Alamein a year later. A third of Rommel's command had been destroyed. The same number of prisoners had been taken as in Second Alamein: 36,000. They had reduced the German tank strength to thirty, as against twenty-two at Second Alamein. Yet this equal victory had been won by an army incomparably weaker than the Eighth Army in October, 1942—118,000 men as against 220,000. And Rommel's forces, by contrast, were stronger in *Crusader* than in Second Alamein: 100,000 men against 96,000, and with adequate supplies of fuel and munitions instead of paralyzing shortages. Eighth Army in *Crusader* suffered 18,000 casualties in three weeks as against 13,500 in the twelve days of Second Alamein.

In spite of the British achievement in *Crusader*, the officers and men who won this the Eighth Army's first victory are not entitled to the figure '8' on the ribbon of the Africa Star. The principle behind this official ruling has never been disclosed.

*   *   *

There followed three weeks of anticlimax, as Rommel fell back steadily behind skilful rearguards with the British close behind him. At Gazala Rommel deployed and offered battle. Beween December 11th and 15th Ritchie attacked him in front with 4th Indian Division while 4th Armoured Brigade felt their way over difficult ground past the Axis right flank. Finding himself turned, with his ammunition scarce and the Italians shaky, Rommel decided to retire on El Agheila. Behind his anti-tank guns, he retreated with deliberation and was never in serious difficulty, except through heavy attack by the Royal Air Force. He feared a repetition of O'Connor's march to Beda Fomm, and therefore kept the main body of his armour south of the Jebel Achdar. An attempt by British armour to cut the coast road west of Antelat was beaten in detail by 15th Panzer on December 23rd. On Christmas Eve, 1941, Benghazi fell, a ruined and empty white town under the winter clouds, a painting by Chirico. On December 26th Rommel stood at Agedabia reinforced to seventy tanks. In the nineteen days since he had begun to retreat from Sidi Rezegh he had received forty new tanks as against only thirteen in the equivalent period after Second Alamein.

Auchinleck and Ritchie now considered whether to risk an immediate attack with the forces available in the forward area. If successful it would force Rommel in disorder through his fortified bottleneck at El Agheila, a position which in British hands would serve either as a sally-port for a renewed offensive into Tripolitania or as a barbican for captured Cyrenaica. However, the remaining tanks were almost worn out, and manned largely by green replacement crews. The risks were obvious. Like those that faced O'Connor they were accepted with spirit. But the courage of Auchinleck and Ritchie was rewarded by a minor disaster. A frontal attack by the Guards Brigade was repulsed. The flanking manoeuvre of 22nd Armoured Brigade met a German counter-stroke that destroyed sixty-five British tanks. On January 5th/6th, 1942, Rommel retreated to El Agheila and the second British Libyan offensive came to a halt, but only, it was hoped, for rest and reinforcement. On January 17th the surrender of the last Axis garrison in the Egyptian frontier defences ended the long epilogue of the *Crusader* battle.

*　　*　　*

The Commander-in-Chief, Middle East, General Sir Claude Auchinleck, now found himself caught in a series of interlocking dilemmas. Like O'Connor a year before, and Montgomery a year after, he recognized that to drive the enemy to Agheila was only a partial and unstable success. True victory lay at the end of a second march, in Tripoli. But Auchinleck faced O'Connor's difficulties without Montgomery's advantages. In O'Connor's time it had been Greece that had bled the desert forces into weakness and into the defensive on indefensible ground. Now it was the Far East. On December 8th, 1941, Britain had declared war on Japan. On December 12th, while Rommel was still standing stubbornly at Gazala, the Prime Minister had informed Auchinleck that reinforcements of two divisions, four light-bomber squadrons and a consignment of anti-tank guns destined for him must be diverted to the far East. At the same time as Auchinleck was thus weakened, his command was extended to include Iraq and Persia and the troops already there; he was now responsible for the northern defence of the Persian Gulf oilfields in the event of a Russian collapse in the Caucasus. Two days after Eighth Army entered Benghazi, Auchinleck had learned from the Prime Minister that he was also to lose four fighter squadrons to the Far East; he was asked to send a hundred Stuart tanks. The Commander-in-Chief, with an Indian soldier's appreciation of the dangers of Japanese success, offered fifty light tanks and 110 Stuarts, organized and manned as a complete armoured brigade group. Auchinleck's loss of strength went on: 6th and 7th Australian Divisions were dispatched hastily eastwards, while some tanks had to go to Malta where invasion was now expected.

For Auchinleck therefore in January 1942, the prospects for a renewed offensive against Rommel and into Tripolitania were dubious. There were neither troops nor transport to prepare for a fresh advance and at the same time establish a firm base and balanced dispositions for the repulse of a German counter-stroke. However, the elimination of the Axis from North Africa was a tremendous strategic prize, opening the way either for a blow at Italy or for massive reinforcement of the Far East. Auchinleck was not afraid of risk; like Wavell he commanded at a time when there were no certainties for a soldier. His intelligence staff in Cairo were absolutely sure that no reinforcements had reached or could reach Rommel in time for him to anticipate our renewed offensive. Auchinleck therefore decided to attack Rommel at El Agheila as soon as possible.

There remained for him the matter of the command of Eighth Army. The *Crusader* battle being over, it was time to end Ritchie's temporary appointment and ask for an army commander of appropriate talents and seniority from England. But this was now not so easy. When the Prime Minister had announced Ritchie's appointment on December 11th, 1941, he did not say that it was temporary. Ritchie was thus accepted by press and public as the new *permanent* British desert leader; the man who had carried *Crusader* to a triumphant conclusion. How could Auchinleck now send him back to Cairo without serious effects on morale and on public opinion? Even on strictly military grounds, Ritchie seemed well-established and successful. Of his conduct of the second half of *Crusader*, Auchinleck wrote later, 'I was satisfied with Ritchie'. He had shown the vigour, self-confidence and emotional stability required for high command; his record on the staff was good. It might be better to leave him where he was. He had, after all, experienced corps commanders to advise him, and in the event of real difficulty, the Commander-in-Chief himself could intervene.

So Ritchie stayed on. There was, perhaps, a subtler, personal reason for Auchinleck's decision. He had enjoyed his ten days of battle during *Crusader*; pitting his wits and will against an enemy in the field was a richer professional experience than the military diplomacy that was the lot of modern commanders-in-chief. With Ritchie, his old staff officer, as a kind of proxy he could retain a close interest and control in the Western Desert battles while commanding in chief in Cairo. This arrangement had worked well in the closing stages of *Crusader*; why not in the future?

The decision to retain Ritchie as Eighth Army commander after *Crusader* was Auchinleck's second great error of judgment in the Middle East. Like his first—the appointment of Cunningham—it stemmed, in General Galloway's words, 'from his inability coldly to consider whether a man was really up to the job'. Auchinleck's judgments of professional ability were too often coloured by his personal liking for the person concerned. His warm-heartedness and his sense of loyalty as a man sometimes betrayed him as a general.

For Ritchie himself the real test—and opportunity—lay ahead; *Crusader*, after all, had been another man's battle. He set to work to prepare Eighth Army for an offensive into Tripolitania; magazines and workshops in the forward area, supply routes from Benghazi and Tobruk. He was strongly advised to prepare a defence system at Gazala in case Rommel should move first. Resting on the categorical assurances of GHQ intelligence that Rommel was not being reinforced, Ritchie refused.

> I was told [said General Sir Frank Messervy, now temporarily commanding 1st Armoured Division before El Agheila, in the place of Lumsden, who had been wounded] that my role was to reconnoitre and make every sort of preparation possible for a further major offensive. General Headquarters wouldn't believe there were large German tank reinforcements—which infuriated the forward troops who had actually seen them. That was why we were on the wrong foot when he advanced.

These reinforcements had arrived in two convoys escorted by Italian battleships, which had been able to move freely in the Central Mediterranean since the British Force K, based on Malta, had been sunk in mid-December. On January 12th, 1941, Rommel held a conference at his headquarters on the possibility of an early counter-stroke. German intelligence, through wireless intercepts, was able to give him an accurate account of the British order of battle in Cyrenaica. In the forward area was 1st Armoured Division, trained under Alan Brooke's direction as C-in-C Home Forces and fresh from England (the British seemed to fight the war with relays of green troops); near Benghazi was the 4th Indian Division; 7th Armoured Division was as far away as Tobruk. The whereabouts of 1st South African, 2nd New Zealand and 70th British divisions were not known, except that they were out of the forward area. Rommel could put in the field 117 German tanks (including light tanks) and 79 Italian, against 150 gun-armed tanks in 1st Armoured Division.

In the evening of January 21st, 1942, he began one of his most brilliant displays of military agility and opportunism. He advanced in two columns, one on the Via Balbia and one inland through the desert. British forward troops fell back or were overrun. Wireless intercepts informed Rommel correctly that the bulk of 1st Armoured Division under Messervy lay east of Agedabia. He decided to shift his weight to the coast road, drive through Agedabia and get between Messervy and Benghazi. Many of Rommel's tanks were now stranded through lack of fuel, but as usual he used time as a weapon with which to belabour the slow British. He personally led the remaining mobile group of his command, Group Marcks, on a race into Agedabia (taken on January 22nd) and on towards Antelat and Saunnu.

To Ritchie, in his headquarters at Tmimi, Rommel's advance presented itself as a reconnaissance in strength that would be followed by retirement next day. However, Antelat and Saunnu fell; Rommel now issued orders for the complete encirclement of 1st Armoured Division. The attempt, made on January 23rd, failed because of a 'serious lapse of staff work' at Afrika Korps Headquarters by which 21st Panzer did not occupy the Saunnu area until some time after Group Marcks had moved away to close the ring round 1st Armoured on the east. The bulk of 1st Armoured retreated through this gap at Saunnu in some disorder and not without heavy loss. 'There were petrol echelons, workshops, supply lorries of all kinds streaming past at full speed in disorderly array like a hunting field,' said a British account.

The rout worsened next day as Rommel swept on with match-less dynamism. Six miles north of Saunnu he smashed a large force of British tanks; in the words of a German staff officer:

> These were overwhelmed by Panzer Regiment 8, closely sup-ported by anti-tank guns and artillery; it soon became apparent that the British tank units had no battle experience and they were completely demoralized by the onslaught of 15th Panzer. At times the pursuit attained a speed of fifteen miles an hour, and the British fled madly over the desert in one of the most extraordinary routs of the war.

Map 10. Rommel retakes Western Cyrenaica
January–February 1942

By the end of the day Rommel was in Msus, and considering a leap to Mechili. First Armoured Division had disintegrated. It said little for their training in England. Ritchie received this flabbergasting news with a combination of stubbornness and indecision. In General Messervy's words,

> Ritchie was all haywire by then. All for counter-attacking in this direction one day and another the next. Optimistic and

trying not to believe that we had taken a knock. When I reported the state of 1st Armoured Division to him at a time when he was planning to use it for counter-attack, he flew to see me and almost took the view that I was being subversive.

It was Ritchie's first battle crisis and it had occurred only a month after he had been 'pitchforked' into his first command for twenty years. He was not properly equipped to cope with it. He understood now the difference between coolly working out appreciations for other men to act upon, and thinking on your feet at Rommel's speed while your army waited for its orders. It was the difference between walking a plank placed on a drawing-room carpet, and the same plank placed over a two-hundred-foot crevasse. It is not surprising that General Godwin-Austen, 13th Corps, which included both 1st Armoured and 4th Indian Divisions, noted that Ritchie had 'a great air of decisiveness, yet was really rather indecisive'.

Upon receiving reports of Rommel's advance Auchinleck flew up to 'hold Ritchie's hand'. Although he now provided sureness of control, Auchinleck also was outwitted by the brilliance of Rommel's manoeuvres, which here raised the German commander to the level of Marlborough or Napoleon. Rommel lay at Msus, where he equally threatened Benghazi or, through Mechili and Gazala, Eighth Army's communications with Egypt. Which way would he go? This was one question. There was another: the true strengths of the opposing forces. Remembering the early days of *Crusader* both Ritchie and Auchinleck were inclined to doubt the stories of rout and disintegration that reached them, and to underestimate Axis strength. Godwin-Austen, on the other hand, who was the last man to become flustered or alarmed, had no doubt that if we were to extricate ourselves from a fast-closing trap, both divisions of his corps must fall back on Derna, 4th Indian on the coast from Benghazi through Barce, 1st Armoured Division (now a wreck) via Mechili. When asked by Ritchie for advice, he therefore recommended a general withdrawal. Ritchie consented, and Godwin-Austen issued orders accordingly. Nevertheless, in Godwin-Austen's words, Ritchie 'had a tendency to ask your advice and having received it act in the opposite way'. In another flush of optimism he decided to fight for Benghazi, countermanded Godwin-Austen's orders and began to issue tactical orders directly to 4th Indian Division. 'I approved of this change of plan,' wrote Auchinleck later. Ritchie now tried to prepare a counter-stroke by both divisions of 13th Corps against the Germans at Msus.

On the map it was the right thing to do, but the balance of forces made it quite unreal. It was anticipated by a further display of brilliant manoeuvre by Rommel. On January 27th he feinted towards Mechili, and tricked both Ritchie and Auchinleck into moving their armour to the east, thus un-covering Benghazi and 4th Indian Division. With his character-istic agility Rommel changed his direction, lunged to the coast and cut off the Indians. Gallantry, as so often in the history of British arms, redeemed error; and the Indians cut their way out, with insignificant loss. Benghazi fell on January 29th with the enormous quantities of stores and petrol built up for the British invasion of Tripolitania. As Rommel entered the ruined town he received Mussolini's signal authorizing him to advance to it. At last convinced of the reality of the danger, Auchinleck and Ritchie led Eighth Army back to Gazala, reached on February 4th. For a time, a retreat to the Egyptian frontier seemed to them a possibility. Rommel, now a Colonel-General, followed with light forces, having outrun his supplies.

The uncertainty of Ritchie's leadership in the last fortnight led to one further result: Godwin-Austen asked Auchinleck to relieve him of his command, 'as he felt,' in Auchinleck's words, 'that General Ritchie had displayed a lack of confidence in him by issuing orders directly to his subordinate commanders'. Auchinleck, as he had to do, upheld his army commander, and Eighth Army lost an able, strong general and a much-loved man.

The campaign had once more come to rest. Eighth Army at Gazala and *Panzergruppe Afrika* round Tmimi settled down to a long period of tedious preparation and training. It was time for Auchinleck to think again about Ritchie's continuance as Eighth Army commander. He had his doubts now. He ordered Brigadier Dorman-Smith, who had remained commandant of the Haifa Staff College since Wavell's time, to visit Eighth Army, ostensibly to check on staff techniques, but actually to take the pulse of the Army and to sound divisional commanders as to their opinions about recent operations. On February 16th, Dorman-Smith arrived at Eighth Army and began his tour. He found general dissatisfaction among higher commanders at Ritchie's leadership, and a loose and amateurish approach to organization and tactics in which slang words like 'swanning', 'boxes' and 'jock-cols' had become charged with tactical significance. On his return to Cairo, Dorman-Smith talked also to Godwin-Austen and learned fully what had lain behind his request for relief.

Auchinleck invited Dorman-Smith to join him in a picnic on the shores of Lake Fayoum, where they could talk freely and privately. They were old intimates. Dorman-Smith had been Director of Military Training in India when Auchinleck was Deputy Chief of the General Staff. They had worked very closely together on the modernization of the Indian Army.

Upon the results of this picnic for two depended the course of the next six months of the war in the Middle East. It took place on March 1st, 1942. The day was cold and the scene depressing: the large, sluggish lake overlooked from the north by a line of desert cliffs, and bordered on the south by the allotments and ditches of the Egyptian countryside. Here the cars were stopped. Dorman-Smith told Auchinleck exactly what he had found in Eighth Army. He said that Ritchie was 'not sufficiently quick-witted or imaginative enough for that command'. He strongly recommended to Auchinleck that Ritchie should be replaced. Dorman-Smith therefore suggested that Ritchie should return to Cairo as Deputy Chief of the General Staff, and London should be asked to find a successor. Auchinleck was deeply perturbed. He replied to Dorman-Smith:

"I have already sacked one army commander. To sack another within three months would have effects on morale."

Personal motives, partly unconscious, distorted Auchinleck's sight of the bleak prospect of public interest. He was a simple man with old-fashioned principles of straightforwardness and plain-dealing. He liked subordinates who appeared to him open and trustworthy. These qualities he knew Ritchie to have. What kind of an army commander would London send him? He had had experience in England of unprincipled intrigue by ambitious subordinates. When the next battle in the desert opened, he could reason, Ritchie would have had time to settle in and master his job; so far as tactics and organization were concerned, he, Auchinleck, could supervise him closely.

So Ritchie stayed on. This decision, proceeding from a flaw in the character of a great man, was to prove a disaster to Auchinleck, Ritchie and Dorman-Smith, and nearly so to the Middle East.

CHAPTER TWO

FROM FEBRUARY to May 1942, the armies rested motionless in the gravel wastes of Gazala. For the troops the long days stretched full of boredom and discomfort. There was nothing to interest the eye but the blank swell of the brown desert; nothing to do but lay mines, dig foxholes and uncoil wire under a sun that grew ever more fierce; nowhere to go but the sea, in a bouncing three-tonner full of whirling sand, for a weekly bathe. A gallon of water a man per day served for drinking—connoisseurs alleged they could tell the difference between Buq Buq or Sidi Barrani or Bardia water—making tea and washing. Petrol was therefore often used for laundry. Sweat and dust permanently stifled the skin, and started desert sores. The flies clung in dense, lazy constellations. The coolest place was inside a tank. Behind the army, the three-tonners pitched perpetually in line ahead from horizon to horizon as they brought up petrol, food, ammunition, cigarettes, mail and Naafi stores. Although on the move, it was not much more enlivening to be a truck driver: day after day they sat over their hot engines, driving for twelve hours in second gear over the vacant desert, naked feet pressing the accelerator to the floorboard.

While the army made the best of its boredom, its senior commanders were digesting the lessons of the mobile battles of the winter. They had apparently learned much, not only from the Germans, but from their own mistakes. General Gott's report on 7th Armoured Division operations in *Crusader* stated that

> tanks require the support of Field Artillery, Anti-Tank guns, and Motor Infantry. The higher proportion of these supporting arms to actual tanks in his Panzer Divisions gave the German a distinct advantage—To our own tanks, the value of good support from 25-pounders was demonstrated time and time again—Therefore, it would appear that in the future the

Armoured Brigade Group should take the place of the Armoured Brigade.

The Commander-in-Chief, General Auchinleck, agreed that the basic ideas and organization of our armour in *Crusader* had been proved unsound: and he set about a radical reorganization of the British armoured forces for which he has never received general credit.

> It seemed to me [he wrote later] that our pre-war divisional organization was too rigid and lacking in flexibility to be really adaptable to the conditions of modern quick-moving warfare in the Desert, or even elsewhere . . .

In particular the British practice of large armoured divisions strong in tanks and weak in infantry and other arms was wrong; it encouraged the idea that the armour was an 'army-within-an-army'. He was also worried by the parochialism of spirit caused by the ancient prides of regimental tradition. Auchinleck therefore broke down the division (whether armoured, motorized or infantry) into self-contained brigade groups with their own artillery and engineers. These groups remained under the command of the divisional general. In the case of the armoured divisions, he replaced the two armoured brigades and a support group by a single armoured brigade group and two lorried infantry brigade groups. This organization (with one lorried infantry brigade) later became standard throughout the British army.

These changes were intended to coerce the separate arms of the British service into thinking and working together in the German style. They were reinforced by a radical overhaul of the training system in the Middle East: Auchinleck created the post of Director of Military Training, and appointed to it Major-General Harding (now Field-Marshal Lord Harding), who had been O'Connor's Brigadier General Staff. Thus, between one battle and another, Auchinleck attempted to repair the reckless conservatism of twenty years. But was there time to change the habits of minds long trained to the static and rigid?

*   *   *

On February 26th, the Prime Minister was writing again: what were Auchinleck's intentions in the Desert? A detailed memorandum gave the answer; Auchinleck was determined not to embark on another ill-prepared offensive like *Crusader*, with poor equipment and an untrained army thrown hastily together. He would attack when his reforms in training, organization and tactics had been thoroughly completed, and when he had a superiority of three to two over the Germans in armour. This superiority he considered was the minimum necessary to make up for the Germans' greater experience and superior equipment. Given his commitments to the Northern Front (Turkey, Iraq, Persia, the Caucasus), Auchinleck did not think he could launch an offensive until May 1st, 1942 at the earliest.

Auchinleck also informed London that in the event of a German offensive:

> I was determined not to allow Tobruk to be besieged a second time . . . I did not consider I could afford to lock up one and a half divisions in a fortress. Admiral Cunningham agreed, particularly since the siege had proved so costly in ships, and so did Air Chief Marshal Tedder, who doubted whether he had sufficient aircraft to provide aircover.

Auchinleck later hinted that the offensive might be postponed because of delays in completing the railhead and dump at Belhammed.

Churchill was not satisfied; telegrams rained on Cairo throughout March, April and May.

> The PM for the biggest possible political reasons

said Auchinleck later with a reverberating reticence

> realized the tremendous desirability of beating Rommel at the earliest possible moment. The Command in the Middle East realized it just as much, but it was their duty to relate this to the resources available.

The new Director of Military Intelligence in Cairo, Brigadier de Guingand, considered 'that in this case the Commander-in-Chief was pressed too hard, and as one who was in daily and intimate contact with him, I noticed that he was feeling the strain of fighting this battle in order to give his own troops a fair chance'. The battle culminated in a letter from Churchill to Auchinleck on May 10th ordering him to attack in June, or resign. The Prime Minister also suggested that Auchinleck should take personal command of Eighth Army during the coming battle; this Auchinleck was unable to do because of his responsibility as C-in-C for the whole of the Middle East and especially the threatened northern front.

On the German side, Rommel had political troubles of an exactly opposite kind. Conscious of the superiority of his troops and equipment, he wished to seek a great victory in North Africa; but he needed extra troops and air support. The German High Command however was not interested in North Africa, it was interested in Russia. When Rommel flew to the Fuehrer's heaquarters in March, it was agreed that there should be a combined German and Italian invasion of Malta during the first June full-moon period, after heavy Luftwaffe bombing. At the end of April there was another meeting, at Obersalzburg, between Hitler, Mussolini, Rommel, Kesselring (German Commander-in-Chief, South) and Cavallero, chief of the Italian *Commando Supremo*. Rommel argued in favour of an offensive in Libya in May with the object of taking Tobruk. If the attack on Malta could not take place before June, he wanted his own offensive to come first. He pointed out that the British were preparing their own desert offensive. Hitler and Mussolini agreed to allow Rommel to advance in May, but once Tobruk had fallen, he was to stand on the defensive and release air support in favour of the attack on Malta.

Between February and May 1942 Ritchie had been developing the Gazala area both as the springboard of an offensive and as the defence of Tobruk and Eastern Cyrenaica. This ambivalence was to prove damaging in the defensive battles that followed, for the presence of the huge dumps at Belhammed and Tobruk cramped the mental and physical freedom of manoeuvre of the British armour. When in mid-May Ritchie learned that his offensive was certain to be anticipated by Rommel, he concentrated his efforts solely on the preparation of his army and the Gazala defences for a defensive battle. His final dispositions betray alike his own unoriginality and the inadequacy of the military tradition in which he had been trained. These were, in brief, an attempt to set down in the desert a linear fixed defence (in some depth) full of infantry and guns, with a reserve of armour held behind it, just as if Eighth Army were fighting in France amid rivers and other natural features, and with another army on its flank.

From Gazala on the coast to Bir Hacheim there was a continuous 'mine marsh', within which were 'boxes' or independent strongholds of guns and infantry. The right flank of this line, on the coast, was held by 1st South African Division and 50th (British) Division (Major-General W. H. Ramsden), whose

Map 11. Ritchie's Forward and Dispersed Dispositions
May 26th, 1942

front extended as far south as the Sidi Muftah box. In Tobruk itself (now of course a fortress in dereliction) was 2nd South African Division. These troops were grouped under 13th Corps (General W. H. E. Gott). The left flank of the Gazala line, including the fortress of Bir Hacheim (Koenig's Free French Brigade) and the armoured mass of manoeuvre was commanded by Lieutenant-General Willoughby Norrie (30th Corps). Some depth was given to these defences by further isolated boxes at Knightsbridge, Acroma, El Adem and Bir Gubi.

The organization and layout of Eighth Army showed little understanding of the nature of mobile, mechanized desert war; an imperfect appreciation of the lessons of two campaigns. They marked a regression of twenty years from O'Connor's defensive dispositions at Mersa Matruh against Graziani. O'Connor had held his forces sixty miles behind the line of his forward patrols, protected thereby from surprise and sudden shock. His men were not pegged out on the ground in any kind of fixed defence, but kept on wheels and tracks so that they could manoeuvre freely in any direction. They were organized in loose, fluid, flexible groups. There was no attempt to form a front to the enemy. Ritchie on the other hand had placed the main bulk of his army in his forward area, wrapped up as gifts to Rommel in those 'boxes'. The first sixty miles of a German advance through the desert south of Bir Hacheim would take Rommel deep into Ritchie's rear: Ritchie thus invited surprise and an early decisive clash. He also repeated the error of the *Crusader* plan whereby the army fought in two halves: the mobile armour, and the static infantry and guns. The infantry would watch helplessly from their boxes while the armour won —or lost—its encounter battle with Rommel.

The static and rigid cast of mind of the Eighth Army command is particularly demonstrated by the division of responsibility between the two corps. Given Ritchie's compartmental conception of a fixed defence zone and a mobile mass of manoeuvre, it would have seemed that the logical division of responsibility was to allot all the fixed defences and infantry to 13th Corps and the mobile forces and armour to 30th Corps. This is what Auchinleck strongly recommended to him. Ritchie however simply drew a corps boundary along the map and allotted the Gazala defences north of it to Gott and south of it to Norrie, who in addition commanded all the armour. This was the ortho-dox way, the way in which Ritchie and all his contemporaries had been trained, the static rather than the dynamic; to extemp-orize other solutions required the creative genius of a man like O'Connor.

There were, however, serious weaknesses in Ritchie's disposi-tions considered even in the light of old-fashioned and 'non-desert' military practice. Between Sidi-Muftah, on the British left centre, and Bir Hacheim, the anchor of the left flank of the

Although he had leadership and powers of command, he was thrown into a very difficult position before he had had time to develop methods of command.

This was exact and just. Ritchie did his best, but, as the French proverb has it, the most beautiful girl can only give what she has. Like Cunningham, Ritchie was surrounded by more experienced commanders, including a corps commander actually senior to him. There was Gott, the lone survivor of the great days of Western Desert Force, already a legend in the desert as a British 'Rommel' tirelessly roaming the battlefield to rally and drive on shaken troops, a man of immense prestige. There was Willoughby Norrie, who had been commanding an armoured division when Ritchie was a colonel, and who had behind him the experience of fighting the *Crusader* battle. His knowledge of armour, lately acquired though it was, far outstripped Ritchie's. His too was a strong personality: urbane, cool, easy, he wore his ability, as a gentleman should, slightly carelessly. If he proffered advice on the placing or handling of armour, it might be difficult for a green army commander to refuse it. Caught therefore between Norrie, Gott, Auchinleck and his own inexperience, Ritchie was delicately placed and independence was not easily won. It is not surprising that Dorman-Smith noted 'an air of uncertainty about his face'.

Courage apart, the army therefore suffered. It was—in organization, discipline, doctrine—flabby instead of taut, sluggish instead of agile. There was a tendency to plan, and later to fight, private battles. For example, Richie himself considered that Rommel might attack in one of three directions: along the coast road, along the Trigh Capuzzo, or round Bir Hacheim, with Tobruk as the objective in each case. Two of these possibilities fell in the 30th Corps area. But Norrie believed there was a third possibility on his front: an attack through the twenty-mile gap (mined) between Sidi Muftah and Bir Hacheim. He therefore planned for this as well. Yet Ritchie never knew it.

In fact, Rommel intended to pass all his mobile forces round Bir Hacheim, fight and win a battle, and drive on Tobruk. It was the *Crusader* plan in reverse; but in other senses than geographical. Whereas *Crusader* had been planned in great detail, in the British manner, Rommel took Moltke's view that 'no plan survives contact with the enemy'. If his plan got him into battle, it was enough. After that, Rommel would fight by ear and eye and tactical sense, like a duellist. He entered the Gazala battle with a total of 561 German and Italian tanks of all kinds. But his principal weapon lay in his 280 German medium tanks. However, except for 19 Mark III Specials, these were completely outclassed in guns and armour by the 167 American Grants that now formed the backbone of the British armour, which numbered altogether some 850 tanks. The Grants carried their magnificent 75-mm gun in the hull of the tank: the gun had therefore a very limited traverse, and could not fire from a hull-down position. Apart from the Grants, the British possessed a mixture of British-made 2-pounder Crusaders and American Stuarts. The British apparently enjoyed a qualitative as well as a quantitive superiority on the basis of armour and guns alone. But the British-made tanks forming the majority of Eighth Army's equipment were unreliable, partly owing to poor maintenance, and had a short track mileage. This was a major worry to Ritchie, because it limited training. In anti-tank artillery, which the Germans used as an offensive weapon, Rommel had a crushing superiority, for both his 50-mm and the new, captured Russian 76-mm guns were better than the British 2-pounders, whose solid shot could not pierce the armour of the latest German tanks. New 6-pounder anti-tank guns were on their way to the Middle East, but so far Eighth Army had received only enough to equip the lorried infantry brigades and motor battalions, and not in time to allow training in their use. Rommel also had his magnificent 88s; the British still would not use their 3.7-inch anti-aircraft gun in an anti-tank role.

During the latter half of May 1942, GHQ Cairo intelligence had warned Eighth Army that a German attack was imminent. In view of the proven wild inaccuracy of GHQ intelligence over the past eighteen months, this information, in the absence of evidence from patrols, was widely disbelieved. However, there was now a new Director of Military Intelligence (de Guingand) and a new, reliable source of information in the Axis camp.

On May 26th, 1942, about half past three in the afternoon,

Eighth Army armoured cars reported by wireless a forward movement by much German transport. This information was passed by 7th Motor Brigade to 7th Armoured Division and 30th Corps by telephone. Thereafter the armoured cars radioed back Rommel's positions and strength at half-hourly intervals: fifty-two messages between 1530 hours on May 26th and 0700 hours next morning. At 2130 hours on May 26th, the presence of panzer divisions had been identified. None of this information reached the various units of 30th Corps, because a constant wireless watch was not ordered either by 7th Armoured Division or 30th Corps—that is, the subordinate formations were not ordered to listen to the armoured cars' radio messages. The information, sent on by 7th Motor Brigade by telephone, apparently only reached 30th Corps and 7th Armoured headquarters. Later, when 7th Motor Brigade had to retire before Rommel's advance and itself use wireless instead of telephone, a constant wireless watch was still not ordered, and Eighth Army still lay in ignorance.

Ritchie himself remained as ignorant as the units spread-eagled in Rommel's path. He concluded in the middle of the afternoon of May 26th that the German offensive was under way, but had no idea of its direction.

Under brilliant moonlight, in a planetary silence, *Pranzer-armee Afrika* rolled towards Bir Hacheim, lit now by Luftwaffe flares. Brigadier (now General) Renton of 7th Motor Brigade went on trying to rouse his division and corps. During that night he gained the impression that they thought he was 'a bit panicky in reporting the enemy advance and withdrawing before it, as they were both convinced the attack was going to come in from the North'.

General Messervy, of 7th Armoured Division, now avers that in fact he was not so convinced:

At a 30th Corps conference with Norrie [some time previously], we were all asked our opinions as to the direction of Rommel's coming offensive. I gave it as mine that Rommel would come round our left flank, and that therefore we should dispose the armour to fight as a corps and not piecemeal. Lumsden (1st Armoured Division), Ritchie and Gott thought it was impossible to come round the left flank; he would try and break through our centre. Therefore the eventual disposition was 7th

Armoured Division on the left and the other armoured division miles away on the northern flank—the idea being that when Rommel did attack, and his direction known, there would be time to concentrate.

Messervy therefore accepted Renton's messages as proof of a major German attack:

> I reported them to corps, asking permission to take up our battle stations which had been planned in case of an attack from the left flank. But this was refused by Norrie, who wanted to wait until Rommel's main blow was known. By morning it was too late . . .

In the small hours of May 26th/27th, 1942, therefore, voices were raised in urgent argument along the British field telephone wires as Rommel, with 500 tanks behind his armoured car, drove towards Bir Hacheim. But the arguments accomplished nothing: Eighth Army did not move.

At half past six in the morning of May 27th the *Panzerarmee* was level with Bir Hacheim and beginning to swing north towards Tobruk. The next intimation of Rommel's advance received by Eighth Army was more urgent than a radio report. In the unfinished Retma box the garrison breakfasted late and leisurely among piles of unlaid mines, enjoying a glorious May morning. A few days before it had been rumoured that a *British* offensive was in the offing but that it was unlikely that Rommel would attack. Beween Retma box and 7th Armoured Division HQ there was a direct telephone line, but no message came down it about the German advance. An air of pleasant relaxation held the Retma garrison.

> Then [in the words of an eyewitness] some gunner started banging away like mad. Thinking it was trigger-happiness, I was about to have it stopped, when we saw something moving in the desert away to the south, about four miles off. It was the whole of Rommel's command in full cry straight for us.

Bir Gubi, east of Retma, was the rallying or pivoting point of Renton's 7th Motor Brigade. When he arrived there he found that 7th Armoured Division headquarters had given permission for half the garrison to go to Tobruk for a swim. There were not enough of them left to fire all the guns.

Rommel swept on and over and through 7th Motor Brigade

and 3rd Indian Motor Brigade. Next in his path, like a township in line for a tornado, was 4th Armoured Brigade.

News of the massacre of 3rd Indian Motor Brigade and the scattering of 7th Motor Brigade now reached Ritchie at Gambut and told him, with a shock like a sudden blow in the kidneys, that the great German offensive had already arrived, from the wrong direction, and before Ritchie's army had been alerted and posted in its battle stations. Now Norrie too was

Map 13. Gazala Battles 1942
Phase A, May 27th–28th

convinced about Rommel's intentions. All over the sunlit morning desert the units of 30th Corps scrambled to get themselves on wheels and tracks. But it was now too late to concentrate in the prepared defence stations, and as General Messervy put it, 'it became an awful muck of a battle. The armour never really recovered its poise.'

Fourth Armoured Brigade was caught by 15th Panzer while still readying itself for a move; it lost heavily in tanks and its command organization was wrecked. Rommel drove on to the north. General Messervy himself was surprised by the headlong speed of Rommel's advance: he and his divisional headquarters were caught, overrun and scattered by the Afrika Korps. Messervy was taken prisoner. By mid-morning of May 27th, 1942, 7th Armoured Division was no longer a coherent fighting force. Its men fought as they had in *Crusader*, blindly and instinctively; shooting Germans wherever they could. Norrie and 30th Corps knew nothing of the disaster to 7th Armoured Division, for with the capture of its headquaters there was no one to tell him. A silence walled him—and Ritchie—off from events at the battlefront. Rommel was clearly moving at some speed, however, and Norrie and 30th Corps headquarters removed to the shelter of the El Adem box; this move, made in haste, further loosened the cohesion of the corps. Norrie ordered 22nd Armoured Brigade to drive southwards to support 4th Armoured Brigade; he did not know that the 4th had been already shattered. Before 22nd Armoured Brigade could move Rommel drove into it in a whirling cloud of dust and gunfire. The Brigade, surprised, was also thrown into disorder. However, it fought hard all the way back to Knightsbridge, the box behind the centre of the Gazala line that controlled the crossroads of important tracks.

In the Gazala defences, news of Rommel's storming advance behind them had now arrived. General 'Strafer' Gott rang up Ramsden (50th Division) and said: "There's bad news on the blower from the south." It was Ramsden's first knowledge that any kind of German advance was under way. He went out to the rear of his position and through glasses saw packed German transport near Knightsbridge.

At Gambut, Ritchie spent a hot and anxious time. In the absence of accurate up-to-date reports he was not merely unable to control the battle, he was unable even to picture clearly what was going on. Meanwhile the instinctive courage of the British troops saved the day. Without any very definite plan, they closed through the smoke, dust and heat haze on to Rommel's columns and fought them to a standstill. The heavy Grants, in battle for the first time, shook the German tank crews. Fresh armoured brigades unknown to German intelligence joined the fight. Rommel and his commanders began to be anxious; the British armour, supposedly destroyed in the morning, was fighting with a violence never seen before. Their blind advances were now falling into a wide gap that existed between Rommel's armour at Knightsbridge and his supply trucks at Bir el Harmat. When night fell, Rommel's as well as Ritchie's battle was slipping out of control. He had achieved none of his objectives and he lay almost out of petrol far behind the British defences open to a counter-stroke. If the British armour had received him in their ordained battle stations, as a corps, Rommel would undoubtedly have been as decisively beaten that day as he was to be at Alam Halfa. Even now prudence suggested that he should retreat to secure his communications. Characteristically he opted for another attempt to break through to Tobruk.

It was the moment for a prompt rupturing British counter-stroke. However, it was only on the morning of May 28th, when such a counter-stroke should have been under way, that Ritchie learned of the wreck of 7th Armoured Division and the dislocation of 30th Corps. For a time he could not believe the accuracy of the reports: it was the first example in this battle of his stubborn optimism. With Ritchie's knowledge twenty-four hours behind events no swift British counter-action could be expected, especially in view of the state of 30th Corps.

During another day of fragmentary fighting, Rommel pushed on farther into danger: Afrika Korps beyond Knightsbridge towards the coast, 90th Light Division near El Adem. Far behind at Bir el Harmat lay the Italian 20th Corps and all Rommel's supply echelons. Already, however, superiority of German skill, training and anti-tank artillery was beginning to tell in a way devastating to the morale of British troops. Once again the British found their equipment wanting. 'On the second day of the battle,' said General Renton afterwards, 'the German armour was scattered all over the desert immobilized for want of petrol, a sitting target. But our 2-pounder anti-tank guns could not damage them.'

On the third day of the battle Rommel saved his army by his personal leadership. During a *khamsin* he himself led his supply trucks up from Bir el Harmat through a gap in the British forces. By nightfall the *Panzerarmee* was concentrated and supplied. Ritchie, who by the rigid systems of British command was sitting remote from the battle in Gambut, had missed his first opportunity of winning a great victory.

Rommel now abandoned his plan of driving to the sea at Tobruk; his forces were too shaken and the long supply lines round Bir Hacheim, still held by the French, were too vulnerable. He must consolidate and regroup. His method illustrated the originality of his genius. He proposed to break through the British minefields between Sidi Muftah and Bir Hacheim from the eastern or British side in order to shorten his communications, and pull his army back into a bridgehead at the east of the gap.

This moment of disengagement and retreat was highly dangerous, but the British made no significant or co-ordinated effort to interfere. By nightfall Rommel was in a safer position inside British minefields, in the shelter of anti-tank guns and with two cleared corridors behind him for his supply trucks. He held a bridgehead through the left centre of the Gazala line. This move was interpreted by Ritchie as a crushing German defeat. How should it be exploited?

There now began a series of wearisome and indecisive conferences between Eighth Army commanders; a series that lasted throughout the Gazala battles. 'Ritchie,' recalled General Messervy (who had escaped twelve hours after capture and rejoined Eighth Army), 'was rather stupidly optimistic in remarks and demeanour, but uncertain beneath it all. He was always saying "Ah, now we've got him", when it was clear we hadn't.' While the British talked, Rommel was all driving energy and singleness of purpose, preparing for a second sally towards Tobruk; while the British talked, the British 150th Brigade box, controlling one of Rommel's supply corridors, was taken against bitter resistance. No real attempt was made by the British to save this commanding position. 'Relief of the 150th Brigade locality (Sidi Muftah) failed because of piecemeal efforts and disorganization of armour,' wrote General Ramsden (50th Division). General Messervy said: '150th Brigade was down and out before Ritchie realized it.'

Rommel now controlled the centre of the Gazala line. Bir Hacheim was completely isolated and under furious land and air attack. During June 1st, 2nd and 3rd Rommel lay in his bridgehead—'The Cauldron'—preparing his army for further attack and untroubled by the British in any way. For neither Ritchie nor his committee of senior commanders could make up their minds what to do. They could agree however that Rommel was beaten. Lumsden for example believed that Rommel's bridgehead was in fact a gap. Ritchie wrote to Auchinleck: 'I am much distressed over the loss of 150th Brigade after so gallant a fight, but still consider the situation favourable to us and getting better daily.' Various plans for counter-attack were pressed on Ritchie in the long, hot committee meetings: by 1st South African Division out of the Gazala line along the coast; by Briggs' 5th Indian Division round Bir Hacheim on Rommel's communications; by the armour and infantry straight on to Rommel's bridgehead. The uncertainty and slowness of British policy began to creep paralyzingly through the veins of the army: General Ramsden recalls Gott returning from the conferences and saying: "I *think* Ritchie is going to do this or that."

Eventually Ritchie agreed to Briggs' idea of a drive (with motorized infantry) on to Rommel's communications. After Ritchie had left this particular meeting to go on a visit the plan was attacked, especially on administrative grounds. Another gained general acceptance—direct assault on the German bridgehead by 5th Indian Division and 22nd Armoured Brigade (Stuarts), with an army tank brigade ('I' tanks) coming in from the north. 'I was put in joint command of it with Briggs,' said General Messervy afterwards. 'It would more normally have been under a corps commander.' So much for Auchinleck's warning that Norrie must use his armour as a corps commander. General Messervy adds: 'I accepted the idea (of the Cauldron attack) and thought it might come off.' When Ritchie returned, the new plan was presented to him. He consented and wrote to Auchinleck: 'I have decided I must crush (the enemy) in the Cauldron . . .'

This operation was the first planned and concerted move undertaken by the Eighth Army in a battle now eight days old; it would be launched when Rommel had been snug in his gap in the minefields for four days. It was organized and led, not by the Army Commander, not by a corps commander, but by two divisional commanders exercising alternate control. It was delayed for further preparation for twenty-four hours.

Everyone was confident that German resistance would be easily overcome. Norrie reported to Ritchie that Messervy and Briggs 'were full of beans, and happy'. However, the techniques of combined operations by tanks and infantry had been lost since O'Connor's time. Operation *Aberdeen* proved a shambles. The infantry went in first, at three in the morning of June 5th, 1942, under cover of darkness. They made an encouraging advance. After daylight, 22nd Armoured Brigade not having come up, the infantry were furiously counter-attacked. Then the 156 Stuarts (the lightest of Eighth Army tanks) of 22nd Armoured Brigade advanced three miles beyond the British infantry and were fired upon by Rommel's concentrated army artillery. They fell back behind the infantry, who were now attacked by German combined groups of all arms and massacred.

It had taken Eighth Army four days to think up *Aberdeen*; it took Rommel half a day to plan and launch a counter-stroke against *Aberdeen*'s left flank, which rested on an uncovered minefield. The German attack routed the British assault forces and captured Messervy and his headquarters for the second time. Meanwhile the northern British attack on the Cauldron was struck in the flank by 21st Panzer Division and driven into a German minefield covered by furious anti-tank fire. On the first day of *Aberdeen*, Ritchie had lost 110 tanks. Eighth Army signalled Auchinleck that while the operation had not been 'wholly successful', there were 'signs that the enemy (was) not entirely happy'.

Next day, June 6th, Messervy—who had escaped again—tried to rescue the British forces still marooned in the Cauldron. It was another day of marching, waiting, orders, counter-orders, cancelled orders and piecemeal effort, ruthlessly exploited by clever German tactics. When at last Ritchie's counter-stroke had been written off, it had cost 168 cruiser tanks, 50 'I' tanks, four regiments of artillery, an Indian brigade and 7th Armoured Division Support Group. Yet Ritchie signalled Auchinleck that night that, in his belief, the enemy had 'suffered considerable losses' and that 'the enemy's position is not too easy'.

What is the explanation of Eighth Army's apparent combination of smugness and inertia? Strafer Gott, of 13th Corps, considered for example that 'June 6th has been a profitable day'. Norrie, of 30th Corps, was responsible for the forward battle;

he was undoubtedly cool and experienced and able; but had he the driving energy, the ruthless killing urge that the situation demanded? Had Whiteley, the Brigadier General Staff, Eighth Army, the quick, creative intellect needed at the head of the staff? Messervy, a great likeable Airedale of a man, was dashing and brave enough; but was he—was any Eighth Army commander—the cold professional, the clever military scientist that could be found among Rommel's officers?

It was the turn of Bir Hacheim. This fortress, once the left

Map 14. Gazala Battles
Phase B, May 31st–June 5th, 1942

flank peg of the Gazala defences, was the last impediment to Rommel's resumed drive on Tobruk. For ten days under fierce attack, it now was assaulted by a major part of the *Panzerarmee* and the Luftwaffe. Once Bir Hacheim fell, Rommel would be able to roll up the Gazala line as far as Knightsbridge; Eighth Army would have to form a front parallel to its communications. Rommel therefore pushed on the attack in person. On the British side, nothing decisive was done either to relieve the fortress or evacuate it. This inactivity stemmed from the usual reason; the committee could not make up its mind.

There was endless shilly-shallying over Bir Hacheim,
later said General Messervy, whose own exercise of command
was by no means always fortunate:

> They were put under us—an absurd thing, a static fortress
> under an armoured commander. Bir Hacheim fell because
> Ritchie had not really made up his mind what his main plan
> was going to be. There was a token advance towards Bir
> Hacheim, but it was too far away.

Meanwhile the men of the Free French garrison continued
a magnificent but futile resistance. General Koenig, the garrison
commander, however, was so much in favour of evacuation that
he refused to accept supplies. While the German attack grew
closer and closer to the web of foxholes, barbed wire and mines,
and the French soldiers, stunned by endless bombardment and
lack of sleep, fought on, the indecision continued. Koenig
pleaded that he had no water or ammunition; finally Ritchie
ordered the garrison to break out on the night of June 10th/11th.

It was the end of the Gazala line. It was the end of Ritchie's
chances of victory.

CHAPTER THREE

AFTER THE fall of Bir Hacheim Ritchie pulled his left flank
back to the line of the Trigh Capuzzo, parallel with the
Mediterranean coast and at right angles to the remaining half
of the Gazala line. This new left flank position was also parallel, and close, to the Eighth Army's main lines of communication.

It was a situation pregnant with disaster. If Rommel broke
through again, the Eighth Army might easily be pinned against
the coast between Gazala and Tobruk and annihilated. Ritchie,
however, preserved his robust optimism; he believed he could
halt Rommel on his new line; and halting an offensive is a
victory. The line was tactically strong. There were the heavily
fortified boxes of Knightsbridge and El Adem, and from north
of Knightsbridge to the 69th Brigade box in the Gazala line
were minefields and more defences. The decayed perimeter of

Tobruk supplied a further, if feeble, guard to the left flank. Ritchie had been able to make up a good deal of his losses in tanks from the large British reserves. In the shelter of the Trigh Capuzzo defences was an armoured force of 250 cruisers and 80 'I' tanks. To Rommel now remained only 160 German tanks and 70 Italian.

However, the British armour, though strong in numbers, had weathered the battle far more heavily in terms of skill and cohesion than the German. As units were diluted with fresh crews, or amalgamated with other units, the shallowness of British experience and training, and the unsuitability of the ancient cavalry regiments as a basis of organization and replacement were revealed once more. The performance of the British armour in the battles for the Trigh Capuzzo line was therefore much poorer than in the early days of Rommel's offensive, though not less courageous. The German armour, more skilled at the start, began now to achieve a dangerous ascendency. General Messervy of 7th Armoured Division wrote afterwards of the Gazala battles:

His (the German) handling of armour, anti-tank guns and mechanized formations in co-operation was, with the *schwerpunkt* idea, much better than our rather dispersed idea of fighting ... We were given area commands, not functional commands —which kept fluctuating. We never fought as a division— always getting different brigades, trained in different ways.

Ritchie himself continued to display that curious personal blend of complacency and indecision. The remains of the Gazala line, held by 1st South African Division and 50th Division, was a deeply turned salient; he looked upon it as a bastion. He still could not hit upon a basic battle plan, and this want of purpose began to be appreciated more and more widely in the ranks of Eighth Army, with damaging effects on morale.

One felt there was no real theme in the battle,

said General Messervy later.

It seemed to us at the time that after Bir Hacheim fell we should have fallen back immediately to a strong position El Adem–Bir Gubi. But Ritchie's intentions were not very evident to us.

About this time Messervy met Renton in the desert. Renton asked his superior: "What is the main idea in the battle now?"

Messervy answered: "I wish I knew—the only real order is to fight Germans wherever you see them."

On June 11th, 1942, the German dustclouds were seen moving north again, and the second act of the Gazala battles had opened. Rommel sent 21st Panzer and Ariete against the British centre north of the Cauldron, 15th Panzer, 90th Light and Trieste towards the British left flank at El Adem. As always, Rommel was feeling for the communications of the flank-conscious British. Rommel in attack never worried about his own flanks: a punch protects itself.

On the eve of the renewed battle, disagreement was arising in Eighth Army over the handling of armour. Headquarters Eighth Army issued an instruction that our tanks must fight from the cover of their artillery and infantry in the Trigh Capuzzo defences; there must be no more rash attacks in the open. However, subordinate commanders, tired of waiting for guidance that rarely came, had by now taken to acting very much on their own initiative. Thus both Messervy (7th Armoured Division) and Norrie (30th Corps) separately and unknown to each other conceived plans and issued orders for June 12th.

Messervy wished to get the armour out of the Trigh Capuzzo defences and grouped in the open desert to the south-east, near El Gubi. He saw his two brigadiers, gave his orders, and then went off to confer with the Army Commander before the move was made. However, Messervy ran into 90th Light and spent the day in a dry well.

Norrie meanwhile had issued his own orders for the armour to attack southwards directly into 15th Panzer Division. The only common factor in Norrie's and Messervy's orders was contradiction of the Eighth Army instruction on the handling of armour. Norrie now learned that Messervy had disappeared. Meanwhile Rommel, who learned of Messervy's plan through wireless intercepts, had laid an ambush for it. At noon Norrie placed 7th Armoured Division under the command of General Lumsden, of 1st Armoured Division, and instructed him to attack 15th Panzer Division immediately. Almost simultaneously Rommel ordered 21st Panzer Division to drive into 7th

Armoured Division's rear. This division, caught waiting for orders and unprepared for battle, melted into a confused mass of vehicles ringed by German anti-tank guns and tanks.

Lumsden now arrived with his own division (1st Armoured) to take 7th under his command. It seemed to him an unpropitious moment to mount a joint attack to the south and he told Norrie so. Norrie disagreed; the British armour must break through 15th Panzer to the south; not, as Lumsden wished, fall back to the shelter of the Knightsbridge box.

During that sweltering afternoon, with vehicles and black smoke shimmering in the haze, the British armour, attacked from all sides, suffered the greatest defeat of its history. At the end of the day Rommel had driven its wreckage beyond Knightsbridge like paper before a gale. As night fell Rommel was through the Trigh Capuzzo line between Knightsbridge and El Adem, was holding in strength the escarpment north of it, and was across the by-pass road round Tobruk. The only land link between Egypt and the mass of troops pinned in the old Gazala line was now the Via Balbia, picking its congested way through Tobruk. The unfortunate Lumsden tried to get further orders from 30th Corps, failed to speak to it, and finally was told that he had been placed under 13th Corps. Owing to the general chaos he was to have no contact with that headquarters for twelve hours.

During June 11th and 12th, 1942, Eighth Army had lost 200 cruisers and 60 'I' tanks.

On June 12th Auchinleck paid Ritchie a visit. He found 'the atmosphere here good. No undue optimism and realities of situation are being faced calmly and resolutely'. In Eighth Army headquarters it was believed that the tank battle of the day had not been conclusive, although apparently the British losses had been heavier. Auchinleck and Ritchie therefore agreed that further battle should be offered on the line Gazala–El Adem. Orders were issued accordingly, together with another warning, again to be unheeded, that the armour must fight defensively under our own guns.

Next day Rommel wrecked this plan by isolating Knightsbridge, whose garrison was got away safely after dark. The danger that the whole of Eighth Army, pressed nearer and nearer the coast, might be cut off was now acute.

Map 15. Gazala Battles, Last Stage
June 11th–14th, 1942

This was a time of complete chaos on the ground, in the command structure, in men's minds. Telephone lines carried a dense traffic of anxious consultation. Ritchie, who had tried earlier to display his independence of Auchinleck's continual flow of advice, now felt the need of the Commander-in-Chief's support; Auchinleck, on his part, began to take a closer and closer hand in events in the desert as he sensed the battle slipping away from Ritchie. His signals gradually alter from general advice to specific recommendations that are almost orders.

At 10.30 in the morning of June 14th, Ritchie sent a signal to Auchinleck outlining his new plans. He proposed that the garrisons of the Gazala defences should be immediately evacuated, while a new mobile force of armour and infantry was built up west of the Egyptian frontier defences. He did not tell Auchinleck that Gott of 13th Corps had been *already* ordered to send the Gazala garrisons straight back to the frontier. He intended, Ritchie said, to hold in the meantime a line from the western perimeter of Tobruk through El Adem to Belhammed. Tobruk had a month's supplies and might be cut off for a time. He therefore asked Auchinleck if they should risk a temporary siege, or evacuate Tobruk and draw the entire army back on the frontier.

It seems clear from the terms of this signal and of Gott's orders that Ritchie had now decided on falling back to the frontier defences, with or without Tobruk as an isolated fortress. That is one crucial point; the other is that the idea of ever again holding Tobruk in isolation had been specifically abandoned in January by the three Commanders-in-Chief in the Middle East, and the decision communicated to London.

Now, however, on the same day as this signal of Ritchie's, came one from the Prime Minister:

> Presume there is no question in any case of giving up Tobruk. As long as Tobruk is held no serious enemy advance into Egypt is possible . . .

The situation was already complicated enough, with half-understandings and misunderstandings developing between Ritchie and Auchinleck; but this signal, contradicting policy long agreed, marks the true cause and beginning of the resounding disaster of Tobruk. While Eighth Army scrambled out of

163

the Gazala line and Rommel's dustclouds swept nearer and nearer Tobruk's ruined perimeter, a three-cornered correspondence raged between Ritchie and Auchinleck, and Auchinleck and the Prime Minister, in which firm statements of policy were gradually transformed by qualification into opposites.

Auchinleck's own plan was clear-cut. He rejected equally Ritchie's alternatives of evacuating Tobruk or allowing it to be besieged; he also ruled out a retreat to the frontier (which was by then, unknown to him, already in progress). He instructed Ritchie:

> Tobruk must be held and the enemy must not be allowed to invest it . . . Eighth Army must hold the line Acroma–El Adem—and southwards and resist any enemy attempt to pass it . . . If you feel you cannot accept the responsibility of holding this position you must say so . . .

This of course was highly embarrassing to Ritchie. He consulted Gott; another drawn-out conference. Gott was sure that the army must make for the frontier; if Tobruk were held at all, it must be in isolation. Torn between Gott and Auchinleck, Ritchie hit on a British compromise, the reality to satisfy Gott, who was on the spot, and the words to satisfy Auchinleck, who was not. At eight o'clock in the evening (June 14th, 1942) Ritchie signalled the Commander-in-Chief that he

> had ordered Eighth Army to deny to the enemy the Western and Southern perimeter of Tobruk, the Tobruk–El Adem road and El Adem to the South. You may rely on us to do our utmost to achieve this . . .

Auchinleck could not know that 1st South African and 50th Division, the only fresh and intact formations, were en route for the frontier, and that the new line was to be only thinly held by the wreckage of earlier defeats. As regards the investment of Tobruk, Ritchie was also disingenuous. He summed up his policy in two alternatives: to fight alongside Tobruk to prevent its investment, or, if that failed, to allow it to be temporarily invested rather than risk a hasty evacuation. 'If this is a correct interpretation of your orders,' he concluded, 'I accept responsibility.'

Meanwhile Auchinleck had been considering Churchill's telegram.

The centre of the drama now moved from Ritchie's head-quarters to GHQ Cairo, where all important decisions were henceforth made. Throughout June 14th there was a conference of intense anxiety in the long, bright, map-walled war room. It was a very hot Cairo day. Auchinleck discussed the telegram with Corbett (his Chief of Staff), de Guingand (his Director of Military Intelligence), and Dorman-Smith (Deputy Chief of the General Staff). Should they flatly disobey the Prime Minister's orders, reminding him of the January decision, with which London had never disagreed? Discipline ruled this out. Should Tobruk be held in isolation after all? This would invite disaster. Its defences were in ruins, the minefields partly cleared—for our own convenience—the artillery control system dismantled. It was no longer a fortress at all. Perhaps the complete answer to Churchill and to the military problem lay in holding Tobruk as part of a line, as Auchinleck had already ordered Ritchie—if Ritchie carried the order out.

At 1.55 in the morning of June 15th the meeting at last broke up. Corbett was ordered to carry personally to Ritchie uncompromising and reinforcing orders that Rommel must be kept west of a line Tobruk–Acroma–El Adem–Bir Gubi.

Corbett flew up to Eighth Army headquarters and, in Ritchie's caravan, gave Ritchie the Commander-in-Chief's orders. This was a bad moment for Ritchie, who knew that there was no hope of the sketchy forces left south-west of Tobruk offering serious battle. The best he could do, he told Corbett, was to hold the old perimeter of Tobruk, with Indian infantry in El Adem and the armour to the south—the bulk of the army was already partly in motion to the frontier. Corbett reiterated Auchinleck's cast-iron orders. Jolted at last out of his calm, Ritchie grew red and angry, banged the table and said of offering battle on the line Tobruk–El Adem: "I'm damned if I will!"

Corbett too grew angry: 'We thumped the desk and shouted at each other. It was most unpleasant.'

That evening (June 15th) Corbett returned to Cairo and reported to Auchinleck and his staff. Meanwhile, Churchill, who had received from Auchinleck a summary of his orders to Ritchie, had dispatched another peremptory telegram about Tobruk:

> We are glad to have your assurance that you have no intention of giving up Tobruk. War Cabinet interpret your telegram to mean that, if the need arises, General Ritchie would leave as many troops in Tobruk as are necessary to hold the place for certain.

This of course was an order, and Auchinleck obeyed it. Corbett's report had shown that in fact Tobruk could now either be invested or evacuated, but not held for long as part of a general line. Auchinleck therefore replied to Churchill on June 16th in language that curiously recalls the disingenuous signals he himself had received from Ritchie:

> War Cabinet interpretation is correct. General Ritchie is putting into Tobruk what he considers an adequate force to hold it even should it be temporarily isolated by the enemy . . . Basis of immediate future action by Eighth Army is to hold El Adem . . . and to use all available mobile forces to prevent enemy establishing itself east of Tobruk.

Thus Churchill had his wish, and paved the way for one of the greatest single disasters ever suffered by the British in the Middle East and Mediterranean in the Second World War. He attempted later to shift the blame from himself to Auchinleck with a disingenuousness only qualified by the weakness of his argument:

> We did not however know the conditions prevailing in Tobruk. Considering that Auchinleck's plan had been to await an attack, and remembering all the months that had passed, it was inconceivable that the already well-proved fortifications of Tobruk should not have been maintained in the highest efficiency, and indeed strengthened.

Elsewhere he stated:

> At home we had no inkling that the evacuation of Tobruk had ever entered into the plan or thoughts of the commanders.

However, London had been informed by a copy of Auchinleck's Operation Instruction No 110, dated January 19th, 1942, that:

> It is NOT my intention to try to hold, permanently, Tobruk, or any other locality west of the frontier.

This instruction was sent on by General Kennedy, Director

of Military Operations at the War Office, to General Alan Brooke, Chief of the Imperial General Staff, on February 6th with a note agreeing with Auchinleck's intention: 'In my opinion, it would be right to avoid such detachments in the future.'

It is impossible therefore to believe that Churchill was never told of this decision—neither at that time nor when the question of Tobruk came up in June. Given that all in London had known and accepted that Tobruk was never again to be used as a fortress, it is highly illogical and unjust to suggest that Auchinleck ought to have diverted men, weapons and materials to fortifying it.

The Prime Minister's last-minute reversal of policy long accepted by the three Middle East C-in-Cs and the CIGS was perhaps partly for reasons of home morale, partly the product of another of his waves of patriotic emotion, caused this time by Tobruk's legendary fame. There is a curious reference in *Jan Christian Smuts*, by Smuts' son. The author, in dealing with the effects of the loss of Tobruk and its South African garrison on public opinion in South Africa, refers to demands for an inquiry into the reasons for its fall:

> It was common knowledge that we would not again commit the dangerous error of trying to hold this [Tobruk] or any other isolated strongpoint. The minefields and other defences of Tobruk were therefore never properly prepared for a siege. It was therefore obvious to all on the spot that Tobruk could never be held. The last-minute decision by the highest authority to hold it came as a complete surprise to us. The decision must either have come from Mr Churchill or some other very high body. *The fact that my father, while opposed to the decision, never pressed the inquiry, may perhaps be significant.* [Author's italics.]

While the fate of Tobruk was being decided, the troops in the Gazala line had begun on June 14th to try to escape from Rommel's closing trap, a process known at the time as the 'Gazala Gallop'. Their sole eastward route was the Via Balbia, and all that stood between it and Rommel was a line of small boxes hastily manned and supported by bits and pieces of 1st Armoured Division and 32nd Army Tank Brigade. Against this thin, desperate line, so true to British military traditions, Rommel personally drove the Afrika Korps. All the day, as the South Africans slipped away along the Via Balbia, the line stood firm and, when at last at nightfall Rommel broke it, his troops were so exhausted they lay down in the breach and slept. Rommel watched helplessly as the rest of the South Africans escaped under the muzzles of his silent guns.

The 50th British Infantry Division was placed too far south in the Gazala defences for it to escape by the Via Balbia, even if that narrow road could have carried the volume of traffic. The division—under General W. H. Ramsden—therefore broke out westwards into open desert and motored right round Bir Hacheim, behind Rommel. 'The journey back to the frontier was calm,' said General Ramsden afterwards. 'We stopped in the desert for a brew-up.' In the afternoon Ramsden reported to Ritchie at Maddalena, whence Eighth Army headquarters had now removed. They sat in a car and Ritchie explained the situation and how Tobruk was to hold out as a hinge for a counter-move, after reorganization of the army. Despite the fast flowing current of rout and confusion, Ritchie remained 'calm and collected'.

'At that moment,' said Ramsden, 'I really admired him.'

Four days later Eighth Army headquarters was back to Sollum. Here Ritchie was visited by Auchinleck and Dorman-Smith. 'There was a general optimism and belief that Rommel would take his time over Tobruk, and that we had leisure to rearm and regroup,' recollected Dorman-Smith. 'Ritchie still said he would not allow Tobruk to be invested. Auchinleck was disturbed by this atmosphere; he thought it was not yet the moment to relax.'

Ritchie's character was thus sustaining magnificently the cumulative disappointments and dangers. He was perhaps mentally protected in defeat by that very lack of imagination that had denied him victory. But intellectually he was done. His mind could no longer cope with the speed and complexity of events. His indecision displayed itself, for example, over the defence of El Adem, which in Auchinleck's opinion (strongly expressed) was the 'decisive spot'.

Twenty-ninth Brigade was in El Adem,

recounts General Messervy.

I got via Corps an order: on no account was El Adem to be

O'CONNOR DORMAN-SMITH

HARDING GALLOWAY

CUNNINGHAM

NORRIE

GATEHOUSE

GODWIN-AUSTEN

RITCHIE

GOTT

FREYBERG

LUMSDEN

HORROCKS
AUCHINLECK

MONTGOMERY
LEESE

evacuated—they were to fight it out to the last. It was already surrounded. I was told by Norrie that these were the Army Commander's personal orders. Then I had a message: It might be evacuated if I thought it couldn't be held. I said I was quite sure it could not be held for long; then I was told to pass this message on to 29th Brigade. Then I got another order—the Army Commander says it must be held. Then yet another: that it was to be evacuated if the brigade could get out. I passed this on to Denis Reid (the Brigadier), and they got out. This was an example of what was happening all the time.

The bulk of Eighth Army was now behind the Egyptian frontier; although Ritchie and Auchinleck were still exchanging signals about the firm holding of Tobruk–El Adem–Bir Gubi line, it was in fact held by a weak screen of disorganized remnants. The only significant British force left in Libya was the 33,000 men mustering in the rusty perimeter of Tobruk: 2nd South African Division, 11th Indian Brigade, 201st Guards Brigade, 32nd Army Tank Brigade, 268 Medium Regiment, Royal Artillery.

To Gott (13th Corps) and Major-General Klopper, now fortress commander, the problem of organizing the defence of Tobruk in a matter of hours was horrifying. The Italian anti-tank ditch had partly filled with sand, partly been filled, for convenience, by the British; 'it would hardly have interfered with the progress of a garden roller'. The minefields had been breached on the south-eastern side during the British sorties in *Crusader*. Inside the perimeter were scattered uncharted minefields of every nationality. The inner perimeter defences had disappeared. Organization of command, of fields of fire and of signals was derelict.

The survival of the garrison depended, as Auchinleck knew and Ritchie had promised, on a powerful force operating in its support in the area El Adem–Belhammed. But on June 17th occurred another disastrous tank action which ended hope of supporting Tobruk from the outside. With cavalry pennants fluttering in the breeze, as they had at Balaclava, 4th Armoured Brigade (under Messervy's orders), drove westwards towards the German concentration between Sidi Rezegh and El Adem. It was the last charge of the British armour in the Gazala battles, ninety assorted tanks and crews, new to each other, though not to battle. They met the two panzer divisions of the Afrika Korps, and when they had lost thirty-two tanks they went back to Egypt. Eighth Army no longer possessed a battleworthy tank arm.

This defeat, which rendered Eighth Army quite helpless, caused Ritchie to relieve Messervy of command of 7th Armoured Division. In telling Messervy of this decision, Ritchie displayed amid all his worries the courtesy and generosity that formed so strong a part of his personal character: 'Well, Frank, I'm afraid I've lost confidence in you—you seem to be out of luck. Nothing seems to be going right with you.'

On June 18th, 1942, Rommel's forces closed the ring round Tobruk.

Inside the fortress there was an atmosphere of doom. Klopper, the fortress commander, had been a general for a month only; his recent military experience had been in the administration of training in South Africa. The headquarters staff of his division (2nd South African) were also green. As subordinate commanders, Klopper had two highly experienced brigadiers, Willison and Johnson. He never established his personal ascendancy; Tobruk was commanded, in the current British manner, by a debating society. The troops were in every stage of disorganization. Maps were hopeless: Willison's showed him minefields he himself had lifted a year ago; Klopper's was a captured German one dating from November, 1941.

By nightfall on June 19th, Rommel had completed the preparations for his attack. The assault force was made up of 21st and 15th Panzer, Ariete and Trieste. Ninetieth Light Division would fend off British attempts at relief. Rommel chose as his point of entry the same sector of the perimeter as O'Connor: the south-eastern. This was also where Rommel had intended to attack in November, 1941, had he not been anticipated by *Crusader*.

In the small hours of the night before the assault, Klopper received a secret signal from Ritchie outlining Eighth Army's plans to help Tobruk and giving Klopper general guidance. Ritchie considered that Rommel would attack Tobruk as soon as he was ready; but on the other hand he might attack the Egyptian frontier defences instead. Ritchie would risk this, and form a striking force of guns and tanks which could attack towards El Adem, on to the rear of a German assault on Tobruk. If Rommel should march straight on the frontier, Tobruk garrison would make a sortie behind him.

This was Klopper's last word from the Army Commander before the German assault. It was heartening: powerful Eighth Army forces would be operating against the rear of the beseigers.

Ritchie, after signalling Klopper, had signalled Auchinleck in similar terms; but he added an extra piece of information. This was that the creation of the striking force of guns and tanks would be a slow business. Rommel's troops were then readying themselves on their startlines. The Commander-in-Chief replied with sharp urgency:

> I am perturbed by the apparently deliberate nature of your preparations though I realize the difficulties. Crisis may arise in matter of hours not days and you must therefore put in everything you can raise.

There can have been no conscious intention to deceive in Ritchie's signal to Klopper: his personal honesty rules it out. The explanation lay in his utter inability to think and act at Rommel's speed, or even to imagine Rommel's speed. Grappling with that tempestuous commander, Ritchie with his stolid British virtues was as baffled as a two-dimensional being in a three-dimensional world.

The dawn of June 20th, 1942, lightened the sky along the bleak escarpment; the night mists lifted. Then the German barrage fell upon the bunkers of the Tobruk perimeter; the desert burst apart in dust and thunder. The Stukas came with the early morning sun. Orange smoke rolled up against the blue sky as the German engineers signalled their gunners to lengthen the range so that they could move in to breach the minefields and anti-tank defences. Just before seven o'clock the German infantry followed. Before eight, the *Panzerarmee* was one and a half miles inside the Tobruk perimeter.

Within the falling fortress there were the too-familiar decisions and counter-decisions and time-wasting exchanges of visits between commanders. A counter-attack was ordered: the tanks arrived without the infantry two and a half hours after the German breakthrough. Only then did the infantry begin to move. By now, two German panzer divisions were driving for King's Cross, where the Via Balbia and the El Adem road met.

Outside Tobruk Ritchie was visiting his corps commanders: at midday he learned that 'some enemy activity' was in progress, 'apparently against Tobruk'. He immediately ordered 30th Corps to attack through Sidi Rezegh with all available armour and mobile forces. This move achieved nothing: in Axis war diaries it is hardly noticed.

Inside Tobruk, the defence was disintegrating in scenes of apocalyptic confusion and doom. By four in the afternoon the Germans were on the eastern airfield, and driving straight for the town of Tobruk, with all its stores and installations prepared for the intended British summer offensive. Under heavy German gunfire, demolition charges were blown in petrol, water, refrigerations and naval ammunition stores. A dark column of smoke towered through the sunshine into the blue Mediterranean sky.

At seven in the evening 21st Panzer had captured the town. Germans swarmed everywhere through the confusion and noise, performing the housewifely function of mopping-up. Some British units held out for a time, others were quickly overwhelmed.

As the debris of his garrison poured past his headquarters, Klopper signalled and signalled Eighth Army. There was no answer. At five o'clock the desperate Klopper had telephoned Brigadier Thompson, the Area Commander, that fortress headquarters was about to disperse, Germans tanks being close. In the hope of speaking to Eighth Army Klopper nevertheless held on until half past six, when his headquarters started to pack up.

Now at last came a personal signal from Ritchie:

. . . You are having a very tough fight today and I see this afternoon some enemy tanks have got through the outer perimeter. But I feel quite confident of your ability to put them out after destroying as many as possible. I am doing all I can from outside to relieve the pressure on you and our power to help you from outside will increase daily. The turn of the tide will come and feel quite sure of inflicting a crushing defeat on the enemy . . . All good fortune to you personally and the whole of your grand command.

Dusk fell, and men from broken formations crowded wearily

into the precarious security of the western half of the perimeter. In their nostrils was the ubiquitous smell of burning; in their mouths the sour, familiar taste of defeat. Klopper himself had joined 2nd South African Brigade, where he tried to speak to Ritchie on the Army Commander's personal radio-telephone link. But Ritchie was away from his headquarters. Klopper spoke to Whiteley, his Brigadier General Staff, and conveyed the state of the fortress. Whiteley got in touch with Ritchie, then passed on to Klopper the Army Commander's orders to break out tomorrow night; an escape route would be held open.

While Klopper's officers talked and talked endlessly round the questions of whether, and how, to break out, the men settled down to wait with that patient resignation of the soldier, and Klopper himself tried again and again to speak to Ritchie. Midnight passed. At two in the morning of June 21st, Klopper gave Ritchie up, and signalled Eighth Army:

> Am sending mobile troops out tonight. Not possible to hold until tomorrow. Mobile troops nearly nought. Enemy captured vehicles. Will resist to last man and last round.

At three that morning Ritchie returned to his headquarters, immediately telephoned Tobruk and found he could not get through to Klopper. Now it was Ritchie's turn to endure anxiety and frustration before a silent telephone. As dawn crept palely up the sky, he paced up and down outside his caravan, waiting. At last he and Klopper talked. Ritchie gave Klopper leave to capitulate if the local situation warranted it. Klopper told him that 'he was doing the worst'. Ritchie ended the conversation with a characteristically generous message:

> Whole of Eighth Army has watched with admiration your gallant fight. You are an example to us all and I know South Africa will be proud of you. God bless you and may fortune favour your efforts wherever you may be . . .

That morning, June 21st, 1942, a white flag was hauled up over Klopper's new headquarters. It was Sir Claude Auchinleck's fifty-eighth birthday.

* * *

At a quarter to ten, amid the shambles of surrendering

173

troops and burning equipment, Rommel imperiously signalled the *Panzerarmee*:

> Fortress of Tobruk has capitulated. All units will reassemble and prepare for further advance.

It was Ritchie's turn again.

Since the evacuation of the Gazala line, Ritchie had been reorganizing his army in the field defences along the Egyptian frontier. These were similar to those of Gazala—a series of boxes, minefields and wire, stretching thirty miles inland and ending in a wide-open flank. Since there no longer existed a British armoured force capable of offering battle, these positions could be turned by Rommel without difficulty: the result of staying there would be a second Gazala, a second Tobruk.

On June 22nd, Auchinleck and Dorman-Smith flew up to Ritchie's headquarters, now in O'Connor's old camp at Maaten Baggush. Ritchie was still personally unaffected by events, unalarmed by the progressive dissolution of the fighting power of his army and the nearness of final catastrophe. But his remaining military intention indicated a dearth of ideas. Rightly arguing that the frontier defences were, in the circumstances, indefensible, he said that he must 'put distance' between himself and Rommel in order to gain time to reorganize. He proposed therefore to retire at the utmost speed on Mersa Matruh, where he would offer a final battle for Egypt. The New Zealand Division from Syria would garrison the Matruh box together with 5th South African Brigade, with 10th Indian Division farther back along the coast at Baggush.

Auchinleck agreed that Eighth Army was not strong enough to defend the frontier, and he therefore sanctioned retirement on Matruh. However, he pointed out to Ritchie that the considerations that made the frontier indefensible also applied to Matruh. Auchinleck also agreed that only infantry with transport should remain in the field. The process was now under way of forming battlegroups of lorried infantry and guns.

The 'Gazala Gallop' was therefore resumed. Auchinleck himself arranged for Norrie and 30th Corps headquarters, as well as 1st South African Division, to go back even farther, to El Alamein, there to reorganize, and for 10th Corps (from Syria) to hold Mersa Matruh.

On June 22nd, Rommel, now a Field-Marshal, was up to the frontier. On the 23rd he drove south of the frontier defences in a wide sweep towards Sidi Barrani; he reached the coast east of that place at nightfall on June 24th, having covered a hundred miles in twenty-four hours. Eighth Army retreated in a final state of rout and dissolution; one observer said he did not see a formed unit of any kind. Eighth Army losses in the Gazala battles had now reached about 80,000, mostly in prisoners.

Map 16. Ritchie's Dispositions at Mersa Matruh
June 25th, 1942

By nightfall on June 25th, Rommel was in front of the Matruh defences. Ritchie had failed to 'put distance' between himself and the *Panzerarmee*. The final battle for the Middle East was at hand.

The Mersa Matruh defences had not been garrisoned or maintained since November 1940. They were more derelict than those of Tobruk: 'Most of the dug positions,' wrote a New Zealand brigadier, 'had caved in or filled with sand, much of the wire was on the ground, minefields were badly marked, communications non-existent, and the whole plan of defence obscure.' There was the fortified perimeter round Matruh itself, another belt of defences to the west, and an unfinished box at Minquar Sidi Hamza el Gharbi, some thirty miles inland. The whole complex was protected by minefields in two sections separated by a six-mile gap in which were thinly scattered on June 25th fresh mines.

Ritchie's dispositions for this last battle were curious: he had no centre, but two widely separated wings facing north and south. Holmes of 10th Corps, with 10th Indian Division and 50th Division, lay in Matruh, with his back to the sea; Gott of the 13th Corps (now the mobile and 'offensive' wing), lay along the east-west escarpment nine miles to the south, with 29th Indian Brigade in the Sidi Hamza box and Freyberg's New Zealanders—Freyberg had refused point-blank to be shut up in Matruh—ten miles to the *east* at Minquar Quaim. In the empty centre were two tiny battlegroups, Gleecol and Leathercol. In the open desert south of Minquar Quaim was 1st Armoured Division, now, owing to Auchinleck's energy in rustling up reinforcements from all over the Middle East, formidable again in numbers: 159 tanks, including 60 Grants. But numbers did not make a team.

Ritchie now awaited, without flinching, the final action. There was to be no more retreat. Eighth Army would stay at Mersa Matruh alive, or it would stay there dead. If dead, the entire Middle East would fall to the Axis. But that was not the affair of a commander of the Eighth Army. As June 25th slowly passed, Ritchie waited amid the sand dunes for Rommel. Late in the afternoon Auchinleck arrived from Cairo and relieved him of his command.

*   *   *

Ritchie epitomized the cherished and admired qualities of the British Establishment: he was stolid, thorough, rather slow, honest, conventional, courteous, brave and unimaginative. Even if he had had Rommel's experience, he would therefore still have been out-generalled and beaten—unless he had also enjoyed the good fortune of Montgomery in the way of overwhelming numbers and equipment. As it was, he was far too junior an officer for his command, as all but Auchinleck recognized. Placed in an impossible position, he did his duty as best he could, never losing heart, never (except once) losing his self-command and courtesy, never imputing blame to others for the defeats of Eighth Army. Ritchie far from lost personal stature in the course of his military failure in the desert. And the failure itself was not decisive for him. Auchinleck wrote an enthusiastic report on his qualities—though with the recommendation that he was not suited for independent command; Brooke retained his high opinion of him; and when Ritchie returned to England in August he was invited to Buckingham Palace for an audience of the King. In 1944 he was to be a corps commander—and a successful one—under Montgomery in north-west Europe. For a man who in 1937 had been only a major, this was professional success indeed.

PART FIVE

THE VICTOR OF ALAMEIN

Field-Marshal Sir Claude J. E. Auchinleck, GCB, GCIE, CSI, DSO, OBE, LLD

Of General Auchinleck I will only say that he is an officer of the greatest distinction, and of a character of singular elevation.

WINSTON CHURCHILL.

CHAPTER ONE

As he flew back to Cairo from Ritchie's headquarters on June 22nd, 1942, the Commander-in-Chief, General Sir Claude Auchinleck, faced a situation more desperate than any other British commander confronted during the Second World War. It was made worse for him by strong feelings of personal loyalty to Ritchie, and perhaps of culpability. He knew he had to decide—and quickly—whether to replace Ritchie. It would be the second time he had relieved an army commander in the middle of a crisis; this sort of thing did not come more easily with habit. But his visit to Eighth Army headquarters at Maaten Baggush no longer allowed him to deceive himself.

Ritchie had seemed to him surprisingly calm and clear-headed in the face of cumulative disaster. But he—and the rest of his headquarters—seemed to suffer from a numbness of the will. Defeat hung over them like smoke above a burning town. Ritchie now proposed to stake everything in a final battle at Mersa Matruh, almost as though he wanted it all to be over and done with. If he had in fact ceased to believe in the possibility of victory, what hope was there that he would find the generalship to win?

As Auchinleck weighed the consequences of Ritchie's losing the battle of Mersa Matruh and the last field army in the Middle East, the more catastrophic they seemed. The Middle East Command formed the connecting cog round which revolved the great wheels of the allied coalition. It joined Britain to India and the Far East; British and American factories (through Persia) with the soldiers of the Red Army; Africa and Asia. It was Russia's southern flank; it was the moral and physical prop that kept wobbling Turkey out of the Axis and, neutral, protecting both Russia and ourselves. And, above all, in Iraq and Persia, it contained the oilfields without which the British armed forces would be paralyzed.

The Eighth Army once finally destroyed, the Germans would hold the magnificent Delta base within a week. The Mediterranean fleet would have to escape southwards through the Suez Canal; Palestine and Syria, bereft of troops, would fall in a few days; and then—within a month at Rommel's pace —the oilfields of the Persian Gulf would be wrecked or producing for the Axis. Turkey would be unable to resist German pressure to enter the war, and with Anatolia and Persia in German hands, the Red Army's extreme left flank would be uncovered. The second German summer offensive in Russia was already a few days old and moving fast. Sevastopol was falling to von Manstein; Kupiansk, some three hundred miles west of Stalingrad, was being smashed from Russian hands by von Weich's army group.

India too might be exposed to attack by a German force from Persia while the Japanese tried in Assam to repeat the easy triumphs of Rangoon and Singapore.

In one sad and bloody encounter at Mersa Matruh Ritchie could lose the war.

And Ritchie was certain to be beaten; that was the obvious truth that Auchinleck had to accept. In this defeat, and the total disaster which would follow, Auchinleck felt himself deeply involved. Ritchie had been his choice; he had left him in command despite advice earlier in the year.

Should he send up another army commander to fight the battle in place of Ritchie and perhaps to save everything by winning it? Should he go himself? Amid all his anxieties, one thing, dictated by his sense of honour, was immediately clear; he must take the blame. And so, in his house by the Pyramids at Mena, on June 23rd, 1942, he wrote to the Chief of the General Staff in London, accepting full responsibility for all that had occurred, offering to vacate the post of C-in-C if the CIGS wished it, and suggesting Alexander as his successor:

The unfavourable course of the recent battle in Cyrenaica culminating in the disastrous fall of Tobruk impels me to ask you seriously to consider the advisability of retaining me in my command. No doubt you are already considering this and quite rightly, but I want you to know that I also realize the probable effects of the past month's fighting. Personally I feel fit to carry on and reasonably confident of being able to turn the tables on the enemy in time. All the same there is no doubt that in a situation like the present, fresh blood and new ideas at the top may make all the difference between success and stalemate . . . After steeping oneself for months in the same subject all day and every day one is apt to get into a groove and to lose originality. For this theatre originality is essential and a change is quite probably desirable on this account alone, apart from all other considerations such as loss of influence due to lack of success, absence of luck and all the other things which affect the morale of an army. It occurred to me that you might want to use Alexander who is due here in a day or two. Personally I do not think Wilson could do it now, but he might. I have thought over this a lot and feel I must tell you what I think.

Next day he wrote a letter to the Prime Minister which did credit to his magnanimity as well as his integrity:

I thank you personally and most sincerely for all your help and support during the past year, and deeply regret the failures and setbacks for the past month, for which I accept the fullest responsibility.

The Prime Minister telegraphed assuring him of his complete confidence.

These letters written, part of Auchinleck's mind returned to rest, and he was able to consider more clearly the command of Eighth Army.

Ritchie, of course, must go. 'The danger of complete catastrophe,' Auchinleck wrote afterwards, 'was too great for me to leave the responsibility with a subordinate already subjected for several weeks to extraordinary strain.' But even then it was not an easy decision for a man with Auchinleck's sense of loyalty, for Ritchie was, in Auchinleck's words, 'a trusted friend and subordinate'.

Auchinleck's choice of a new army commander fell for a time on June 24th on General T. W. Corbett, his Chief of the General Staff, and fellow officer of the Indian Army. But then he decided that no subordinate could be asked to preside over the coming disaster. He must go himself.

Corbett was to remain at GHQ to transact all routine business of the office of Commander-in-Chief and to prepare for the defence of the Delta. Because Auchinleck felt that the Eighth Army Staff were tired by battle and mentally vitiated, he decided to take with him a close adviser and personal staff officer, but his choice did not fall on any of the obvious men who had already served him in high staff appointments.

He chose instead his Deputy Chief of the General Staff, Major-General E. Dorman-Smith. It was, and is, a highly controversial appointment; and it had a crucial bearing on the outcome of the most dangerous three weeks of the war.

Dorman-Smith was an Irishman of great charm and high intellectual powers. To these abilities were unfortunately added a fatal gift for wit and a short patience with the stupid. Before the war he had enjoyed a reputation in the British Army as an advanced military thinker; he had played an important part in the struggle to mechanize the army. Dorman-Smith had later been associated with O'Connor and Galloway in planning the highly unorthodox battle of Sidi Barrani. He had been Commandant of the Haifa Staff College from 1940 to December 1941, and Deputy Chief of the General Staff in Cairo since June 1942.

Auchinleck had first met him in India before the war when Auchinleck, as Deputy Chief of the General Staff, and Dorman-Smith, as Director of Military Training, had radically reshaped the Indian Army for a mechanized war. Despite his record and the high opinion of such men as O'Connor and Wavell, Dorman-Smith was by now suspected by the orthodox, who regarded him as 'brilliant but unsound'. But it was because of his unorthodoxy that Auchinleck turned to him in a moment of impending ruin:

> I took Dorman-Smith because I knew he had a most fertile, active and a very good brain. I wanted him because I knew he was a man I could talk to—a fresh mind. I remembered him from our time together in India, when we walked every morning before breakfast in the Simla hills.

In fact, Auchinleck and Dorman-Smith constituted a formidable combination: great powers of leadership united with a brilliant and original intellect. Want of either would have lost us the Middle East.

The prospect of personal command in the field did not exhilarate Auchinleck: 'The problem was much too grim and the future much too uncertain for anything of that sort.' At

10 am on June 25th, 1942, Dorman-Smith reported to Auchinleck's office in Cairo. The Commander-in-Chief told him that he was going up to take over Eighth Army and that Dorman-Smith was to accompany him. Auchinleck's mood was sombre, but lightened when Dorman-Smith suggested that they should have a final good lunch at the Mehemet Ali Club. At two in the afternoon they climbed aboard an empty bomber. Rommel's advance guards were already beginning to run blind fingers over the face of the Matruh positions.

It was now, sitting on the floor of the aircraft during the flight to Maaten Baggush and amid the roar of the engines, that Auchinleck and Dorman-Smith talked out the strategy and tactics that were to save Egypt and the oil. To help them there was the valuable information received that day from the Prime Minister in Washington: according to the President's informants in Rome, Rommel was expected to delay his attack on Matruh for three or four weeks, but the Prime Minister's own guess was that the delay might be greater.

Auchinleck was clear that the army must not be pinned to the ground at Mersa Matruh; that battle was already compromised. The army must, if there were time, fall back to El Alamein, where it could be disposed for battle according to Auchinleck's own wishes. But even here there was to be no question of a last stand, because at all costs the army must be preserved in being, even if it meant retreating into the Delta, or up the Nile on Port Sudan. For the Persian Gulf oilfield, not Egypt, was the object he must protect to the last. Supplied through Port Sudan he could lie on the flank of a German advance from Egypt towards Iraq and eventually launch a counter-stroke.

This strategy has since been strongly condemned. It is said that he should have issued an order of 'No retreat' and staked everything on a last battle at the gates of Egypt—as in fact Ritchie had intended. It is difficult in the circumstances of June 1942 to see much merit in the criticism, which Auchinleck himself regards as nonsense; heroic gestures were more opportune in August when all was over.

The aircraft flew on towards Baggush. Dorman-Smith suggested to Auchinleck that their counter-attacks should be aimed at the Italians. To rally them Rommel would have to use his Germans and so disperse his own striking force. This idea

185

Auchinleck accepted. He also agreed that the army artillery should be placed under central control.

In the course of the long flight Auchinleck's mood changed. The sense of defeat that had gripped him on the previous day faded; it had been quite foreign to his character, a stealthy intruder in a moment when all the cumulative pressures had pushed him under.

Early in the evening the aircraft landed on the Royal Air Force field at Maaten Baggush. The sun was throwing long shadows across the salt-sparkling dunes of the coast as the Commander-in-Chief and Dorman-Smith climbed into a dusty yellow staff car and were driven to Eighth Army Headquarters. It had been in these headquarters that O'Connor had planned the destruction of Graziani and his 200,000 men two years ago; it was thus familiar ground to Dorman-Smith.

Auchinleck stepped out of the car and on to the sand and officers saluted. They watched the tall, bull-shouldered figure of the Commander-in-Chief as he strode alone towards Ritchie's caravan. Inside, the two big men—Ritchie was actually the taller—faced each other. Ritchie still showed no outward sign of fatigue or strain; he was, as Auchinleck said, 'a strong and stolid fellow', and Auchinleck found him, as he was to find the rest of his headquarters, 'surprisingly normal'.

No time was wasted.

> I told Ritchie that the situation was such that nobody but I could be saddled with the responsibility and that therefore I was taking over from him.

Ritchie took the news calmly: did he not take everything calmly? There was no tension, no recrimination. The efficient staff officer once again, Ritchie described what he knew of the situation, which, in Auchinleck's words, 'wasn't much'.

The brief conversation over, Ritchie came out of the caravan alone, got straight into a car and drove away towards the Delta. Then Auchinleck, now in command of Eighth Army, went down into that underground operations room that O'Connor had used, and which had remained unoccupied for eighteen months.

Auchinleck was not a fresh man. He had borne the responsibilities of commanding-in-chief in the Middle East—and the ceaseless, ignorant goading of the Prime Minister—for twelve months. The double burden he could never share and only momentarily forget. But others sometimes glimpsed his intense desire to get some sort of relief from the constant mental pressure. General Galloway recalled that the C-in-C:

> might look out of his window and see his ADCs playing some game with a ball in the garden, and would join in. Then he would really enjoy himself, even if only for a few minutes —you and he would forget that he was the Commander-in-Chief.

As Auchinleck entered, Dorman-Smith and the staff looked at him. There were always the others watching—to see whether the chief was tired or angry or despondent or, more rarely, if he had good news. But at GHQ this watching was in a context of wall-map generalities. Here in the shadow of the prison camp and the operating table was the reality of war and, for a general, the reality of command.

Lonely in Cairo, Auchinleck would now be lonelier still, for he had become the leader of desperate and defeated men. It was his job to do the worrying so that every man in the army, from corps commander to private, could sleep easy in his blankets, knowing that defeat would not bear his signature. And here in the desert, the strain of command would be sharpened by want of privacy; there was no secluded commander-in-chief's house where Auchinleck could relax safe from watching eyes for a time in each day; eating and sleeping in the open amid the men, he would have to act out the role of bluff confidence every moment he was awake.

Auchinleck's years spent in small expeditions had given him a very close sense of community with the men in the ranks. This sense was to refresh and strengthen him in the coming battles. He felt strongly that no man must die unnecessarily; the lists of killed and wounded were to lie heavily against his will to continue the fight. It was this true and uncontrived kinship with his soldiers—which he shared with Rommel—that made him seem a warrior of the ancient kind who stood on the field with a pile of enemy dead under his sword and his retainers round him. And in fact his magnificent figure, which wore modern uniform so well, seemed made for armour; the blue eyes for glaring through a visored helmet.

On the evening of June 25th, 1942, he felt, as well as the weight of his new anxieties, a sense of 'relief at being in command, with the soldiers and doing something; at being at last personally responsible'. He had stepped into a crisis within the general crisis. General Holmes (10th Corps, in Mersa Matruh) drove in to report to the new army commander and receive his orders. He told Auchinleck that Rommel was certain to attack the Eighth Army early on the morrow; this news made it certain that the compromised battle of Matruh would have to be fought after all. The prospects for the battle were gloomy. In Auchinleck's words, 'nobody knew where anything was. I was desperately afraid that the troops in Matruh would be surrounded.' Auchinleck therefore made clear to Holmes that in no circumstances was he to allow himself to be bottled up in Matruh; Ritchie's order to stand and fight to a finish was revoked. If the battle of Mersa Matruh went badly, Eighth Army would fall back towards El Alamein. Holmes went back to his headquarters 'alert and confident', but then he was new to defeat.

There was no time for Auchinleck to alter Ritchie's dispositions; there was no reserve; and Auchinleck's ability to control the battle was further blunted by the distance between his two corps in Mersa Matruh and round Minquar Quaim. He realized that he could be hardly more than an onlooker. But in the few hours that remained he could at least impress on his subordinates the style of warfare he expected.

He was an Indian soldier. All his experience was of empty plains and hills; his natural bent was for mobility and manoeuvre. In the First World War he had taken part in the vain attempts to relieve the fortress of Kut-el-Amara in Mesopotamia; it made a permanent mark: 'The Turks should have been manoeuvred out of their positions—not frontally attacked.' Of the great campaigns in history, Stonewall Jackson's Shenandoah campaign with its deception and manoeuvre had made a deep impression on him. As a staff college instructor, as a field force commander on the Frontier, and as Deputy Chief of the General Staff in India during the modernization of the Indian Army, mobility and manoeuvre remained his theme, 'as opposed to anything based on the battles in France in the First World War'. On the evening of June 25th, 1942, he issued to Eighth Army a series of instructions and orders which constitute his written testament as a desert general, and which fore-shadow the revolution he tried to bring about during the July battles at Alamein.

He insisted that the army must keep its mobility. It must work as a team, with units co-operating with each other and co-ordinating their efforts. Rigid corps and divisional autonomy was outmoded at the present time; Auchinleck sharply reminded the proudly separatist arms of the British service that they all belonged to the same army. He went on to tell his commanders how they were to deal with German penetrations of the ancient Matruh minefields.

> He will be at once engaged with all available artillery by the division or divisions nearest the threatened spot. Other divisions, while continuing to watch their own allotted flank and fronts, will move at once to the threatened front and attack the enemy boldly and quickly with all available artillery, this movement being co-ordinated by Corps Commanders.

Auchinleck was particularly concerned about the quality of leadership in Eighth Army manifested during the summer campaign. Now, a few hours before battle, he tried to infuse into his commanders something of the initiative and energy shown by their German rivals. He instructed them:

> An essential part of [my] method of defence is the close control and co-ordination of the action of battle groups by divisional commanders who must make their presence felt on the battlefield. It is their duty to supply the driving power . . . The Corps Commanders must be in the closest possible touch so as to ensure that if one Corps or part of it has to give ground the other is immediately able to take advantage of the situation by rapidly and boldly attacking the enemy in the flank.

His conception of war in the desert, as he pointed out with somewhat acid emphasis, 'called for the maximum of mobility on the part of the troops concerned and the greatest alertness and quickness of decision on the part of all commanders.'

All this was revolutionary and long overdue, but it had no effect on the battle of Mersa Matruh. The old, slow habits of the eighteen months since O'Connor had been captured and the ingrained rigidity and orthodoxy of pre-war British military doctrine could not be eradicated in a few hours; it required a long period of repose, wherein the army could be taken apart and remade. The advantage of such a period was to be bought by Auchinleck in the coming battles, but to be enjoyed by his successor.

That night Auchinleck lay in a sleeping-bag on the sand. He slept well, for although he knew that tomorrow's battle was really out of his control, the oriental fatalism he had absorbed in India gave him peace of mind. Early in the morning, as the bright sun beckoned to Rommel from the East and the desert snails crawled up the camel thorn to drink the dew 'like', as Dorman-Smith expressed it, 'lazy soldiers getting out of their blankets', Auchinleck was awakened, as was to be his habit, with the latest situation report.

All over the desert men stirred, boiled tea over petrol fires and prepared for a day of battle. When the sun was high the *Panzerarmee* came on over the stony ground, dark columns of transport led by squat, white-crossed tanks with gun muzzles nosing left and right for targets. From the shallow weapon pits of the British, they appeared to dissolve and float in the shimmering heat haze.

Rommel's plan for the battle of Mersa Matruh was that of O'Connor for Sidi Barrani; and it was to be as successful. In forty-eight hours Rommel, with 60 tanks and 2500 German infantry, was to rout two British army corps, with 150 tanks, and fling them again along the bitter road to the Nile. But Rommel's plan was more daring in theory than it proved to be in fact. His intelligence placed the tanks of 1st Armoured Division in the British centre, which was in fact virtually empty, and he proposed to drive through this division with the 20 tanks and 600 men of 21st Panzer Division, together with 90th Light Division. When well in the British rear he would fan out in a double envelopment of the British wings at Mersa Matruh and Minquar Quaim.

British intelligence, no more accurate than the German, credited Rommel with 25,000 Germans and 100 tanks.

For the Panzer Army it was an unexpectedly easy day. In the centre 21st Panzer and 90th Light flicked aside Gleecol and Leathercol, lost in those spaces, and rolled on to the east between 10th and 13th Corps. This was the moment for Gott and 13th Corps to drive into the extended German flank and smash

21st Panzer and 90th Light against 10th Corps in Matruh, in accordance with Auchinleck's orders. But Gott's corps did not move; as in all the battles of the summer British formations who were not under attack were the interested but inactive spectators of those who were. The tanks of the 1st Armoured Division, upon whom the outcome of the battle depended, spent the day by Gott's orders so far out of touch to the south of Sidi Hamza that they did not even meet Rommel's feinting force, 15th Panzer Division, as it drove eastwards along the escarpment south of Minquar Quaim.

Night fell on this scene of British passivity and German progress; Rommel was now ready to sweep north and south in his double envelopment. Yet Rommel's advance constituted only a fantastic imposture; he was so outnumbered by the British that by his manoeuvre he had really put his head through an open door which might slam at any time on his ears. He himself lay with his main body between Holmes and Gott. Far away to the south the 20 tanks of 15th Panzer Division risked collision with 150 of 1st Armoured Division. But Rommel's moral ascendancy over Gott and other Eighth Army commanders was now such that he convinced them it was they who were in terrible danger. On June 27th, he and 21st Panzer Division 'surrounded' the New Zealanders, who remained quite still on the ridge of Minquar Quaim as the Germans worked round them. Rommel then went by car across the empty British centre to 90th Light Division; a brief conference, and 90th Light drove east and north to the coast behind Matruh. Now Holmes too was 'surrounded'.

Rommel's shadow of an army had passed deeper still into a trap; but a trap that would never be sprung because the trappers were held frozen in an hypnotic trance. Ninetieth Light lay on the wrong side of a 'fortress' held by five full-strength, semi-mobile brigades; 21st Panzer Division, now in a strength of 14 tanks and 600 men, lay scattered round the full strength and fresh New Zealand Division.

A concise account of the battle suggests an exactitude and tidiness that did not exist. Neither Eighth Army intelligence nor the outgoing army commander had been able to give Auchinleck more than the vaguest picture of his new command—of its dispositions, its numerical strength, its moral state or its equipment. Reports coming through to Auchinleck's headquarters at Baggush during the battle added fresh obscurity to what was already confused; it was impossible for Auchinleck to tell what was really happening. It was thus pointless and even dangerous for him to issue fresh orders. Nor was it possible for him to go up to one of the corps himself, because Ritchie's dispositions had so separated them that once there he would lose all power of decision over the rest of the army.

Therefore, like a calm man lost in the fog, Auchinleck listened to the reports and considered the proper battle he was going to fight at Alamein. Perhaps his principal regret was that he had not been able to meet Gott as well as Holmes beforehand to impress on him personally how the battle was to be fought and to put some backbone into him. But Gott had been unobtainable, roaming as usual somewhere out in the desert in the semi-independent way to which he had become accustomed. And now, though happily Auchinleck did not know it, Gott was losing the battle of Mersa Matruh.

Gott at this time had supped too long on disaster; his optimistic energy had turned into an energetic pessimism. The advance of 21st Panzer Division to the east of the New Zealanders had convinced him that the battle was lost. At a time when Auchinleck expected him to order the combined blow of 1st Armoured Division and the New Zealand Division to the north that would crush Rommel against Holmes' corps, Gott was in fact telling General Freyberg of the New Zealanders that he could withdraw if he so wished. Later in the day, having motored to another part of the field, he had doleful and utterly untrue news for General Lumsden of 1st Armoured Division. Lumsden wanted to move his division up close to the New Zealanders, a manoeuvre which might have saved the battle; but Gott shook his head. The New Zealanders, he told Lumsden, 'did not exist'. He followed this with a formal order to Lumsden to fall back. When Freyberg next spoke to Lumsden by telephone, he therefore learnt that the armour was already leaving him high and dry on Minquar Quaim. Gott's leadership that afternoon had certainly led to mobility, but hardly of the sort intended by Auchinleck.

The news that his left flank had melted eventually reached Auchinleck in the operations room at Maaten Baggush, and told him that the battle was lost. He signalled Holmes in Matruh that Gott had gone and ordered him also to fall back on Alamein. This done, Auchinleck climbed into a covered station wagon and went back himself. This station wagon, with a hole in the roof through which the Commander-in-Chief could stand and talk to his men on the road, was for a few days Eighth Army headquarters; Auchinleck was accompanied by a signals truck and a small staff. Dorman-Smith had left for Fuka the day before in order to prepare for the C-in-C's arrival.

After an unpleasant journey over rough going and under German air attack, Auchinleck and his party bivouacked in the desert. The night spent under the stars, the sleeping-bag laid over a scooped-out body-shaped cavity in the sand, the tea brewed over a petrol fire—these things brought Auchinleck ...ck from the lofty splendour of commanding-in-chief to the ...nd of soldiering he liked best. In the morning his party found ...emselves and their vehicles the centre of an empty circle described by the low desert horizon. They set up their wireless; and this was combined headquarters of Eighth Army and Middle East Forces. During the day the Luftwaffe found some targets to bomb in their piece of the desert.

But if the battle of Mersa Matruh was over so far as Auchinleck knew, it was in fact only just beginning for Freyberg and Holmes. Because of confusion in Eighth Army signals, Holmes did not get Auchinleck's order to fall back to Alamein until twelve hours after Gott's corps had begun their retreat. And because of this signals delay, Holmes launched his own break-out when Gott had already abandoned the battle. On the night of June 27th/28th, under a bright moon, 10th Corps drove southwards in a dense and conspicuous column of guns and transport. Soon the characteristic lofty profiles of the British trucks stood out starkly in the light of flares and tracer as the Germans poured fire into this easy target. Naked on that open desert, Holmes' inexperienced corps fell back routed into Mersa Matruh. It was on the following morning, while sorting out his force, that Holmes learned that they had been left by Gott surrounded and alone.

That night of the full moon had seen another stirring action as Gott's other victims, the New Zealanders, broke out from Minquar Quaim. With the bayonet they hacked a hole in 21st

Panzer Division through which they charged in column, men clinging to every kind of vehicle. As they bucked through moonlight seamed with tracer and splashed with gun flashes, their general, Freyberg, wounded and in bandages, stood in front of a truck shouting:

"By God, another Balaclava!"

It was on the following day, June 28th, that the last bloody encounter of the Matruh battle was fought out between 10th Corps and *Panzerarmee Afrika*. In the white glare of late afternoon Rommel began attacking the surrounded British in Mersa Matruh; but, when night fell, he still lay outside the perimeter. In the utter darkness before the moon rose, 10th Corps prepared for escape. At nine o'clock 10th Corps charged blindly into its besiegers. It was a night of chaos. The British trampled through the headquarters of 90th Light; Rommel's own headquarters were surrounded by burning trucks, which as the only objec to be seen in the pitch dark attracted everybody's fire; the Roya Air Force bombed British troops; and the Germans fired on each other. And then 10th Corps were out in the open, bumping along the escarpment towards Fuka and the passes down to the coast road which Auchinleck had ordered Gott to hold open. But Gott was still elusive, still running a private war without reference to orders; and so when 10th Corps reached the head of the passes, they were greeted not by 13th Corps but by *Panzerarmee Afrika*. There was another brisk action before four-fifths of the corps were able to reach El Alamein. Meanwhile Rommel gathered in 6000 prisoners, 40 tanks and many guns in Mersa Matruh.

The battle of Mersa Matruh, Rommel's most astonishing victory, the battle Auchinleck never meant to accept, was over.

It marked the consummation of a colossal moral ascendancy of the *Panzerarmee Afrika* over the Eighth Army; a matter far more alarming to Auchinleck than the mere fact of defeat. Scattered now between Fuka and El Alamein was the wreckage of two British corps, while close behind them, and sometimes in front of them, came the *Panzerarmee*. It seemed like the last disaster. The Cairo stock exchange and Strafer Gott agreed upon fearing the worst, and all over Egypt panic began to flap its quivering wings. 'Groppi's Horse' and 'Shepheard's Short Range Desert Group' began a highly mobile retirement to the

King David Hotel in Jerusalem. In this sliding, melting world of rout and defeatism Auchinleck stood a lonely and defiant figure, and the troops rallied to him.

Perhaps the most disconcerting factor for Auchinleck was his continued ignorance of the state of his army, for Eighth Army headquarters could tell him nothing.

> No one [he wrote later] least of all I—could say whether the Army could be rallied and reformed soon enough to hold Rommel and save Egypt. This remained in doubt for at least a fortnight.

Therefore, while the race to El Alamein was still going hard, he left his headquarters—now at Ommayid—and drove back towards the enemy, against the current of retreat, to Daba on the coast road. First he superintended the destruction of the immense stores in Daba. Then he went out on to the coast road, because 'I wanted to see what the general state of morale and discipline was among the troops coming back'.

The road stretched away from him through the flat, scrubby desert, a black and shimmering tape, two vehicles wide; fifteen hundred miles away through Sollum, Tobruk and Benghazi was Tripoli. Auchinleck stood in the sand by the roadside, bareheaded, and watched his beaten army stream past him towards El Alamein. It came radiator to tailboard: tanks on transporters; supply trucks; troop carriers; towed bombers without wings, like monstrous maimed insects; trucks loaded with mess and Naafi stores and furniture; guns. A yellow-painted travelling funfair on the move to the next ground. As a scene of disastrous retreat, it was incongruous: instead of the starvation and frost-bite that Corunna, Moscow and Valley Forge have made the traditional trappings, there was the travel agent's sunshine, the Mediterranean's copper sulphate blue between the white dunes. Their faces dried and brown as biscuit, the men passed by him in trucks powdered thickly with dust and hung about with bedrolls and billy-cans.

> The troops were bewildered [Auchinleck recollected later] but completely unconcerned. There were no signs of panic, such as people trying to pass each other. The spectacle was encouraging from the point of view of morale, but there was terrible disorganization, and I could see the army would need refitting.

Yet there was an aspect of the choked traffic on the coast road which surprised, appalled and angered the Commander-in-Chief; it was the superfluous clutter the army was carrying with it in its retreat—the trucks loaded with Naafi stores and furniture and all the other hamper of welfare. It had not been necessary—it would have been impossible—to take all this comfort up the passes of the North-West Frontier; and to Auchinleck it was another aspect of the softness and luxury that he had hated in Cairo. In his anger at the sight he resolved to strip the army down to what it needed for battle; and he, the Commander-in-Chief, would set the example in his own head-quarters. 'I think,' he said long afterwards, 'that we are inclined to carry too much about. We are too luxurious. In Mesopotamia in 1914–18 we lived much more simply.'

His vigil on the roadside had served another purpose: 'I also wanted to show myself a bit, and talk to one or two of the chaps.' Either there, or while standing up hatless in his car, he chatted to as many as he could, from as many different formations as possible—to British, to Indians, to Commonwealth soldiers. If his men impressed Auchinleck, 'The Auk' equally impressed his men. He looked a fighter, big and burly, with a fighter's pugnacious chin and mouth; and they could tell from the way he talked to them that he was a real chap—no tricks, none of 'the old flannel', the 'bull' through which the British soldier can instantly see.

For Auchinleck was a simple, genuine man, brought up by his mother—whom he admired and loved—in an old-fashioned code of manners and principles. Men had always loved the Auk. 'He sometimes appeared severe and formidable,' as General Galloway put it, 'but he had great charm and innate kindness.'

Auchinleck drove back to Ommayid again to prepare for the desperate action that would be under way in a few hours. Yet there was on that day, June 29th, 1942, a fair chance that there would be no such action, for Rommel was trying with all his relentless energy to sweep the British in shreds through the Alamein 'bottleneck' without giving them a pause in which they might recover themselves. The exhausted *Panzerarmee*, dreaming of sleep and of swimming in the creamy breakers that curled endlessly along the coast of Egypt, toiled on through the heat and sand clouds. Above them the sky now belonged to the Royal Air Force, which had at last abandoned distant strategic targets and was dropping a moving curtain of bombs between Eighth Army and its pursuers. With their petrol and ammunition trucks burning, the starved panzers began to slow down.

During June 29th and 30th, 1942, the war in the desert—the war between Britain and Germany—moved to its climax, as both armies raced each other over the last few miles to Alamein. No moment in the war had been or was to be as mouth-drying as this.

Back in the Delta the British were affording an example of British phlegm that could be remembered by the Egyptians with advantage in the future. Behind a smoke-screen of burning paper, the 'Gabardine Swine' (as Auchinleck recollects that base personnel were dubbed) moved out of harm's way with a speed that would have impressed Rommel. The Royal Navy, without bothering to inform the Army, weighed anchor and sailed from Alexandria with such dispatch that the White Ensign was still flying over the deserted camp at Sidi Bishr while Egyptians looted it at leisure. In the Alamein defences the racket of road-drills gave an imitation of the noise of battle as the troops employed the last hours in drilling new weapon pits in the hard rock.

From the open desert the last British stragglers were coming in. Among these was 1st Armoured Division, which had hoped for a peaceful journey but which had instead bumped into two Italian divisions once and into the Afrika Korps twice. During the morning of June 30th, 10th Corps was still streaming east along the coast road past El Alamein and through 1st South African Division, which held the coastal flank. But the stream of vehicles at last dried up; the road stretched empty into the haze before the eyes of the Eighth Army gunners, and somewhere beyond was Rommel.

Auchinleck had now moved from his temporary headquarters at Ommayid to the place behind the Ruweisat Ridge from which he was to direct the battle. To his soldiers he issued a calm and characteristically untheatrical order of the day:

> The enemy is stretching to his limit and thinks we are a broken army . . . He hopes to take Egypt by bluff. Show him where he gets off.

Auchinleck's own personal recovery from the terrible depression and sense of failure of June 23rd–25th was now complete.

"The British pride themselves on being good losers," he remarked to Dorman-Smith. "I'm a damn bad loser. I'm going to win."

About noon visibility grew worse as a sandstorm rose. Whirling dust filled eyes and nostrils and choked the mechanisms of guns—thick as a London fog, but oven-hot. Eighth Army peered into the billowing murk, waiting for it to form into the shapes of tanks crawling on towards Alexandria.

Then something moved out there—tanks, trucks and guns in the blowing sand. It was 90th Light. A salvo crashed out from a battery of British field artillery, the first shots in the First Battle of Alamein.

But no more Germans were seen that day.

CHAPTER TWO

At this time, the British Broadcasting Corporation and the British Press were telling their public that the Eighth Army had retreated into 'The Alamein Line', which apparently stretched like a desert Maginot from the Mediterranean forty miles to the salt marshes of the Quattara Depression. Here, alone in the desert arena, it appeared that there were no open flanks for Rommel to turn with his armour. It is the way of wartime propaganda, manufactured from hour to hour to keep up home morale, to form in the public's mind lasting and false impressions; impressions which over the years become national myths. But the oddest thing about the dream world of propaganda is its influence on the real world of battle. Hitler and Stalingrad is one case of this; Churchill and Tobruk another; the BBC and Alamein a third. On June 29th and 30th, 1942, the British broadcasts about the Alamein Line reached two unexpected audiences. The first was the troops of the Eighth Army, who heard it on the way back from Matruh, and who were surprised to find that the line was just the same old empty desert. The second was Rommel, who believed in it and, because he believed in it, delayed his attack twenty-four hours in

Map. 17. General Map to Illustrate First Battle of Alamein
July 1942

order to prepare more thoroughly, and so gave Auchinleck what he needed more than tanks—time.

In fact, neither under Auchinleck nor Montgomery was the British front at Alamein a continuous web of defences right across the bottleneck. There was always an open flank; at first because the troops were so thin on the ground it was impossible to hold the entire forty-mile front, and later because Auchinleck preferred to leave the southern sector open in order to tempt Rommel on to the British refused left flank along the Alam Halfa Ridge. What defences there were on June 30th, 1942, had been constructed by Auchinleck's orders after June 1941, and improved in haste by Norrie in the last few days.

Between the Mediterranean at El Alamein and the seven-hundred-foot cliffs that line the northern edge of the Quattara Depression was a stretch of various desert as wide as the distance between Croydon and Brighton—about forty miles. This can hardly be called a bottleneck. The northern half was so featureless that almost imperceptible rises in the ground became of great tactical importance. South of these ridges—Miteiriya, Ruweisat—there were abrupt escarpments and bad going that became worse and worse until the Quattara Depression was reached. Auchinleck in 1941 had chosen this unpleasant piece of country as the final defence of Egypt for two reasons: firstly, if the forty-mile-wide neck were held in proper strength (two full-strength infantry divisions and a large armoured force), it could not be turned; and secondly, the jagged ground in the south would very much cramp the movement of armour. West of the Alamein–Bab el Quattara track too the going was bad: Dorman-Smith has described it as 'large flat stones that stood on edge and looked at you, one after the other'.

The fixed defences consisted of three defended localities ('boxes' in the local jargon that Auchinleck hated) placed at fifteen-mile intervals across the neck. The right flank was anchored by the El Alamein locality, which blocked the railway and the coast road; it had been intended as a corps headquarters. Its defences were much like Tobruk's, but with a perimeter shorter by half. In the centre was the locality of Bab el Quattara, in fine defensive country full of cliffs; and in the south was the locality of Abu Dweiss which commanded a way down the cliffs to a track in the Quattara Depression that could be used by cars.

Into these positions had been drifting for the last fortnight troops from all over the Middle East Command: fresh troops such as the 18th Indian Brigade from Iraq; the wreckage of the Gazala defeats, such as 1st South African Division and 50th Division; and more recent survivors such as the New Zealanders and 9th Indian Brigade. Since June 23rd Norrie had been working with desperate speed to sort these troops out and place them; and to do something to fill the vast stretches of desert between the boxes. The South Africans held the extreme right flank, in the Alamein box. A new box had been established between Alamein and Bab el Quattara, at Deir El Shein, west of the Ruweisat Ridge, and had been garrisoned by 18th Indian Brigade. Bab el Quattara was held by the 6th New Zealand Brigade, with 4th and 5th New Zealand Brigades behind them to the east. Far out to the south was 9th Indian Brigade, lacking both a water supply and artillery.

In the breathing space accorded him by Rommel, Auchinleck continued the radical changes in battle technique laid down in his operations instructions before Matruh. It was clear to him that the immobile infantry in the Alamein defences would be as helpless and ineffective as those in the Gazala boxes. Auchinleck therefore thinned them out so that no more remained in the line than could be carried by allocated transport. He also broke down the divisional organization into the flexible 'battlegroup' system that Rommel had used with such success for eighteen months. Auchinleck's battlegroups, extemporized in a time of scarcity of equipment, consisted of lorry-borne infantry surrounding nuclei of 25-pounders. They could do two things in the desert that a British infantry division could not do—move and hit. In particular, Auchinleck took two brigade groups from the South Africans in the Alamein perimeter and placed them in the open desert north of the Ruweisat Ridge. Hence the box was almost empty. But its presence was a psychological factor forcing avoidance on Rommel.

Auchinleck's efforts to cure the arthritis of the traditional 15,000-men British division have aroused enduring controversy. Orthodoxy alleged it was a 'penny packets' policy. But Auchinleck is convinced he is right:

> The 'Battle Group Controversy' is rubbish. In the circumstances existing there was no other way. Infantry and artillery in solid divisional lumps were not and could not be any match for armour, until and unless they were dug in with unturnable flanks. Even so the enemy armour could penetrate and play hell behind unless opposed by our armour, which was not there—to begin with.

swift turning movements are the essence of desert warfare. To do this you must be strong in 'armour', stronger than the enemy or at least as strong. If this requirement is absent you have had it—infantry and artillery are helpless in the Desert without armour, however brave they are—useless mouths who can be outflanked, surrounded and mopped up at will . . .

Auchinleck had his supporters. The New Zealand Brigadier Kippenberger, a hard critic of British command, wrote that 'The brigade group organization had many advantages for desert warfare, particularly in mobility and quick readiness for action'. Since the Second World War, the American, British, French and German armies have all replaced the division as a basic unit by some form of the brigade group.

At Dorman-Smith's suggestion, Auchinleck had now had all the artillery regrouped under his own command as an equivalent of Rommel's army artillery. For the first time in the desert since O'Connor the British were to defend and to attack under the cover of mass gunfire. Auchinleck also formed a new kind of armoured brigade—4th Light Armoured Brigade—composed entirely of armoured cars and intended to exploit breakthroughs at a speed impossible for tracked vehicles.

The armour remained the greatest of Auchinleck's anxieties. He had 150 tanks in 1st Armoured Division, commanded by General Lumsden, but of them only two squadrons were Grants, which were now believed by the British command to be the only British tanks at all fit for battle. The morale of officers and men was shaken after a month of heavy losses and continuous defeat. This was no reflection on the courage of British tank men, but they had seen too many knocked-out tanks with charred objects still sitting in the crew's places, had experienced too often the warm and odorous horror of a comrade's intestines spread over them in the hot imprisonment of the tank. Shaky nerves extended to Lumsden himself. For example, four days after the battle at Alamein began, there was a sharp exchange between him and his corps commander, Norrie, in Norrie's caravan on the Ruweisat Ridge, witnessed by Dorman-Smith. Lumsden pleaded hysterically the strain of battle on his division and 'in terms almost insultingly insubordinate' demanded that the armour should be stationed farther to the rear. The meeting might have ended in a furious row; but Norrie, himself a cavalryman and an officer of great coolness and balance, handled Lumsden with patience and sympathy, and the armour stayed where it was. But Auchinleck intended to use it 'close-hauled' under the cover of his artillery.

In the last two days before the battle began, Auchinleck, Norrie, Dorman-Smith and the staff worked without a break in the heat and flies of the operations caravan. In the absence of an HQ mess, sandwiches filled with oily butter and 'desert chicken' and mugs of tea were brought to them from time to time. There was no question, in those flying, crowded hours, of preparing a tidy, copy-book array. In Auchinleck's words,

> The Eighth Army was rebuilt as far as could be done with the forces available and having regard to the standard of training of newly arrived troops. It was not and could not be a reasoned, measured process.

At the same time he had to prepare against possible defeat. On June 30th he ordered Holmes of 10th Corps to go back and organize the defences of the Delta; next day he issued orders for the conduct of a retreat from Alamein, should that be necessary. For Auchinleck's view was—and is—that to issue a 'No retreat' order at Alamein in the circumstances of the time would have been 'bloody stupid'. He was, after all, Commander-in-Chief as well as Eighth Army commander, and he had to consider the safety of his entire command. Eighth Army must be kept in being, because he recognized, as did the Chief of the Imperial General Staff, that the oil of the Persian Gulf was more important to the war than Egypt. In fact, to stand and fight at all at Alamein was a decision of enormous courage; Wavell, for example, had accepted a staff study in 1941 which recommended that if the Axis forces got east of Matruh, then Egypt would have to be evacuated.

His army placed, Auchinleck waited in his headquarters behind the Ruweisat Ridge, close to the front, for Rommel to attack. He had made his guess as to Rommel's plans: he signalled London on the evening of June 30th that he expected the enemy to make his main effort between Alamein and Bab el Quattara. The British army was therefore disposed to meet an attack on its right centre. He signalled his army at the same time that

> the Army Commander appreeiates that as the enemy has not attacked this evening he will attack at a very early hour tomorrow morning . . . all troops to expect attack from midnight onwards.

The time for attack in fact given in the *Panzerarmee*'s operations orders was 0300 hours.

Auchinleck proposed to defeat any attempt by Rommel to pass round the El Alamein box to the sea by blocking it or taking it in the flank with the South African battle groups. The German force making the expected main blow on his right centre would be struck from the south by New Zealand battle groups—especially at night when the exhausted German armour leaguered—and from the north by 1st Armoured Division from its assembly area at the western end of Ruweisat Ridge.

Rommel proposed to hustle the British into a fresh retreat by bluff and dazzling manoeuvre. Of the great army that had rolled round Bir Hacheim in the bright morning of May 26th, only 1500 German infantry and some 60 tanks remained, together with 30 Italian tanks and about 5000 men of that Italian infantry which was useless in an offensive battle. So starved was Rommel of essential supplies and equipment by the ships of the Royal Navy and the stupidity of the German Supreme Command that four out of five of his soldiers had travelled up from the frontier in captured British trucks. The German Command just could not be made to see what a colossal strategic success might be won in the Middle East by sending Rommel one of the twenty-odd panzer divisions swallowed up in Russia. However, Eighth Army Intelligence credited Rommel with at least 100 German tanks and 25,000 Germans; bluff was in fact his most hopeful weapon. Therefore Rommel planned to repeat Matruh: 90th Light Division and the Afrika Korps would drive through the British right centre, between the Alamein and Deir el Shein boxes; and then, while 90th Light turned north to the sea and cut off the troops in Alamein—which German intelligence thought consisted of the remnants of 50th Division—the Afrika Korps would sweep far to the south behind the British

Map 18. First Battle of Alamein
July 1942, Phases One and Two

centre and left flank to attack them from the rear. It was exactly as Auchinleck had guessed.

Rommel expected his men to move at a brisk pace: Afrika Korps, for example, was to cover thirty miles through the British defences at ten miles an hour. A sign of growing German weakness was the employment of Italians, who had not been used at all at Matruh. A part of them was to line the western face of the Alamein box, part to hold the Ruweisat Ridge when it had been captured. The Italian 20th Corps (*Corpo Armata de Manovra*) would accompany the Afrika Korps and attack the New Zealanders at Bab el Quattara.

The battle plan was typical of Rommel: hasty, reckless, unrealistic and based on poor information. But he counted as always on the moral factor to make nonsense of rational calculation; once he was behind the enemy, the British Command, fearful for its communications, would again lose its nerve and bolt. He did not know yet that he now faced the man who had called his bluff in November 1941.

If there were a moment during the desert campaigns when, as before Valmy, destiny seemed to hold its breath, it was on the night of June 30th/July 1st, 1942. This night, the eve of the battle that, with the defence of Stalingrad, marked the turn of the Second World War, was fine and decked with stars. Later the moon rose, and turned the desert and its waiting armies to black and tarnished silver. By its sad and fatal light the two veteran divisions of the Afrika Korps set out on their approach march, and became deeply entangled in the course of climbing up and down unexpected and deeply shadowed escarpments. As was the Germans' custom when in confusion, they sent up a magnificent display of Very lights of every colour to indicate to each other where they lay. For the watching British outposts it was an odd diversion. The Afrika Korps arrived on their startline three hours late; things had already begun to go wrong with Rommel's battle. When it was light enough on the morning of July 1st, 1942, for airmen to discern targets on the ground, the Royal Air Force savagely bombed the Afrika Korps and threw it into more confusion. At last, and very late, the Panzer Army, with a squealing clatter of tank tracks, began to advance.

Afrika Korps (21st and 15th Panzer Division) on Auchinleck's right centre ran immediately into heavy fire from the Indians in the Deir el Shein box and the South African battle groups farther east. This was a check and a shock: German intelligence had placed these troops much farther to the east, out of their way. Rommel's tired men therefore had to endure heavy fighting instead of the expected morning's motoring. As they struggled towards the east, the fire grew hotter and the whole of the day was spent by both panzer divisions, led in person by the corps commander, General Nehring, in dealing with the Indians in Deir el Shein, in the face of whose stubborn defence the southern German envelopment thus completely broke down.

The northern envelopment did no better. Ninetieth Light Division wheeled round the Alamein box as expected by Auchinleck and was caught in the converging fire of the South African brigade groups on Auchinleck's right flank. Ninetieth Light struggled on through soft sand and shell-bursts; and by midday its attack seemed more promising to Rommel than that of Afrika Korps, stuck at Deir el Shein. He switched his few reserves to their support and in the afternoon he and Bayerlein went up in person to drive on the attack. With Rommel behind them, 90th Light managed to move a little farther to the east of Alamein. The desert about them continually erupted in plumes of sand and lumps of rock as Auchinleck's newly regrouped army-controlled artillery shelled them furiously from all sides. By the late afternoon even Rommel was stuck; he and Bayerlein lay out on the ground with his troops under this fire, unable to move, unable to give an order.

These were the hours when the tactical initiative began to pass from Rommel to Auchinleck. While the Panzer Army and its chief were paralyzed, the British commander was preparing orders for counter-attack.

That night, as 90th Light lay panting in its salient, and Afrika Korps were discovering that their eventual capture of Deir el Shein had cost them eighteen out of fifty-five remaining runners, Strafer Gott at last came into Auchinleck's headquarters. There was a conference in Auchinleck's operations caravan—Gott, tired and stained with defeat; Norrie, cool and able, but carrying his own memories of defeat; Auchinleck, new from Cairo, vigorous and belligerent.

Auchinleck reviewed the day's fighting. It had gone well. Rommel had achieved nothing of his strategic design. His only success had been the destruction of the Indians at Deir el Shein at the price of Afrika Korps' standstill; and Auchinleck took the loss calmly. It might have opened a dangerous breach in his right centre, but the slowness of its fall had given him time to muster fresh forces, and Afrika Korps now faced an even harder task on the morrow.

A greater cause for anxiety was the state of the British armour. This had been intended by Auchinleck to fall upon the Germans investing Deir el Shein and destroy them: it would have been a major success. Instead, one British armoured brigade became hopelessly stuck in soft sand and the other, with eighteen runners, did not get into action until the box was about to fall. This brigade skirmished with 21st Panzer Division and then, by a mistake, was ordered home again.

Auchinleck explained his orders for the following day. It was essential that Eighth Army recover the tactical initiative—strategic defence depended on tactical attack—in order that Rommel should be thrown off his stride. Therefore Eighth Army would launch a counter-stroke on the morrow. The plan, as Auchinleck expounded it in his deep, big man's voice, was bold. While 30th Corps held Rommel's attacks, as it had done all that day, 13th Corps, with the armour, would drive into and around Rommel's right flank, across his communications and on to the coast road at Sidi Rahman. The object of the manoeuvre was Rommel's complete destruction.

This conference with Gott and Norrie on the evening of July 1st, 1942, ended the drift and confusion in Eighth Army. It established Auchinleck's personal authority over his corps commanders; this was specially important in the case of Gott, who had been so disheartened. It opened the resolute and clever fighting by which Rommel's will to victory was bent, at first slowly, then more and more quickly until finally it was broken.

The oppressive awareness of being mastered by a superior will and superior forces would come to Rommel gradually through the dense medium of a confused battle, with its clash of isolated units, its false and true reports, its small defeats and little victories. But on the evening of July 1st and despite the setbacks of the day Rommel was still buoyant and sanguine. He signalled to Rome and Berlin that he had won a great victory and that he was on the road to Alexandria. There only remained the task of turning this lie into fact.

During those night hours when exhausted men hunger desperately for sleep, he tried to drive his divisions along their original thrust lines, but in vain. The Afrika Korps, on Auchinleck's right centre, could not move because the Royal Air Force had bombed their convoys of supply trucks to a standstill. It was quiet in 90th Light's part of the desert, but the division did not move either. Its men wanted sleep more than victory, more than food; and because it was a quiet night, they slept. Towards dawn they returned reluctantly from the womb of sleep to the cold white sand of Egypt and began again to struggle towards the east, round the Alamein box. Out of the darkness came the murderous concentric fire from Auchinleck's army artillery, the tracer curving towards them, and 90th Light were stuck again.

By first light on July 2nd Rommel had had to submit a little to Auchinleck: he had abandoned his plan of a double envelopment. Instead Afrika Korps was to join 90th Light in a single envelopment of the El Alamein box. Subsequent reports that both German panzer divisions were concentrating about Deir el Shein gave Auchinleck hope that his own plans for the day would bring a decisive victory, for Rommel's concentration towards the north had exposed his right flank.

The day—the endless day of a battle—slowly passed in the tiny army headquarters behind the Ruweisat Ridge. Distantly the smoke rose and drifted across the brassy sky.

From the west, where the mirage turned desert and crawling armies to a glittering liquid, sounded the iron rattle, the dull violence of a major action. The reports came in, the flags moved on the map in the baking metal oven of the operations caravan; did they truly represent what was happening out there beyond the mirage?

There were other doubts for the C-in-C. Would his troops and their officers remain steady in the face of a dangerous encirclement of the Alamein box? Most of the men on his right flank were South Africans under Pienaar, who was under pressure from his own government to avoid white South African losses. If they should give way, the army would be in great danger. And how was his own attack going? Gott had seemed very tired last night; was he driving the attack as hard as he should? If it were successful, the danger to the Middle East might be over before nightfall.

The day died at last, and gradually the truth began to shape itself as the reports were sifted. Auchinleck's counter-stroke had failed; yet, not so much failed as never been made. To prepare and launch such a stroke in a few hours had proved beyond the powers of British staff work and leadership alike. Instead of a sudden terrible blow coming out of the desert, there was a slow and laborious accumulation of pressure. The New Zealand Division, which provided most of the infantry, was commanded by a young brigadier instead of the wounded Freyberg, 'that tremendous dynamo', as Auchinleck expressed it. Gott, the corps commander, could not find the bounding energy of leadership the bold plan required. The armour, instead of passing to the south of the German armour, met it head-on along the Ruweisat Ridge, and in that collision both Rommel's and Auchinleck's plans were smashed.

Yet with the road to the Delta still barred, the day was Auchinleck's; and German war diaries after six weeks of triumphant reporting became competitive essays in tear-jerking. They were fluent and moving on such topics as battle fatigue, the incessant British air attacks, and the universally powerful British defences. Rommel himself sensed the change in the climate of the battle :

> General Auchinleck, who had meanwhile taken over command himself at Alamein, was handling his forces with very considerable skill. . . He seemed to view the situation with decided coolness, for he was not allowing himself to be rushed into accepting a 'second best' solution by any moves we made.

A tank state informed Rommel that he had only twenty-six runners. His supply lines, stretched to Benghazi and Tripoli, were dislocated by bombing. His men, he knew, were exhausted, and British resistance, instead of collapsing, was sharpening.

He gave himself one more day in which to gain a victory, failing which the Panzer Army would have to pass to the defensive.

Auchinleck on the other hand was still thinking in terms of a massive counter-stroke to Rommel's rear. Having forced Rommel to commit all his Germans on the coastal flank, he now felt himself able to bring the New Zealanders at Bab el Quattara and the Indians at Abu Dweiss in to his centre; instead of a curtain of troops across the Alamein neck, he would now have his army concentrated closely under his hand. There was a mass of manoeuvre at last.

Next day Rommel struck again. The panzer divisions struggled on, calling upon each other for help, shelled, bombed, and disgruntled. The fruit of all their efforts still lay just beyond their reach, on the other side of the unexpectedly revived British: modern cities and ancient vices, hot baths and white beds, the pleasure of women, final victory. It was therefore with the energy of desperation that Rommel, cursing and exhorting, and his *Panzerarmee* strove to split the British and motor the last few miles into Alexandria. At ten to one in the afternoon Rommel signalled:

I demand energetic attack by the whole of DAK.

At twenty past he was up in person to inform them that 'the Commander-in-Chief orders that the attack must be carried out with the utmost energy'. The Panzer Army fought their way eastwards along both sides of the Ruweisat Ridge and by late afternoon, with the sun behind them, had reached Alam Baoshaza, well to the south-east of Alamein.

On the map in Auchinleck's caravan this might appear a deep and dangerous penetration, but the Auk was unmoved. It had, he knew, been made against the bitter and deliberately mobile defence of his battlegroups and of 1st Armoured Division; his sense of the battlefield told him that the Panzer Army had little left to give. At the end of the day the Germans had stopped in a paralysis of exhaustion, and Auchinleck was still between them and victory.

Meanwhile the Italians in the south had suffered a bloody reverse. As Ariete Division tried to outflank the New Zealanders (who had not yet moved north from Bab el Quattara), it was struck from the east by tanks of 1st Armoured Division and from the south by the New Zealanders. By midday Ariete had lost almost all its artillery and all but five tank runners.

At four minutes to 11 pm on July 3rd, 1942, Rommel

acknowledged temporary defeat by ordering his army to dig in and await a British counter-stroke.

Auchinleck sent an encouraging signal to his men that evening:

> From C-in-C to all ranks 8 Army. Well done everybody. A very good day. Stick to it.

It was on this day when the Panzer Army was panting in prostration under Auchinleck's guns, that the Prime Minister in London chose to attack Auchinleck and his men to the Chief of the Imperial General Staff. Of this, Brooke wrote later:

> I had an uphill task defending him and pointing out the difficulties of his present position. Also the fact that any rash move on his part at the present time would very quickly lose us Egypt. However, PM was in one of his unpleasant moods, going back over old ground, and asking where the 750,000 men in the Middle East were, what they were doing, and why they were not fighting.

It was still, as Wellington would have said, a near-run thing. As Auchinleck went among his troops in the lulls of the battle to revive the offensive, optimistic spirit in them and their officers, he was conscious that he stood almost alone against a drifting current of defeatism that was perhaps as dangerous to the Army's defence of Egypt as Rommel. An anecdote illuminates this loneliness. On July 1st, the Afrika Korps radio had jubilantly warned the ladies of Cairo and Alexandria to 'make ready to receive them tonight'. Dorman-Smith thought he would use this news item to amuse the Auk and take his mind off his anxieties. He went to Auchinleck's caravan and said:

"Sir, I'm afraid we are attempting the impossible."

Auchinleck rounded on him, grim and surprised.

"What do you mean?" His voice was thick with sudden anger. "Do you say this? I always thought you believed we could pull this thing off."

Dorman-Smith went on to explain about the Afrika Korps' message to the ladies of Alexandria and to suggest that for Eighth Army to try to defend *their* honour was a hopeless task since they hadn't any. Auchinleck was mollified, but not amused:

"Don't be a damn fool, Chink."

As well as conducting a touch-and-go battle, and rallying and reforming his army in the middle of it, he had his continued vast responsibilities as Commander-in-Chief, Middle East, not made easier by a lack of consistent advice from London on strategic priorities. There was for example the news from Russia, worse every day and heavy with impending threat to Auchinleck's northern front. Kupiansk had fallen on the day Auchinleck had arrived at Eighth Army; then another gigantic German blow was struck from the region of Kursk; and on July 1st the 2nd Panzer Army smashed a gap in the Russian defences through which the whole of von Weich's army group began to roll towards the Don. Next day the third German attack was launched by von Bock with three armies and three panzer armies between Byelgorod and Kharkov. The Russian front in the Ukraine had thus broken like glass under a hammer; and for Auchinleck, who knew that Persia and Iraq—with their essential oilfields—were held by troops hardly numerous enough to assure civil order, the news of this developing threat to his rear was deeply disturbing. It was not less so to the higher direction of the war in London: the Chief of the Imperial General Staff and his staff were busy working on plans for dealing with a German arrival at the head of the Persian Gulf.

Yet despite his double burden, Auchinleck outwardly retained his cool nerve and his big-man's calm. He had settled in now at his tiny headquarters behind the Ruweisat Ridge. Here, in an area of featureless and unpleasant desert, were the caravans of the Commander-in-Chief, his operations and communications staff, an operations room, a mess lorry (but no mess) and some slit trenches. Auchinleck's caravan had a let-down lean-to shelter; beneath this, in sleeping-bags on the desert ground, slept the Commander-in-Chief and Dorman-Smith, his Chief of Staff—the first in the history of the British Army.

It was not every man's idea of an army headquarters. Some of the staff and the Press bitterly criticized its austerity and discomfort, its distance from anywhere but the front, the number of its flies and the scarcity of its headquarters staff and equipment. For the first time since Auchinleck and Tedder had established in 1941 very close co-operation of army and air force through a combined headquarters, the Eighth Army and the Desert Air Force headquarters were apart; the Air

Force had gone back to Burg el Arab on the coast. It was an amicable arrangement: Tedder felt he could not risk his elaborate communications network in a place so near the fighting, while Auchinleck had equally valid military reasons for staying there. He wrote later:

> In the conditions prevailing and the desperate nature of the situation, it seemed to me essential that the Commander should be as close behind the line as he could be without risking dislocation by capture or bombardment. Ruweisat Ridge was in my opinion the key to the whole position.

He was only half a mile from Willoughby Norrie's 30th Corps headquarters; it was easy to confer without either of them being taken far from home.

Auchinleck also had a characteristic personal reason for not joining the air force:

> To have gone to Burg el Arab would have taken me out of the atmosphere in which I wish to live, for the sake of my own and the army's morale.

The critics especially disliked Auchinleck's headquarters' exposure to air attack; there was one air raid in which Auchinleck and Dorman-Smith fell out of a caravan into a slit trench a few seconds before a German cannon shell tore a hole in the floor where the Commander-in-Chief had been standing.

If there were valid reasons for siting the Army HQ behind Ruweisat, there were others, springing deep from Auchinleck's character, for making it so austere. The memory of the circus on the Daba road remained with him; and he, the Commander-in-Chief, would set the army an example of plain living. His headquarters staff had the same water ration as the troops; he himself had a basin wash once a week. He wished also to regain that sense of kinship with his men he had known in the hills of India; to draw strength from the awareness that he was no longer a uniformed diplomat, but a soldier again. He wrote later of the simplicity of his headquarters:

> It had an effect on me. If I had been sleeping in a bed I would not have felt the same. As it was, I felt a sense of community with the chaps.

Amid the unceasing worries of the battle Auchinleck left undisturbed the anomalous situation in regard to Brigadier White-ley, Brigadier General Staff of the Eighth Army, and General Dorman-Smith. Dorman-Smith was in the first place the channel through which Auchinleck transacted business as C-in-C; but he also acted, as Auchinleck intended, as his closest adviser on the battle; as *de facto* Chief of Staff. Whiteley was tired by the long summer battle and Auchinleck suspected that he and the rest of the Eighth Army staff, with their placidity and conventional minds, had had a share in the slowness and clumsiness of British reaction and action. Auchinleck therefore began to issue orders through Dorman-Smith rather than through Whiteley; and this developed into a custom. This duplication was bound to lead to bad feeling within the army, especially as Dorman-Smith had no official post. In retrospect it seems clear that Auchinleck should have faced the implications of his temporary arrangement, and recognized Dorman-Smith's functions by appointing him formally Chief of Staff, as was de Guingand later. But Auchinleck was immersed in the crowded events of a battle and he left the arrangement alone. In his own words, 'It worked'.

On July 4th, 1942, as the Americans celebrated their first wartime Independence Day and the British had been fighting in the desert for over two years, the stillness of perfect balance held the Alamein battlefield. Rommel, checked in his first rush, was preparing to deploy the *Panzerarmee* again for a fresh attempt on the last sixty miles to Alexandria; Auchinleck was preparing another counter-stroke. In the evening he had Norrie and Gott in to hear his orders; it gave him a fresh opportunity of judging Gott, that romantic legend of the desert. He was not as impressed as some: 'A very curious character. He was a tradition in the Army, especially with the junior officers. I thought he was tired at that time.'

As Gott and Norrie listened, Auchinleck expounded his plans:

> Our task remains to destroy the enemy as far east as possible and not let him get away as a force in being. This can best be achieved by containing the enemy's eastern and southern flank and attacking his rear. It is important that the enemy should be given no rest . . . Eighth Army will attack and destroy the enemy in his present positions.

He added: 'Speed of action is essential.'

His plan was simple: the whole of Gott's 13th Corps and 7th Motor Brigade, 4th Light Armoured Brigade (newly formed out of spare armoured-car units) and a squadron of Stuarts would drive into Rommel's right rear and roll *Panzerarmee Afrika* up towards the coast at Ghazal and Sidi Rahman.

It was a more hopeful conference than his first. That morning Dorman-Smith had been down to see the first German prisoners—they were 'absolutely whacked'. And in fact the German morale was the main object of Auchinleck's manoeuvres:

> The whole idea was to get Rommel over to the defensive—upon troops so long victorious and on the verge of Alexandria, the moral effect would be disproportionately great.

Auchinleck had piped a lively tune for July 5th, but Eighth Army could not manage more than a bear-like shuffle. It was beyond the compass of the military doctrine, the training and the mental agility of the Eighth Army, exhausted by battle, to organize in the course of a night an attack imbued with the Commander-in-Chief's offensive energy. What Auchinleck had conceived as a killing blow became in fact a slow tightening in pressure between July 5th and 9th, as 13th Corps felt its way cautiously round Rommel's right flank.

Among some of the Commonwealth troops that formed the majority of Eighth Army, there was at this time a sullen reluctance to move. In the New Zealand Division, one brigadier's opinion of the plan for 13th Corps was that 'it doesn't look real'. The same brigadier described as 'fanciful' an attack by ninety-nine tanks and an infantry brigade on the fifteen German tanks of 15th Panzer Division. Thus it was that this officer was able to describe July 6th, when his division and the rest of 13th Corps should have been driving hard for the coast, as 'a really quiet day'.

The only gleam of light in this scene of inertia was shed by the flashing advance of 4th Light Armoured Brigade. Its armoured cars broke right through the German defences and wheeled north-westwards towards Daba, far in Rommel's rear and a nodal point in his precarious supply lines. The cars were taken to be tanks, and because the Germans had no anti-tank or other shells left, a shiver of alarm went through the *Panzer-armee*. But with the mass of 13th Corps inert behind it, the dash of 4th Light Armoured Brigade was a gesture in the air; and Auchinleck's second counter-stroke had failed.

Yet the failure was only relative. The pressure of 13th Corps on Rommel's southern flank was enough to alarm the German commander and make him bring 90th Light to the south from its salient by El Alamein. At the same time Rommel was being forced to deploy Italian infantry for the first time since the beginning of the battle of Gazala. Therefore Auchinleck had succeeded in pulling the tactical initiative further out of his opponent's hands. But Rommel was still confident that Egypt would be his. Reinforcements would reach him soon: 164th Infantry Division from Crete, and a shipment of 260 tanks. On July 8th, having stood on the defensive for four days, Rommel decided that his best hope lay in attacking the New Zealanders at Bab el Quattara, taking their box and driving far to the east towards the Delta, while Auchinleck was left in the air at Alamein.

But Auchinleck too was planning another stroke. It was now his policy to gain and keep the tactical initiative by a series of attacks upon different parts of Rommel's army—like a tennis player placing the ball so that his opponent is constantly running for it. This time he was going to use his personal reserve, the newly arrived and fresh 9th Australian Division, to break through the German defences on the coast road, west of El Alamein, and force the *Panzerarmee* off its communications into the desert. To draw Rommel's attention from the coast, Auchinleck therefore pulled back 13th Corps and evacuated the Bab el Quattara box—a manoeuvre that by the odd coincidence of war exactly fitted into Rommel's own plan. Jubilantly the German commander congratulated himself on July 9th on the success of his new offensive which had opened with a British retreat and the 'capture' of a magnificent box; the road to Cairo, he thought, was at last open.

That night, as Rommel slept in a concrete shelter in the Quattara defences, wrapped in impending triumph, the massed guns of Auchinleck's army artillery shook and tore the German positions west of Alamein; it was, so one German officer said, like a barrage of the First World War. In the morning, the Australians went in.

The Italians of the Sabratha Division broke and bolted, discarding all impediments to mobility, such as their armament. The hill of Tel el Eisa, which commanded the western approach to El Alamein and which was to be immensely important to Montgomery, was taken. Almost all Sabratha's divisional artillery was captured. The Australians and light armour drove on towards the larger objectives given them by Auchinleck—Daba and the Sidi el Rahman track.

This was a moment when Rommel was near disaster. In his own words 'the enemy was now in hot pursuit westwards after the fleeing Italians and there was a serious danger they would break through, and destroy our supplies'. It was the finish of Rommel's own ambitions in the south; his plans cancelled, he hurried north with part of 15th Panzer Division in time to help a scratch force from the *Panzerarmee* Headquarters stop the Australians. Since Auchinleck had no reserves with which to maintain the momentum of the attack, Rommel was able to prevent catastrophe—but by using German troops earmarked for an offensive. This had been the first of those blows on Italians that Auchinleck and Dorman-Smith had discussed during the flight from Cairo to Baggush.

Two days later Auchinleck attacked again, and this time the Trieste Division was routed; once more Rommel prevented a complete breakthrough only by draining Germans from his southern flank. He counter-attacked the Australians in the Tel el Eisa salient, and saw his men fail in a choking sand-storm and heavy gunfire on July 13th. Both sides now made up the accounts of war. Auchinleck's claims were modest: fifteen guns and over a thousand prisoners. The failure to achieve a general breakthrough was a disappointment, but hardly a surprise in view of his complete want of reserves. But he preferred to give large rather than limited objectives, 'to keep the troops going'. In his opinion orthodox British doctrine of attack placed too much emphasis on the attainment of certain linear objectives upon which the attacking force then halted for fresh orders; he preferred Liddell Hart's concept (taken over by the Germans) of the *Schwerpunkt*, or drive without limits along a given axis.

Rommel's estimate of the results of the battle of Tel el Eisa was gloomy: 'This British drive along the coast had brought about the destruction of the bulk of Sabratha and a large part of Trieste, and important sectors of the country had fallen into enemy hands.' He now had utterly to abandon his own proposed offensive in the south because, with the unsteadiness of the Italians, '. . . . the situation was beginning to take on crisis proportions'.

A growing sense of impotence and frustration began now to tell on the spirits of German commander and soldier alike. Rommel confided his bitter disappointment to his wife in his letters, and awarded Auchinleck a tribute: 'During the past few days the British Command has been showing considerable enterprise and audacity.' On the British side there was a sense of easing tension which showed itself in small things, such as the permanent mess, with tables and chairs, that was installed at Auchinleck's headquarters.

The improvement was even sensed in London, for the Prime Minister, who had fallen silent in the face of catastrophe, now began again to send Auchinleck exhortatory and minatory telegrams. They did not help; they were, in Auchinleck's words, 'a cause of considerable anxiety, an added burden'. General Ramsden, who took over from Norrie at 30th Corps on July 7th, noted that 'Auchinleck was obviously labouring under pressure from the PM'. But Auchinleck impressed the newcomer by his strength and coolness: 'He inspired confidence even in the most precarious circumstances.' He slept well at night. The only hint of concealed strain that his colleagues noted was sudden and formidable outbursts of anger; but these quickly subsided into his usual gruff charm.

The climax in the long and wavering battle at Alamein for the control of Egypt and the Middle East was now at hand. In the next four days, between July 13th and July 17th, 1942, Auchinleck defeated Rommel's last attempt to crown his Gazala victories with the conquest of Egypt; and forced him back on to the general defensive. On July 13th and 14th the Germans came slowly on with the white glare of the afternoon sun behind them and the massed guns of the Eighth Army before them; 21st Panzer Division against the Alamein box, while their comrades at Deir el Shein waited for its fall before beginning their postponed drive on Cairo. When night fell on July 14th, 21st Panzer Division had failed, and it was time for Auchinleck's next blow at the Italians.

Map 19. First Battle of Alamein
July 1942, Third and Last Phases

It was a cold and dark night, the Ruweisat Ridge like the back of a great beast stretched under the stars. It was quiet, and men snuggled gratefully into their blankets. Then the night exploded in flares and tracer as the New Zealanders and 5th Indian Brigade attacked along the Ridge with the bayonet. At the glint of steel, the Italians of the Brescia Division broke.

The whole of the Ruweisat Ridge fell to Auchinleck's troops, who now cut into the rear of the Brescia and Pavia Divisions and (according to Rommel) took most of them prisoner.

South-east of Deir el Shein the Axis line also collapsed, as the British overran German anti-aircraft batteries and broke into the Deir el Shein box itself. Brought yet again to the edge of rout by a blow on his Italians, Rommel saved himself yet again by using his Germans to patch the front. Twenty-first Panzer Division abandoned for good its attack on El Alamein, came down to Deir el Shein and retook some of the lost ground.

A battle between evenly matched opponents is like a tug-of-war. At first there is a period of intense and prolonged effort during which the knotted handkerchief does not move. Then it begins to shift; at first slowly, and then with increasing ease and speed until the moment of victory. By July 16th, 1942, Auchinleck was giving the easy, the assured, the winning pull, and Rommel was moving helplessly with it.

By Auchinleck's wish rather than his own, Rommel now had all the Afrika Korps grouped in his centre, round Deir el Shein; therefore he decided to attack in the centre and recapture his lost ground. But he was anticipated by another of Auchinleck's night attacks; the Australians drove along the coast road to take the important ridge of El Makh-Khad. Next day they trampled through the Trieste and Trento Divisions and began to roll up Rommel's front like a ceremonial carpet, north to south. Rommel hurried northwards with every last German reserve in his army. He managed to prevent a general rout; but from now on his mind turned not on how to achieve victory, but how to prevent retreat.

His great summer offensive was over, and it had failed.

He wrote to his wife: '. . . it can't go on like it for long, otherwise the front will crack. Militarily, this is the most difficult period I've ever been through.' In three weeks at Alamein he had seen the triumphs of Gazala, Tobruk and Matruh made bootless; all his straining effort had won him only empty desert and a cruel mirage of victory parades amid the fountains of Cairo. This moment of sudden defeat following upon easy triumph broke Rommel; ahead of him lay the dogging ill-health that is born of disappointment and frustration—desert sores, the infected liver, the duodenal ulcer. The old Rommel, that dynamic optimist, was never seen again.

Rommel's agony of mind was made worse by his clear awareness of what Auchinleck was doing.

> The enemy [he wrote to his wife] is using his superiority, especially in infantry, to destroy the Italian formations one by one and the German formations are too weak to stand alone. It's enough to make one weep.

On July 17th, 1942, therefore, Auchinleck had won a historic battle. It had been as desperate, difficult and gallant as Wellington's repulse of Napoleon at Waterloo, but for Auchinleck there was no Blücher with 40,000 fresh men to come up on the flank and turn defeat into rout. Nevertheless Auchinleck had saved the Middle East, with all that this implied for the general course of the war. It was the turning point.

CHAPTER THREE

ON JULY 18th, 1942, the war in the desert had died away for a moment. It was a time to sit in the narrow shadow of a tank or truck and dream of bright clouds towering up an English summer sky; to close the mind against white light and hot dust and remember the smells of damp and growing things. But in the Axis lines exhausted, toiling men were learning the differences between winning and losing a campaign: instead of cool sea bathes, laying mines almost too hot to touch; instead of drinking iced lager, uncoiling barbed wire. As they worked, and looked back on Gazala and Tobruk, they learned that all victories are vain but the last, and *that* the generalship of Auchinleck had denied them. For the Eighth Army the day after Rommel's defeat was perhaps one of strangeness; the battle so many had thought was lost, had been won. To prosaic

British soldiers, it began to appear that there were many advantages about the Alamein positions which Gazala and other places in Rommel's country had lacked: regular supplies of NAAFI cigarettes and beer, and when things were quieter, a spot of leave in conveniently adjacent Alex.

But in Eighth Army headquarters, a dusty metal mockery of a hamlet amid the stones and sand, Auchinleck could not relax with victory; he faced a new and unpleasant dilemma.

An immense German offensive was now rolling through the Ukraine; several panzer armies (each one larger than Rommel's command) formed the van of an army of more than a million men; and the Russians appeared helpless before this weight and power. Two German threats had now developed: one to Stalingrad, whose western bastions at Kletskaya and Kalach were already enveloped in German fire; and the other to Rostov, the fortress which covered the Caucasus and Auchinleck's northern flank. The Russians judged Stalingrad, covering the heart of European Russia, to be more important than Rostov and they had begun to pull their troops round Rostov back towards the Volga. Thus it was that Auchinleck received top-secret information from the British Military Attaché in Russia that the whole of the Caucacus was expected to fall to the Germans within a month, bringing them to the borders of Persia. Troops must, then, be found for Persia and Iraq; but there were none, except those of Eighth Army and of green divisions still on ships sailing slowly round Africa. According to earlier staff studies of the time necessary to move an army from Egypt to Persia and deploy it there, such an army should have been in transit by July 14th. Clearly the troops for Persia must be drawn from Eighth Army and without delay; clearly this could only be done after Rommel had been destroyed or immobilized.

The case for an immediate British offensive was implacably put by the Prime Minister in a telegram of July 12th, hard on the heels of 'an unpleasant wire'—so unpleasant that Brooke and Ismay tried without avail to prevent his sending it, and whose contents have understandably never been made public.

You . . . no doubt realize that it is practically impossible to send six or even four additional divisions from Home or United States to the northern theatre before the end of October.

The only way in which a sufficient army can be gathered in the northern theatre is by your defeating or destroying General Rommel and driving him at least to a safe distance. If this were accomplished before the middle of September, the Australian divisions could return to their station in Palestine and Iraq ...

Because of the time needed to transfer these troops, of which Churchill had taken insufficient account, Auchinleck realized therefore that as Commander-in-Chief he must now take a decision which as Army Commander he might judge to be rash: to launch an immediate offensive with his poorly trained and battle-worn army. Thus it was that in July 1942, as in 1940 and 1941, the campaign in the desert was directly and fatally affected by dangers elsewhere in the vast Middle East Command.

While the troops enjoyed a brief lull after July 17th, the Commander-in-Chief was preparing his offensive. It took him —there was no more time—four days. Auchinleck proposed first to drive into Rommel's extended centre on July 21st: 'We should thereby have a chance to sever his communications and roll up the northern part of his armour ...' When this attack by 13th Corps had drawn in Rommel's reserve, a second blow by 30th Corps in the north three days later would drive the German left flank off the Miteiriya Ridge, the key to the defence; the armour would then break through before Rommel could disengage himself from the earlier battle with 13th Corps. The whole of both corps would join in the general pursuit, with the armour in the van. First Armoured Division was to run for the Fuka bottleneck; 7th Armoured Division also for Fuka, but by another route; and the armoured cars of 4th Armoured Brigade far ahead to Charing Cross. It was not, and could not be, a set-piece battle and a sure success; it depended on Eighth Army displaying the Afrika Korps' kind of nimbleness and thrust. The doubt was there; could a British army, trained and officered in quite another, older tradition, find the élan?

Auchinleck tried hard to evoke it; Gott's orders to 13th Corps were full of thrustfulness:

All commanders must be prepared to act with extreme vigour. Without waiting for precise orders, they must act within the spirit of these (general) orders and carry out the pursuit relentlessly to the complete destruction of the enemy forces.

Auchinleck issued his orders for the battle at a smart pace—operation instructions on July 17th, orders for the pursuit on the 20th, and orders covering army-air co-operation on the 21st. The pace was too fast for the slow-working staffs of lower formations (German staff work, because of greater experience and better training, was always faster and more lucid than British), and detailed organization for the offensive was poor and confused.

July 21st passed slowly for Auchinleck, as his army moved into position. The awareness never left him that he had committed himself to a hazardous enterprise; his want of reserves to follow up initial successes was a special worry. There was the painful irony that he could best achieve his own strategic objects —continued safety of Egypt and the destruction of Rommel— by leaving Rommel in peace at the end of his stretched communications, until Eighth Army was rested and reinforced; it was not *Panzerarmee Afrika*, but the Germans at Rostov, a continent away, that had forced him to gamble.

His features were now beginning to show the effects of a month of such moral, physical and emotional strain as no other Allied general in the Second World War except possibly Gort experienced. Like Wellington in Goya's portrait after Salamanca, Auchinleck had become gaunt and tense; his blue eyes gazed hollowly and implacably out of his loneliness. Above all in his mind, as he waited for the long day to pass, was the question of conscience that he asked himself before all his battles: 'Are the chaps who are going to attack going to have a reasonable chance—if not, you are just murdering them.' But this time the answer was not his to give. The possibility of failure weighed with him least of all (it could not now endanger Egypt, for Rommel had had all the attack beaten out of him), although he knew that the blame would fall on him rather than on the politicians.

Just before dusk, like a starting gun severing the tension before a race, a rolling bombardment by his massed artillery opened his last desert battle. Under its cover the infantry of 13th Corps went forward—New Zealanders to the edge of the El Mreir depression, Indians through the defences of the Deir el Shein box. Now it was the armour's turn, working closely with the infantry and sappers, to break out of the bridgeheads and to protect the infantry against German tanks. But combined attacks against minefields and fixed defences had been out of fashion for a year now in the desert; and the technique had been forgotten. As 13th Corps fumbled with the unaccustomed problem, the great flaw in Eighth Army—between armour and other arms—cracked wider, and in an abyss of misunderstanding and recrimination, the attack was lost.

First Armoured Division, supposed to be up with the New Zealanders at first light on July 22nd, was still not there in broad daylight, despite the New Zealanders' urgent night signal that the Mreir Depression in front of them was full of German tanks. German artillery wrecked the New Zealanders' anti-tank guns, and then the squat tanks rumbled out of the depression and over the helpless New Zealanders. In the Indian sector it was the armour that was massacred. General Gatehouse, who had taken over command of 1st Armoured Division the night before (Lumsden being wounded) criticized the battle plan, but Strafer Gott insisted that 23rd Armoured Brigade should make its attack. It was the brigade's first action. Auchinleck had used it because there was no other, knowing that it was physically soft, having just come off the troopships after the long voyage from Britain; without desert training; and equipped with obsolete 2-pounder Valentines. But it had received a thorough training in armoured fighting in the United Kingdom and the task given it was within the compass of this training. As it went into action, Gatehouse too was wounded; his place was taken by Brigadier Fisher.

The brigade's performance was a surprise and a tragedy. It began by having a complete wireless breakdown. Out of the control of the army command as a consequence, it charged as if it were after a fox, full of exultant courage and devoid of tactical cunning. Gravelled on a minefield, 23rd Armoured Brigade was shot to pieces by furious and accurate German anti-tank fire. Of 97 Valentines, 11 returned. It was an astonishing indictment of the state of armoured training in Britain after three years of war.

Auchinleck took the news of this disastrous day with outward calm; but like Wellington in the Peninsula he was beginning to wonder if anybody in his army could be trusted to carry out his orders with professional competence and zeal. Clearly the army needed the most thorough weeding-out and retraining; and that would require time.

Yet the attack had achieved its object despite the confusion; Rommel had been alarmed because it had reached 'dangerously far behind our front' and had 'demanded the use of our last reserves'. The German armour had therefore seeped away from the Miteiriya Ridge to meet the attack; and Rommel was off-balance for Auchinleck's second and principal blow. As the British tanks moved secretly northwards towards Miteiriya, the Prime Minister was drafting a telegram to Auchinleck to 'hurry the Auk on to attack' and, in tranquil, air-raid-free London, 'pouring out questions as to why the Auk could not have done this or that'.

Auchinleck himself was facing a new crisis. General Morshead, commanding 9th Australian Division, which was to make the infantry attack on the Miteiriya Ridge, had objected to his orders.

Auchinleck was visiting 30th Corps HQ with Dorman-Smith after lunch on July 22nd, when General Ramsden, commanding 30th Corps, told him the news. Ramsden was a lean Yorkshireman, steady and forceful, who always wore a huge automatic taken from a German officer in the previous war. Ramsden explained that Morshead had been questioning his orders for July 24th, saying that his division had done enough attacking. 'His main reason,' in Ramsden's words, 'was *no* confidence in our armour.' Ramsden said that he had done his best 'to stop this bloody-mindedness without result'. Morshead, he told Auchinleck, had insisted that 'he must refer to his government'.

For Auchinleck, this occurrence in the middle of a carefully-timed battle was his most serious problem so far in commanding an army drawn mostly from Commonwealth countries other than Britain, where divisional commanders were subject to political pressure from home, and in turn could appeal to their own governments if they disliked their orders. It was the ultimate test of his quality as a man and a commander. At first it shattered his self-control; in Ramsden's words, 'he went through the roof' in a sudden terrible anger fuelled by all the accumulated strain of a month of crisis. He ordered Ramsden to have Morshead report to him immediately. Ramsden, looking at the big man in his anger, reflected that an interview at that moment would not be fruitful. He suggested that Morshead should come up for tea.

Auchinleck thought for a moment, and in that moment the swift rage abated with equal swiftness. The Australians must be got into action and anger would not do the trick. He took Ramsden by the arm and, in his usual deep voice, agreed that Morshead should come for tea. Time passed, Morshead arrived; Auchinleck was gruffly charming, they all, in a thoroughly British Commonwealth manner, had tea. By now Auchinleck, with his usual sympathy, had seen the other man's point of view:

> Morshead was a fine fighter and had done all that he had been asked and that was a great deal. He had been asked because he had a fine fighting division—the penalty of being good. He was of course quite entitled to represent that his division had had about enough of it—particularly as an Australian commander responsible directly to his own government. His was a difficult position.

Then they walked across the sand to the operations caravan. When they were seated, Auchinleck began to persuade Morshead. He referred to 'your wonderful division, comprised of the finest fighters in the world'. He promised that the 69th British Infantry Brigade would be moved to Miteiriya to conduct the second and most dangerous phase of the attack. Morshead succumbed; and, rather like Wellington on his knee to Cuesta before Talavera, Auchinleck had saved his battle.

A year later he wrote of such episodes in a letter to Ramsden:

> I have often wondered since how you ever got anything going at all! The story must be told some day; it was a comedy but very nearly a tragedy!

He bore Morshead no malice; on the contrary he admired him then, and afterwards, as 'a first-class soldier'.

He had solved another of his problems; but the switching of 69th Brigade, as well as the time spent in talking Morshead round, had imposed a delay of two days in the attack; it was now to begin on July 26th. As Auchinleck and Dorman-Smith walked back from Ramsden's operations caravan, Dorman-Smith asked him whether the attack should be called off, as there was now time for Rommel to regroup to meet it. But

Auchinleck said the attack must be put in—for reasons of a wider strategic and political kind than a mere assessment of the prospects of success on the Miteiriya Ridge. As if to confirm this decision, Rostov fell on July 24th and the Germans began to pour down into the Caucasus.

The second phase of the battle opened with one of Auchinleck's night attacks (an Indian custom) in the evening of July 26th. The Australians fought all night under the moon. By dawn on the 27th they had broken into the German front and taken Sanyet el Miteiriya. South African sappers had cleared gaps in the minefields on the Australians' left, and through them the British 69th Infantry Brigade began to drive on towards the Miteiriya–Deir el Abyad track. In Ramsden's corps headquarters, Auchinleck heard the news of this promising beginning and then drove back to his own headquarters to wait in suspense for the next developments.

After two hours there was a telephone call: it was Ramsden.

> I told the Auk that it was useless to go on with Miteiriya Ridge battle . . . because gaps in the minefields for the passage of our tanks had NOT been cleared as ordered.

While the British infantry were cutting deeper into the German defences, 2nd Armoured Brigade, which should have been up with them as both their spear and their shield, was still on the British side of the minefields. Brigadier Fisher considered the gaps not to be sufficiently cleared for his tanks. When they had been cleared, and his tanks had passed through, 69th Brigade had already been cut off and mauled by German armour and infantry as Rommel came into action with the Afrika Korps. The British armour was able to rescue the infantry eventually, but all tactical and strategic surprise was gone, and the attacking forces had fallen into that cursing confusion that the British soldier knows so well. Ramsden therefore wanted to know if he should continue the attack. Auchinleck had no reserves, nothing more to give.

'I told Ramsden to call off the battle.'

The epic days were over.

*   *   *

In London, in the endless underground conferences from which men emerged white yet kippered by tobacco smoke, the Prime Minister was continuing to make those grand gestures over the map with his cigar that passed for strategy; continuing to abuse men the reality of whose difficulties he refused to acknowledge. On July 30th, 'the PM's impatience with what he regarded as the inexplicable inertia of Middle East Command had become uncontrollable'.

For in England Auchinleck's decisive success in repulsing the *Panzerarmee,* so clear to Rommel himself then and to the historian today, had passed without notice or appreciation. This strange and unfortunate neglect is a reflection partly on want of perspicuity in high circles in London, but mostly on Auchinleck's poor sense of personal public relations. On July 25th, for example, he had written a full private letter to Brooke about the battle so modestly couched that an ignorant reader might, like the American Ambassador with Wellington's Waterloo dispatch, be uncertain whether it recounted victory or defeat.

In the desert Auchinleck, himself still full of aggression, had had to accept that he just had not the strength to beat Rommel out of his ever-stronger fixed defences.

The weakness of the Eighth Army relative to the front which had to be held or closely watched, prevented me from forming a real reserve, in which troops could be rested, reformed and trained for fresh assaults on the enemy; and there were no more formations in the Delta or further to the east on which I could call.

But he was not dissatisfied with the results of his month of battle, which were admirably summed up by the man he had beaten. Rommel wrote:

Although the British losses in this Alamein fighting had been higher than ours, yet the price to Auchinleck had not been excessive, for the one thing that mattered to him was to halt our advance, and that, unfortunately, he had done.

General Bayerlein, Rommel's Chief of Staff, agreed with his chief:

All of Auchinleck's counter-attacks were tremendously successful. If Rommel had not been beaten then, he would have advanced deep into Egypt. When Rommel lost Tel el Eisa and Ruweisat, he and all of us knew we were lost.

He significantly added:

> It is a pity that no one in Britain recognized the marvellous, though smaller, battles Auchinleck won.

And General Sir Brian Horrocks, whose name is so closely associated with Field-Marshal Montgomery's command, has written:

> It can be argued with justification that this heroic stand was the turning point of the war.

On July 27th, 1942, as the gunfire died away along the Miteiriya Ridge, General Dorman-Smith submitted to Auchinleck an appreciation of the present and future prospects of the war in the Middle East.[1] After discussion, Auchinleck accepted this appreciation. It is one of the most crucial documents of the Second World War and it deserves the closest study. Yet, except in the writings of Captain Liddell Hart, it has been generally neglected. This is not strange, for it upsets the legend of how the desert war was transformed by the arrival of Montgomery; it gives the lie to those in the army who thought that Dorman-Smith was 'unsound', and Auchinleck's 'evil genius'. It forecasts the date of the battle of Alam Halfa and Rommel's plan of battle; and it describes the defence (unaltered by Montgomery) by which it might be defeated. It then looks further ahead to the Second Battle of Alamein, and describes, in outline, the offensive plan which should be adopted, which was adopted, and which was unaltered, though developed, by Montgomery.

The appreciation took into account the reinforcements which might reach Rommel in the next few weeks, and considered that

> though the Axis forces are strong enough for defensive action, they are hardly strong enough to attempt the conquest of the Delta except as a gamble and under strong air cover.

On the other hand,

> none of the formations in Eighth Army is now sufficiently well

[1] See Appendix B for the complete text

231

trained for offensive operations. The Army badly needs either
a reinforcement of well-trained formations or a quiet period in
which to train.

Therefore

seeing that we are hardly fit at present to do any attacks, our
best course is the defensive combined with offensive gestures
from time to time . . . until we are strong enough to attack . . .
which will not be till mid-September at the earliest.

The Second Battle of Alamein began on October 23rd.
In the meantime, the appreciation continued,

Rommel will certainly try to attack before the end of August . . .

Rommel actually began his advance on the night of August
30th/31st.

. . . and as Eighth Army defences gain in strength and depth he
will be more than ever tempted to avoid them and seek success
in manoeuvre. This may well land him in serious difficulties in
the soft desert . . . Eighth Army may have to meet an enemy's
sortie developing into manoeuvre by the southern flank . . . We
must therefore organize a strong mobile wing . . . well trained
in harassing defensive technique.

The appreciation now went on to sketch the plan on which
Montgomery was in fact to fight the Second Battle of Alamein:

Eventually we will have to renew the offensive and this will
probably mean a breakthrough the enemy positions about El
Alamein. The newly arrived infantry divisions and the armoured divisions must be trained for this and for pursuit.

Three days after Auchinleck had discussed this appreciation
and approved it in its final form, he asked his corps commanders,
Gott and Ramsden, and Corbett (from Cairo) to come to his
headquarters for a day's conference. The instructions issued
that day, July 30th, 1942, were Auchinleck's last achievement
in his twelve months in the Middle East; they formed the
basis of final victory in the desert.

Firstly, Auchinleck said that there were to be no more British attacks at present. Then he reviewed the reinforcements that were on the way to Egypt; reinforcements on a scale and of a quality that none of the officers in that caravan had before seen. Two new and additional armoured divisions—8th and 10th—had arrived and were being re-equipped with Grants and the powerful Shermans for which the Prime Minister had asked the American President. One hundred self-propelled 105-mm guns were also expected. The American tanks had still to be fitted with wireless and sand filters, and the men of the new divisions needed thorough training. All this would take till mid-September, which therefore fixed the earliest possible date for the offensive. Auchinleck would then have, however, four armoured divisions instead of two; and their equipment—Grants, Shermans and 6-pounder anti-tank guns —would be for the first time in two years in the desert vastly superior to the German. As well as the extra armour, an infantry division—44th—had arrived and was being trained, and another—51st—was on its way. Given the present complete British air superiority, it would be a battle fought on very different terms from those of *Battleaxe*, *Crusader* and First Alamein.

Auchinleck and his officers now got up from the table and faced the battle map on the wall of the caravan. Auchinleck pointed out that by mid-September Rommel too would have been reinforced and that his defences would be well laid out, protected by minefields. The Commander-in-Chief explained that at the moment he favoured the set-piece attack near El Alamein itself which had been sketched in the appreciation before them. It was the kind of static, rehearsed battle in which the good qualities of a British army—endurance, steadiness and discipline—would shine, while its poor qualities—want of dash and agility—would not signify. 'I considered,' wrote Auchinleck later, 'this operation offered the greatest chance of success.' The alternative was the traditional desert plan—the armoured striking force rolling round through the southern flank and across the enemy's communications. Auchinleck ordered Gott to prepare an outline scheme for this; but Ramsden was to start immediately on detailed plans for the northern breakthrough.

Now Auchinleck laid down his new policy in organization and training. In his opinion, every desert battle from *Battleaxe* to those just over showed that the traditional British organization of infantry and armoured divisions was quite unsuited to modern mobile warfare. Whether in desert manoeuvre or in close attack and defence, the co-operation of tanks, infantry and artillery was far below the standard of the easy and supple teamwork of the Germans, and often did not exist at all. As Auchinleck remarked later:

> We were not as well trained as the Germans—a fault of our pre-war training. We don't really train for war in peacetime in England—we play at it.

He wanted the distinction between armoured and infantry divisions abolished in favour of an all-mobile Eighth Army made up of divisions each with its ratio of tanks, guns and lorried infantry. In this way the co-operation of all arms would be made permanent through the very structure of the division, under its divisional commander. Auchinleck thus set in motion the complex machinery of training and organizing a new model army—three days after the close of the July battles.

He concluded his conference by reviewing the measures for defeating a forlorn-hope German offensive at the end of August. The El Alamein positions were now well fortified. The west-to-east ridges of Ruweisat and Alam Halfa, which Auchinleck regarded as keys of the defence, had been already prepared with a defence zone thirty miles deep. But he emphasized to Gott and Ramsden that 'the essence of the defensive plan was fluidity and mobility and the maximum use of artillery fire'. The bulk of the army artillery, with an escort of lorried infantry, would fight alongside the armour. If Rommel tried to drive far to the east, instead of attacking Alam Halfa, he would be struck in the flank.

The conference broke up, and Auchinleck and his officers stepped out into the sunshine conscious that at last the easier days of the war were on the way. They could reckon that they deserved some free-wheeling; they had peddled uphill long enough.

Meanwhile there was an air of relaxing tension in the desert. The day had ceased to be composed of twenty-five hours and the headquarters mess had more time for sport: 'Our chief amusement,' said Auchinleck afterwards, 'was fighting scorpions

Map 20. Auchinleck's Plan for Alam Halfa
August 1942

against tarantulas. Kisch (Engineer in Chief of the Eighth
Army) had a black spider and I had a scorpion. We used to have
fights in a tin box after dinner.' There was time too for swimming in the Mediterranean, in whose warm embrace cares and
fatigue melted away; time for him to get away from that prison
of an ops room for long walks.

He took a day's leave in Cairo, and wandered strangely among the sleek civilians, along the brilliant streets; had lunch in a club where deft Sudanese in white robes of pavonine colours passed as quiet as wraiths along the marble terraces. In the Sharia Adly Pasha he turned into a bookshop, prophetically named *La Librairie la Renaissance d'Egypte*—he had always been a great reader—and bought a new copy of a childhood favourite, Macaulay's *Lays of Ancient Rome*. Perhaps the eye of the man of Alamein fell first on these lines:

> And how can man die better
> Than facing fearful odds,
> For the ashes of his fathers
> And the temples of his Gods.

A week later, after swift events and intrigues, he had been relieved of his command.

CHAPTER FOUR

AT THE end of June 1942, the Coalition Government lost a by-election at Maldon in Essex by a colossal turnover of votes. It was an expression of the heavy groundswell of public criticism of Churchill's war direction.

This was the middle year of the war, the dangerous, weary year that lay between the splendid and exhilarating defiance of 1940–41 and the victories assured by Allied superiority still to come. In Churchill's own words:

> We had had a succession of misfortunes and defeats— Malaya, Singapore, Burma, Auchinleck's lost battle (sic) in the desert; Tobruk . . .

He was now in the greatest political danger he was to know in the course of his wartime premiership; and on July 1st, as battle was joined at Alamein, he rose in the House of Commons to answer a vote of censure that attacked him while excusing the generals; the motion was 'That this House, while paying tribute to the heroism and endurance of the Armed Forces of the Crown in circumstances of exceptional difficulty, has no confidence in the central direction of the war.' The Prime Minister won by 475 votes to 25, against an attack so inept as to suggest it might have been rigged as a dummy. But the groundswell of public discontent continued. 'During this month of July, when I was politically at my weakest,' a striking offensive victory was required. When at the end of the month Auchinleck cabled to say that he was not going to launch another offensive for at least six weeks, Churchill decided to go to Cairo in order, in his own words, to settle this issue: 'Had General Auchinleck or his staff lost the confidence of the Desert Army? If so, should he be relieved, and who could succeed him?' But subsequent events were to suggest that he had already made his mind up.

Auchinleck received these tidings at his headquarters behind the Ruweisat Ridge. Dorman-Smith advised him to receive the Prime Minister in Cairo, in full panoply of Commander-in-Chief, Middle East—before anyone else could get the Prime Minister's ear. But Auchinleck, with his complete disdain for intrigue, stayed with his army until asked for.

On August 3rd Churchill and his entourage arrived in Cairo; the Prime Minister talked with Smuts, who had flown up from Cape Town; and in the afternoon Auchinleck, having been asked for, went up to Cairo to explain the military situation. On the morning of August 4th Churchill saw General Corbett, the Chief of the General Staff, Middle East Command. In a letter to Major-General J. N. Kennedy, Director of Military Operations at the War Office (dated August 5th, 1942), Corbett described the end of his interview with the Prime Minister:

> When I was leaving, I stressed what in some ways is perhaps the most important factor. General Auchinleck has been through a great ordeal. Once again, his Army Commander has been unable to cope with the situation. All these terrible events have naturally bitten deep into his soul, and he is now busy regaining confidence in himself . . . I explained all this to the PM, and said perhaps the greatest disaster of all would be the loss of General Auchinleck, and that he needs a helping hand to assist him back on to solid ground.

On the 4th also Wavell arrived from India; and the Prime Minister was able to play the role he loved, that of Marlborough 'riding the whirlwind and directing the storm', with Wavell,

Auchinleck, Alan Brooke, Admiral Harwood, Tedder, Casey (the Minister of State) and Smuts. They discussed many matters but, since Auchinleck was present, not the one uppermost in Churchill's mind—Auchinleck's relief and successor.

For, before even visiting Eighth Army, the Prime Minister had made up his mind to dismiss Auchinleck; and he first offered the Middle East to Brooke who, from *The Turn of the Tide*, seemed less concerned with the justice or military validity of the decision than with debating with himself whether he should take Auchinleck's job or not. He decided not, partly for fear that Auchinleck might think he had come to the Middle East 'to work his way into his shoes'.

In the early morning of August 5th, Auchinleck stood with his staff on the airstrip near Eighth Army headquarters and watched a figure in a siren suit and topee emerge from an aircraft into the white sunshine. For a moment they faced each other—the politician and the soldier. Then hands were shaken cordially—neither Churchill nor Brooke gave a hint of what they had already decided; Auchinleck began the unconscious but ghastly charade of showing them his army and explaining his plans.

From Auchinleck's point of view, this was above all a time for smart public relations work. The Air Force knew this, so when the Prime Minister went on to them for lunch after 'a long and invigorating day with Eighth Army' [sic], he found 'the food had all been ordered from Shepheard's Hotel . . . a gay occasion in the midst of care—a real oasis in a very large desert'. But Auchinleck was too honest or too simple a man for press-agenting; the Prime Minister's breakfast that morning was just the ordinary Eighth Army mess issue. Before he sat down to it he had been driven round Ramsden's corps, giving his two-finger sign. An observer has described the soldiers' responses: 'the last stage of the route along the ridge was thinly lined with phlegmatic soldiers who seemed to be in two minds about the warmth of the reception they were going to give the Old War Horse.' Also before he had his breakfast, Churchill had another and this time detailed discussion with Auchinleck about his plans for the future. The discussion took place in Auchinleck's caravan in the presence of Dorman-Smith. Again Churchill pressed for an early offensive, 'his pudgy fingers stabbing at the map, as he threw in imaginary divisions here and there.' On his way to enjoy the Air Force's shrewd hospitality, the Prime Minister had a long private talk with Strafer Gott, who was his personal choice as Army Commander when Alexander succeeded Auchinleck in the Middle East Command.

Meanwhile at a lower level, certain men of the Gazala defeats were quietly telling members of the Prime Minister's entourage that Auchinleck, Dorman-Smith and other officers were responsible for *their* mistakes. This was believed.

Next evening, after consulting Smuts and Alan Brooke, the Chief of the Imperial General Staff, who agreed that changes should be made in the Middle East command, the Prime Minister sat down to make the stroke that had the effect of diverting much of the discontent at the Government's war leadership on to Auchinleck and his immediate staff officers.

> Prime Minister to Deputy Prime Minister. 6 Aug. '42, 8.15 pm. As a result of such inquiry as I have made here, and after prolonged consultations with Field-Marshal Smuts and CIGS and Minister of State, I have come to the conclusion that a drastic and immediate change is needed in the High Command ...

After giving details about the splitting in two of the Middle East Command, the Prime Minister came to the meat:

4. General Alexander to be Commander-in-Chief the Near East.
5. General Montgomery to succeed Alexander in TORCH.
6. General Gott to command the Eighth Army under Alexander.
7. General Corbett to be relieved as CGS Middle East.
8. General Ramsden to be relieved as GOC XXXth Corps.
9. General Dorman-Smith to be relieved as Deputy CGS.
10. It will be necessary to find two corps commanders for the Eighth Army in place of Gott and Ramsden.
11. The above consitute the major simultaneous changes which the gravity and urgency of the situation here (sic) require. I shall be grateful to my War Cabinet colleagues if they will approve them. Smuts and the CIGS wish me to say they are in full agreement that amid difficulties and alternatives this is the right course to pursue. The Minister of State is also in full agreement. I have no doubt the changes

will impart a new vigorous impulse to the Army and restore confidence in the Command, which I regret does not exist at the present time ...

Returning to Cairo on August 21st, after the purge, he amplified this charge:

I am sure we were heading for disaster under the former régime. The Army was reduced to bits and pieces, and oppressed by a sense of bafflement and uncertainty. Apparently it was intended in face of heavy attack to retire eastwards to the Delta ...

It was these events, and the interpretation placed on them by Churchill, which led to a general belief that Auchinleck had been an 'unlucky' general who had been relieved of his command in the midst of disaster.

At the end of June, as Auchinleck himself had recognized, Ritchie's defeat exposed Auchinleck to dismissal. But Churchill had not dismissed him. Now Auchinleck had magnificently redeemed his errors. Thus the military case for relieving him was infinitely weaker than it had been. How weak was shown when Dorman-Smith sued Churchill for libel in respect of the phrase '. . . and restore confidence in the Command, which I regret does not exist at the present time.'

The case was settled out of court, Churchill agreeing to insert a footnote in future editions of his *Memoirs*. This footnote, of the greatest historical importance, reads:

The references to the officers whose names figure in this list are factual only. Neither they nor my later remarks are to be taken as imputing personal blame to any individual. These were the principal changes in Commands and Staff when General Auchinleck was replaced by General Alexander. Major-General Dorman-Smith only became Deputy Chief of Staff on June 16th, 1942; he thus bears no responsibility for the fall of Tobruk or the defeats at Gazala. From June 25th to August 4th he acted as General Auchinleck's principal Operations Officer at Headquarters Eighth Army during the operations described in Chapter 24. My appreciation in that chapter of the handling of the Eighth Army is supported by Rommel's remarkable tribute.

Running deep in this sad and unpleasant affair is the memory of the fall of Tobruk. The news had broken on the Prime Minister in circumstances of the greatest personal humiliation —from President Roosevelt's own lips while Churchill was a guest at the White House.

To Churchill, with his old-fashioned way of seeing history as a procession of great names and great events, the fall of a legendary fortress like Tobruk rang louder in the mind than the complicated truths of strategy. Politically he was right; he considered the result of the Maldon election to be a by-product of Tobruk. Tobruk was the memory that he had come to Cairo to exorcize; and yet ironically the fall of Tobruk had been his responsibility.

On August 7th, Gott, Eighth Army Commander designate, was shot down and killed while flying to Cairo. The second choice had always been Montgomery; Churchill cabled to London; and Montgomery stepped on to the stage. Auchinleck still did not know he had been dismissed. In his ignorance, he thought Churchill's visit was going well for him. His first meeting with the Prime Minister had been 'cordial enough', though with characteristic modesty, he admitted 'one had the sense of having let him down—I was C-in-C and the ultimate responsibility [for the Gazala defeats] was mine'. On August 4th he had discussed with Brooke, apparently successfully, the future of the Middle East Command—the strategic appreciation of July 27th, the appointment of Montgomery (Brooke and Auchinleck preferred him to Gott) under himself as C-in-C. On 7th he sent Dorman-Smith to discuss with Brooke the question of reorganization of the divisions. Brooke acted out his part with skill; Dorman-Smith never suspected that he and his chief were already dismissed. In the evening Auchinleck went for a walk with de Guingand, the new Brigadier General Staff at Eighth Army, and discussed his plans 'with great enthusiasm'.

Next day, Auchinleck received the news at last, in his battle headquarters behind the Ruweisat Ridge, but from neither Churchill nor Alan Brooke; in the Prime Minister's words, '. . . having learnt from past experience that that kind of unpleasant thing is better done by writing than orally, I sent Colonel Jacob with the . . . letter'. Colonel Jacob (now Sir Ian Jacob) flew up to Alamein, drove to Eighth Army Headquarters, and walked to Auchinleck's caravan. As he wrote in his diary that day: 'I felt as if I were just going to murder an unsuspecting friend. After offering the condolences of the Prime Minister and CIGS on the death of General Gott, I handed the C-in-C the letter I had brought. He opened it and read it through two or three times in silence. He did not move a muscle and remained outwardly calm and in complete control of himself . . . I could not have admired more the way in which General Auchinleck received me and his attitude throughout. A great man and a fighter.'

The letter said:

Cairo, August 8, 1942

Dear General Auchinleck,

On June 23 you raised in your telegram to the CIGS the question of your being relieved in this Command, and you mentioned the name of General Alexander as a possible successor. *At that time of crisis for the Army, His Majesty's Government did not wish to avail themselves of your high-minded offer.* [Author's italics]. At the same time you had taken over the effective command of the battle, as I had long desired and had suggested to you in my telegram of May 20. You stemmed the adverse tide, and at the present time the front is stabilized.

The War Cabinet have now decided, for the reasons you yourself had used, that the moment has come for a change. It is proposed to detach Iraq and Persia from the Middle Eastern theatre. Alexander will be appointed to command the Middle East, Montgomery to command the Eighth Army, and I offer you the command of Iraq and Persia, including the Tenth Army, with headquarters at Basra or Baghdad. It is true that this sphere is today smaller than the Middle East, but it may in a few months become the scene of decisive operations, and reinforcements for the Tenth Army are on their way. In this theatre, of which you have special experience, you will preserve your associations with India. I hope therefore that you will comply with my wish and directions with the same disinterested public spirit you have shown on all occasions. Alexander will arrive almost immediately, and I hope that early next week, subject of course to the movements of the enemy, it may be possible to effect the transfer on the Western battlefront with the utmost smoothness and efficiency.

I shall be very glad to see you at any convenient time if you should so desire.

> Believe me,
> Yours sincerely,
> Winston S. Churchill.

As he read and reread this letter his mind might well have been moved to bitterness. But he accepted it without recrimination.

I knew as soon as Jacob arrived what he was bringing. I had guessed the night before when there was the gathering in Cairo (Churchill, Smuts and CIGS) to which I was not invited. Nevertheless, it was a shock. There was the regret at losing the finest job a general could have at the time. But it came during a lull; if it had happened in the middle of the battle, it would have been far worse. It was worse for me afterwards when I had actually handed over, and began to think about it.

He was quiet at dinner that night, and afterwards asked de Guingand to come for a walk. "He put his arm in mine and said: 'Freddie, I'm to go'."

On the following day he handed over command of Eighth Army temporarily to Ramsden, and quitted the battle headquarters from which he had won his victory. He never saw the desert again. In Cairo, he met the Prime Minister for an hour's conversation, which, in Churchill's words, 'was bleak and impeccable'. Auchinleck refused the offer of the Persia-Iraq command, which he magnanimously describes as 'very generous of Churchill'. He refused it 'because I had, like another people, a certain amount of pride and I did not think that I should have the same professional control over others after having stepped down in command. Anyhow, it was difficult to start all over again.' In particular he pointed out that the Commander-in-Chief of the new command would depend for troops, base facilities and even many headquarters services on his colleague in Cairo; and he did not consider the scheme would work out. As events proved, it did not.

Auchinleck now remained in Cairo to await Alexander and Montgomery; the date of transfer of responsibility was fixed for August 15th. In the meantime, the machinery that Auchinleck had set in motion on July 30th for the remodelling of

Eighth Army and for the planning of the new offensive, had been dislocated by the Prime Minister's visit and the prolonged comings and goings of various officers. Ramsden, who was planning the breakthrough at El Alamein, had twice acted as temporary Eighth Army commander; Gott, the other corps commander, had first been army commander designate and then killed. De Guingand, the new BGS at Eighth Army, had been there only since August 3rd; Dorman-Smith had returned to Cairo. It was the temporary dislocation consequent upon all this that was interpreted by some as a general want of leadership and purpose in Auchinleck's command. As Churchill put it:

> . . . no plain plan of battle or dominating willpower had reached the units. So serious did this appear that General Montgomery insisted on taking command of Eighth Army as soon as he had visited the front . . .

On August 10th Alexander arrived in Cairo, and on the 12th Montgomery. Until August 15th, Auchinleck was both Commander-in-Chief and in personal command of Eighth Army, though he had put General Ramsden in temporary command during his absence in Cairo. Montgomery had thus no official status in the Middle East at all; as an officer on duty in Cairo, he came naturally under Auchinleck's command. But as a matter of courtesy and in keeping with the usual custom of the service, Auchinleck took the opportunity of Montgomery's early arrival to invite him for an interview in which he could explain the general situation at Eighth Army and the plans for its future. This interview took place in Auchinleck's map room at GHQ. Montgomery made an odd assertion in his *Memoirs* that Auchinleck's plans at that time were of retreat into the Delta in the face of German attack, and even up the Nile. The appreciation approved by Auchinleck on July 27th, Auchinleck's conference with his corps commanders on July 30th, and his explanation of his plans to the Prime Minister and to Brooke on several occasions (in the presence of other witnesses), make it clear that Montgomery's assertion is not supported by fact. Montgomery's own chief, General Alexander, in his official dispatch, disavows Montgomery's version of Auchinleck's plans:

The plan was to hold as strongly as possible the area between the sea and the Ruweisat Ridge and to threaten from the flank any enemy advance south of the ridge from a strongly defended position in the Alam el Halfa ridge. General Montgomery, now in command of Eighth Army, accepted this plan in principle, to which I agreed.

To clinch the matter, Montgomery's publishers, with Montgomery's consent, issued a statement[1]—to be printed in later editions of the *Memoirs*—acknowledging that his account of the interview gave a false impression.

Though Montgomery was not due to take over Eighth Army for three days, Auchinleck suggested as a courtesy that a smooth transition of responsibility would be helped by Montgomery's going down to see Ramsden, the temporary army commander, and learning something of his new command. Auchinleck added, in his own words,

Had there been an emergency, I should of course have taken over command of Eighth Army from Ramsden up to the time of formal transfer of responsibility.

On August 15th, 1942, Auchinleck handed over the Middle East theatre to his friend Alexander. At the same time Montgomery entered into command of the Eighth Army, which had technically been vacant since Ritchie's relief. Auchinleck now sent to the Eighth Army his last order of the day:

It has been a great honour to have held direct command of the Eighth Army for nearly two months, and it is with great personal regret that I now leave you on the arrival of your new Army Commander. During these weeks you have stopped the enemy; and, in spite of your heavy losses and the inevitable disorganization consequent on a rapid withdrawal from the frontier, you have forced him on the defensive, taken 10,000 prisoners from him and destroyed or captured many of his guns, vehicles and other equipment. You will, I know, join me in acknowledging the great and glorious part our air forces have played in helping us to achieve these results. Without their aid the story would have been very different. I thank you with all my heart for the magnificent way in which you have responded to the heavy calls I have made on you and for your unfailing cheerfulness and tenacity in the worst circumstances.

[1] Reproduced as Appendix A to this book.

I know you will continue in the same fine spirit and determination to win under your new Commander. I wish you luck and speedy and complete victory.

He stayed on in Cairo for a while. The fate of Dorman-Smith and Corbett, who had fallen with him, greatly distressed him. They were not given any reason for their dismissal; the first explanation was provided by Churchill's memoirs after the war. It was against all the traditions and practice of the army for subordinate officers to be dismissed at the order of a politician; a precedent which had been resisted as long ago as Wellington's time at the Horse Guards, and which should have been resisted by Alan Brooke, as professional head of the Army. In Auchinleck's own words: 'I felt terribly about what happened to Dorman-Smith and Corbett—far worse than I felt about myself. Their treatment was entirely unfair.' But his subordinates were thinking, on their side, only of him. General Corbett wrote to the Deputy C-in-C in India:

The grim ordeal of the desert battle ends in providing Rommel with a triumph which I prayed he would not be allowed to enjoy. I am to go, as is right with my Chief . . . I am desperately sorry for Claude. He is, as you know, as simple as he is great. . . .

Auchinleck and Dorman-Smith dined together on the terrace at Mena House. It was cool for an August night in Cairo. Two tables away a young Hussar officer was flirting energetically with a pretty young British nursing sister. It was an odd, sad occasion: both Auchinleck and Dorman-Smith looked back to that other ceremonial meal, six weeks ago, before they had flown up to Eighth Army. Then it was all about to begin; now it was all over.

A contemporary observer in the Middle East wrote:

The overall direction of the War does not inspire much jollity in men who have consistently been chased by superior numbers with better equipment. Besides they like Auchinleck and do not see why he should be kicked out for General Alexander and some new Army Commander from England.

General Ramsden, who served under Auchinleck and Montgomery, writes of Auchinleck as a commander:

The Auk was being continually pressed from home, he was

not given the goods, and was frequently distracted by affairs in Iraq, Syria, etc.—in short, his command was too big and too much was expected of him. Yet he was a most attractive commander; with a great sense of humour, individually a born leader.

An enemy opinion was:

If Auchinleck had not been the man he was—and by that I mean the best Allied general in North Africa during the war —Rommel would have finished the Eighth Army off.

And, now he was gone, Churchill himself could safely acknowledge that he had demanded too much of Auchinleck:

I doubt if the disasters would have occurred in the Western Desert if General Auchinleck had not been distracted by the divergent considerations of a too widely extended front. . . .

The benefits of this belated (by two years) recognition of the obvious accrued to Alexander and Montgomery, for, as Churchill put it, 'I should be most reluctant to embarrass Alexander with remote cares at a moment when all our fortunes turn upon the speedy and decisive defeat of Rommel'. Alexander's Middle East Command was therefore but a shrunken remnant—Egypt, Syria and Palestine—and his cares not plural, but single: 'to take and destroy at the earliest opportunity the German–Italian Army commanded by Field-Marshal Rommel.' In truth, the hard days of the war had gone, along with the men who had borne their heat and shock.

What must be the judgment on Auchinleck as a man and as a commander? Perhaps General Sir Alfred Godwin-Austen touches the truth:

His outstanding fault was, I should say, his inability to believe that every soldier was not as brave as he.

PART SIX

MILITARY MESSIAH

Field-Marshal The Viscount Montgomery of Alamein, KG, GCB, DSO

Just his conceptions, natural and great;
His feelings strong, his words enforced with weight . . .
View the whole scene, with critic judgment scan,
And then deny him merit if you can.
Where he falls short, 'tis Nature's fault alone;
Where he succeeds, the merit's all his own.

CHARLES CHURCHILL,
The Rosciad.

CHAPTER ONE

WITH SIR Claude Auchinleck's victory in the First Battle of Alamein, the history of the Desert War passes into a long though sometimes bloody anticlimax. For the Axis had now lost the war in the Mediterranean. In retrospect, both Italians and Germans were to recognize that their hopeless renewed offensive at Alam Halfa and their subsequent obstinate clinging to the Alamein position were alike disastrous attempts at wish-fulfilment. Kesselring, German C-in-C in the Mediterranean, wrote that 'given our full knowledge of the gamble, the attack ought never to have been begun'. Mussolini agreed:

> When (Rommel) had twice attacked unsuccessfully before Montgomery's offensive he should have withdrawn at once to Mersa Matruh . . . I told (Hitler) we had lost the initiative from June 1942 onwards, and that a nation which has lost the initiative has lost the war.

The matter had been clinched when, on July 25th, emboldened by Auchinleck's success in halting Rommel, the British and American war leaders had decided to invade French North Africa in November with large British and American forces, an intervention which in Rommel's words 'spelled the end of the army in Africa'.

But if the desert fighting after First Alamein is a kind of epilogue, it is, by a paradox, also the first act of the famous career of Field-Marshal the Viscount Montgomery of Alamein, KG; and this is what makes it interesting.

It is not easy to look back beyond the veteran Field-Marshal, with all his honours and victories, at Lieutenant-General B. L. Montgomery, in August 1942. Yet his performance as a Lieutenant-General in the desert, when he was unknown and untried, is the key to an objective assessment of his abilities.

The difficulty of seeing him then as he really was, rather than as a superhuman figure, does not lie in want of documentation. However, in most of this documentation the haphazard facts of real life have been pruned into an artistic symmetry.

*   *   *

Bernard Montgomery was perhaps the first individual to adopt as a personal principle of conduct and judgment the Stuart doctrine that the king can do no wrong. If he admitted to an error, it was always minor, and served, like a touch of black in a colour scheme, to throw up his general infallibility. At Sandhurst he was a member of a gang that persecuted cadets they disliked; as a climax, Montgomery set light to a cadet's clothes and burned him severely enough for him to be sent to hospital. He not only tells this story in his memoirs, but tells it with relish. Such an attitude illustrates another trait—his lack of judgment in regard to conduct outside a battlefield. It would seem that he has always been so wrapped up in himself and his own view outwards to the world that he has little sympathetic understanding of other people's minds and emotions; and the results of this want of comprehension of the reality of so many things outside Montgomery have been wild strokes of misjudgment fatal to a man less professionally talented.

At the end of a lecture to Home Guard officers he told them that he was now going to present a play he had written himself. 'While the audience watched fascinated, four soldiers dressed in German uniforms entered carrying umbrellas. As they opened the umbrellas a loud report echoed through the hall, and this, apparently, was to illustrate the arrival of parachutists in England. The four soldiers then lined up on the platform and announced solemnly: "We'll cut the throat of that bastard Montgomery".'

In France in 1940 as GOC 3rd Infantry Division he published an order on troops' morals and the prevention of venereal disease so offensive that both the Anglican and Roman senior chaplains bitterly complained, and Montgomery only retained his command by grace of General Brooke, his corps commander, who required him to publish an apology.

In Tunisia the American General Bedell Smith said in fun he would give Montgomery an American aircraft if Montgomery reached a certain town by a certain date. Having done so, Montgomery claimed his plane. The affronted Americans pointed out that the bet had been only a casual joke. But Montgomery insisted on his plane with complete American crew, got it, and could not be made to see why the Americans were furious with him.

Yet paradoxically Montgomery, though unpredictable to the point of eccentricity in his general judgment and even conduct, was in war devoted to ideals of precision, punctuality, caution and close control; his plans were shaped and explained with the exactness of a watchmaker. As an instructor at the Staff College at Camberley he 'had the unique gift of making complicated matters appear quite simple'. His schemes there showed a tendency towards overwhelming superiority of force rather than manoeuvre; and one daring student observed that he 'took a sledgehammer to crack a walnut'.

Montgomery's teaching, which so embodied the clear and precise nature of his military temperament and the solidity of his knowledge, did however reveal in the professional sphere his unawareness of, or lack of interest in, other people and their reactions. A student noted that a typical scheme of Montgomery's dealt with 'our side's' plans with comprehensive exactitude and elaboration; but the 'enemy's' intentions and reactions were not imagined, either as a source of danger or opportunity. Montgomery was the steam-roller, the enemy the gravel road. Had this tendency also roots in his profound desire to dominate; and dominate absolutely rather than conditionally?

In preparation for a call to great command, Montgomery spent his life immersed night and day in that narrow world which he knew so well and in which his understanding acted so judiciously. The world outside, except for his brief and tragic marriage, remained a world of shadows. His want of true friends, of hobbies, of intellectual interests has been noted by himself as much as by his colleagues. He wished only to fit himself for success in his profession; yet his *Memoirs* indicate that by a tragic irony he thus fixed, in a favourite word, his own ceiling, for as he moved up from the battlefield to the council chambers of the Allies, his narrow professionalism and want of understanding of humanity sometimes betrayed him.

Yet in simple ways he could be touched. When General Godwin-Austen visited him in Sicily in 1943, Montgomery gave him

a letter to a humble girl in England with a ring. He also gave me a letter he had received from the girl. This said (I quote from memory) 'Dear Monty, I see you have changed your beret. If you still have your old beret, may I have it? My man was one of yours, who was killed at Alamein, and I send my wedding ring. But if you've not got your old beret, please keep the ring.' Monty had written a very nice letter to her returning the ring, and was insistent that I posted it in England in case it went astray. He was particularly anxious about this, and reminded me several times.

The same powerful will to dominate which informed his conduct and his military thought also drove him up in his profession for, as an able man should be, he was ambitious. But for his abilities to be rewarded they must first be recognized; and the flair for public relations was revealed early and employed constantly. The development of this flair is a subtle interplay of his natural eccentricity (with the consequent circulation of 'Monty' stories) and the cold calculation of the battlefield-side of his mind.

To rebuffs he was cheerfully insensitive, even if he admitted their justice. In the 1930s when Montgomery was a battalion commander in Egypt, he had a brush with his brigadier, Pile:

> Both Monty and Franklin (another Battalion Commander) had recently been instructors at Camberley. The GOC in C, BTE, Lieutenant-General Sir Jock Burnett-Stuart, carried out extensive and valuable training exercises in the desert. In one of the night exercises both sides reached a state of complete confusion, which was the time when you began to learn something. Franklin and Monty were on opposite sides in this particular exercise, and late on in the night these two Battalion Commanders conferred together and decided, without reference to Brigadier Pile, to call off the exercise and march home. When Pile heard of this he was livid. He sent for both officers and gave them a tremendous ticking-off. Monty said afterwards: 'I fully deserved it . . . fully', but, quite unperturbed, turned up for a previous invitation to lunch the following day with the Brigadier and the whole proceedings passed off pleasantly.

Montgomery's first major command was 8th Infantry Division in Palestine during the Arab rebellion in 1936–9. He now showed clearly his character as a man and a commander. Though chasing elusive rebel bands, he insisted on methodical operations from 'a firm base, a firm base'. He also revealed a tendency to look upon the troops and operations under his command in a very personal, or even egostical manner. An incident of the time illustrates this, as well as his genius for advertising his actions in the proper quarters.

General Godwin-Austen recalls that one day Montgomery was coming on a routine visit to the Border Regiment, part of Godwin-Austen's brigade; he, Godwin-Austen and Lay, commanding officer of the Border Regiment, met at Megiddo. Lay had just heard the news that Abdul Karim, a much-wanted rebel leader, had been killed and was lying in Sannur village. He suggested that the Divisional Commander might prefer to see this gentleman rather than carry on with a routine tour. Montgomery asked:

"Abdul Karim? Who is he? Who is he?"

Lay explained, and all set off for Sannur. The dead rebel, the flies buzzing above him, was surrounded by Palestine Policemen (who had of course identified him) and troops. Montgomery strode to the body, and then snapped:

"A notebook!"

He took one of a dozen proffered, and wrote busily. Then he announced to those round him:

"This is what I've written. Major-General B. L. Montgomery, at Sannur, to GOC-in-C Palestine and Transjordan. Today *my* troops shot and killed Abdul Karim, the rebel leader. *I* have identified the body and pronounce it to be that of Abdul Karim. . . ."

Towards the incompetent he was as ruthless, swift and remorseless as a sabre-stroke. In his area of Palestine there was a certain inefficient member of the *civil* administration. Montgomery told one of his brigadiers, Brigadier (now General) Ramsden, that he was going to sack this man; Ramsden was to be in Montgomery's office at 9 am on the morrow. Here Ramsden was shown a report for the High Commissioner drawn up by Montgomery. It began:

This civil officer is one hundred per cent wet and one hundred per cent inefficient . . .

At 9.30 the official turned up, was given the report to read, and became purple with outrage. Montgomery asked him to initial it to show he had seen the report, before it was sent to the High Commissioner. He refused.

"All right," said Montgomery, "I'll send it *without* your initials. Ramsden, you're a witness."

Montgomery's departure for England was an early essay in his technique of public relations. The night before he was due to be invalided back to Egypt in an aircraft on the first stage of his journey he sent for Ramsden and instructed him to have all his brigade officers at the airport, by the plane, for his departure. The morning came and Montgomery was taken on a stretcher to the door of the plane between an avenue of his officers while he waved his now-famous wave.

The German invasion of France and the Low Countries, that most brilliant of all campaigns in the Second World War, provided Montgomery with his only taste of action against great odds and better equipment. While it is true that the British Expeditionary Force did not feel the full violence of the German onslaught until the battle was nearing its end, nevertheless Montgomery and his 3rd Division showed what could be effected by six months of hard training and a thoroughly professional approach to war. Neither Montgomery nor his men were perturbed by disaster. Montgomery on the contrary seemed to be enjoying himself in a quite nerveless manner. The worse the news, the more arrogantly confident he seemed. At one of his last conferences before the army fell back into Dunkirk, he concluded his orders to his officers by announcing:

"Gentlemen, we'll shatter the boche—shatter the boche!"

But now there was to be no more fighting for Montgomery for more than two years. From June 1940 to August 1942, the years of desperate struggle in the desert, he commanded in the home army in England, first 5th Corps and then South Eastern Command. Apart from his methods of hard training, the chief interest of this period lies in the prototype of Montgomery's plan for an offensive battle; a prototype that failed disastrously because the essential ingredient of the later offensives—overwhelming force of guns, tanks and airpower—was missing. It was the Dieppe raid.

Combined Operations Headquarters Planning Staff began work on an Outline Plan about the middle of April 1942. At an early stage, the Commander-in-Chief, Home Forces, delegated his authority in the matter to the General Officer Commanding-in-Chief South Eastern Command, Lieutenant-General B.

L. Montgomery 'who', in the words of the Canadian official history, 'thereafter took the responsibility for the military side of the planning and himself attended some of the later meetings of the planners'. The plan adopted had much in common with Second Alamein, with Mareth, with Enfidaville, the Sangro, Caen and Arnhem. It consisted of a main blow with tanks frontally delivered against the powerful German beach and port defences of Dieppe, with subsidiary flanking attacks designed to reach round behind the town. On May 11th, 1942, the Chief of Combined Operations submitted this outline plan to the Chiefs of Staff Committee, informing them that it had the concurrence of the GOC-in-C, South Eastern Command. Only now that the master plan was accepted did Canadian officers begin work on the details.

About the middle of July 1942, Montgomery ceased to be responsible for the military side, and on August 18th when the raid took place he was in Egypt. But the master plan remained essentially unchanged. The main frontal attack broke down before furious German fire, all tanks being lost on the beach. The subsidiary attacks made better progress but were too feeble to get inland. In any case the gullies up the cliffs were impassable to larger forces. After the disaster it was concluded, as the Navy suggested beforehand, that such a frontal assault as had been made required overwhelming air and gun support for success.

The failure of the Dieppe raid was partly owing therefore to bad luck and bad management on the day, but partly owing to the nature of Montgomery's master plan, and, though he himself was not there, Dieppe must constitute in a real sense Montgomery's first defeat, and a proof that Montgomery's conception of an offensive battle as a head-against-the-wall frontal trial of strength could only succeed where the enemy could be borne down by overwhelming weight of metal.

Dieppe is also interesting as the first example of Montgomery quietly brushing himself clean of so unfortunate an occurrence as a defeat. There is no discussion in his *Memoirs* of the master plan and the reasons for its failure. He briefly suggests that loss of secrecy (the Canadian official record disagrees) and the elimination of preliminary saturation bombing, among other things, caused the repulse.

In the summer of 1942, when the war was nearly three years old, Montgomery had still to hold a high command in battle. The opportunity, to fit himself for which he had sacrificed most of the usual human pleasures and interests, eluded him. He could console himself that from June 1940 had begun 'my real influence on the training of the Army in England'.

But at last Montgomery's opportunity came, by the accident of the death in an aircraft crash of Strafer Gott, Eighth Army Commander designate. Montgomery flew to Cairo on August 10th, 1942.

*　　*　　*

In the morning of August 12th, Montgomery, incoming Army Commander, and Auchinleck, outgoing Commander-in-Chief, met in Auchinleck's map room in GHQ, Cairo. It was a tense interview. On one hand, there was the buoyant fellow from England who had endured no battle strain for two years, eager to enter his inheritance; on the other the man whose supreme and successful efforts had just been crowned by dismissal. The two men were utterly dissimilar in every respect but their resolution in battle. As they talked, Auchinleck big and burly, Montgomery's chin on a level with Auchinleck's decorations, the spark of mutual dislike leaped between them.

Then Montgomery went down to Eighth Army. He had a vested interest in the Prime Minister's legend that in the Middle East all was incompetence and ruin until the Cairo Purge, after which instead genius and unclouded victory reigned; and he set about propagating it with conspicuous skill by putting his own name to the best of Auchinleck's plans, while assigning to Auchinleck and his officers the blame for the hiatus in leadership and planning caused by the fortnight-long comings-and-goings of the Purge.

Personally, he made a deep and energizing effect on the army, battle-worn as it was and bewildered by the apparent want of leadership since July 30th. Always arrogantly self-confident and relentlessly energetic, he was above all things fresh, and, as de Guingand wrote of Auchinleck's arrival in the Middle East in 1941, 'he was like a breath of fresh air'. However, it would be wrong to place too much emphasis on the moral effects produced by the new army commander: for in the words of the Official History, Auchinleck 'had retained to a remarkable degree [his army's] admiration and confidence'.

Montgomery heard the acting Army Commander, General Ramsden, explain the situation and future plans; then told him:

"All right, I'll carry on here. You can go back to your corps."

Montgomery was to display an increasing high-handedness that he would have been the last to tolerate in others. Now, in Eighth Army Headquarters on August 12th, 1942, he signalled GHQ, Cairo that he had assumed command of Eighth Army, two days earlier than he should have done and in complete disobedience of orders. This gesture was of no importance militarily—he did nothing during those two days that he could not have done as an army-commander designate—but it throws a bleak light on his character as a man. It could serve only to wound Auchinleck in his last two days of command. Sixteen years later his pleasure in his action was undiminished; he made a point of saying in his *Memoirs* that on August 13th, 1942, 'it was with an insubordinate smile that I fell asleep: I was issuing orders to an army which someone else reckoned he commanded!' However, he did not issue them from Eighth Army headquarters, because he 'decided to leave the HQ quickly in case there were any repercussions'. Montgomery need not have worried; his signal never reached Auchinleck.

Montgomery set about impressing himself on his command, which now became 'my men', 'my army'. The army headquarters staff learned that he would hold a conference at a certain time and *that air cover would be provided*, an innovation for such an occasion. Unfortunately, Montgomery was so late all the air cover had gone home.

He spent a long day with General Ramsden visiting 30th Corps, conspicuously new in long shorts and white knees. But he was full of bounce, full of an almost childlike pleasure at being in command in the desert. He showed Ramsden a new wristwatch. "See this wristwatch? New one for the desert, new one for the desert!"

Later on it was a fine picnic basket—"I bought it for the desert!"

The day's tour began at 9th Australian Division; this visit had far-reaching effects on military iconography. An Australian liaison officer saluted and remarked to him: "It's a hot day, sir."

Montgomery, in a general's red-banded cap, replied: "Quite right, it is a very hot day—a very hot day. This is quite the wrong sort of hat to wear—far too warm."

"You should have one of ours, sir."

"A very good idea—a very good idea."

A selection of Australian slouch hats was provided for him to try on. Eventually he picked one, but remarked: "No badge—I can't wear a hat without a badge." So he was given an Australian badge. At the end of the day he had collected hats and badges from the South Africans and the Indians. His *Memoirs* show that behind this apparently spontaneous acquisition of distinctive headgear lay calculated policy.

He disliked Auchinleck's battle headquarters because it had no beds, no amenities and plenty of flies; and the crisis that had caused Auchinleck to place his HQ behind the Ruweisat Ridge being over, Montgomery moved back to join the Desert Air Force headquarters at Burg el Arab, in accordance with the year-old custom of shared headquarters. Here, under a marquee, he held his famous 'no-bellyaching' conference. His officers listened, without coughing, to a crisp, simple and emphatic lecture delivered in a metallic voice, a nasal drawl with strongly lisped 'R's. Afterwards Major-General Brian Horrocks, an old colleague of Montgomery's who had just arrived from England to take over 13th Corps, came up to his fellow corps commander, smiling that toothy smile later so well known to television audiences. "Ramsden," he said, "Isn't he *marvellous*?"

Montgomery had heard Auchinleck explain his plans; he had heard Ramsden repeat them; he had seen on the wall of the operations caravan a map of the Alam Halfa dispositions; and he had had long conversations with de Guingand, lately Auchinleck's Brigadier General Staff, and fully versed in Dorman-Smith's Appreciation of July 27th and Auchinleck's orders of July 30th. These now became *his* plans; nowhere, in two books and a television performance, does Montgomery hint that the Battle of Alam Halfa was fought on a plan conceived by Dorman-Smith, approved and initiated by Auchinleck, and from fixed defences largely dug before Montgomery left England. He wrote in his *Memoirs*:

I decided to hold the Alam Halfa Ridge strongly . . . It was obvious to me that Rommel could not just bypass my forces and go off eastwards to Cairo; if he did so, I could have descended on his rear . . .

And General Alexander writes in his official dispatch:

The plan (Auchinleck's) was to hold as strongly as possible the area between the sea and the Ruweisat Ridge and to threaten from the flank any and every advance south of the ridge from a strongly defended prepared position on the Alam el Halfa Ridge.

Again, Montgomery writes in his *Memoirs*:

I then decided that my extreme south flank should be mobile; the 7th Armoured Division would hold a wide front and, as the attack came, would give way before it. When the attack swung left-handed towards the Alam Halfa Ridge, the 7th Armoured Division would harry it from the east and south . . .

And in Dorman-Smith's Appreciation of July 27th:

Eighth Army may have to meet an enemy's sortie developing into manoeuvre by the southern flank. . . . We must therefore organize a strong mobile wing . . . well-trained in defensive harassing technique.

On August 19th Montgomery was able to dazzle both the Prime Minister and the Chief of the Imperial General Staff with the swiftness with which he had evolved his plans for the future. He made a striking success. When he had dealt with the coming defensive battle, Montgomery turned to his own offensive and described how he wished to break through the enemy position about El Alamein. He said the offensive could not take place in under six weeks, owing to the need for thorough training and for breaking in the new Shermans. This was exactly what Churchill had heard from Auchinleck. It had clinched Auchinleck's dismissal, but Churchill swallowed the delay from his new general. Brooke said of Montgomery's performance: 'One of the highlights of his military career. He had only been at the head of his command for a few days . . .' and Churchill wrote later: 'A masterly exposition of the problem . . . he accurately predicted Rommel's next attack . . .' The Prime

Minister's visit did much to dissolve his earlier doubts about Montgomery. Unlike Auchinleck, Montgomery had a perfect grasp of public relations. He made tremendous efforts to see that the discomforts of war in the desert did not affect Churchill. He gave up his own caravan for the Prime Minister to sleep in, and placed it near the sea for ease of bathing. There was wine and brandy at dinner in the mess.

In the fortnight that elapsed between his taking command and the opening of the Battle of Alam Halfa, Montgomery developed Auchinleck's plans in two ways; he had tanks dug in along the Alam Halfa Ridge and he ordered the green 44th Division up from the Delta. However, this division was not used in the battle. Montgomery's main personal contribution was the cast-steel control, sure and precise, that he exercised over the battle. There was to be no loose fighting. He warned Ramsden, of 30th Corps:

"It will be an Army battle, Ramsden—an Army battle."

The Eighth Army faced an easy task. Strongly and cleverly posted, it had 767 tanks fit for action, of which 713 were in the forward area. Of these 164 were the heavy Grants. Against this array, posted defensively, Rommel could muster only 200 gun-armed German tanks. All British armoured and infantry divisions fought for the first time equipped with the new 6-pounder anti-tank guns. The British enjoyed complete air supremacy. Rommel was so starved of fuel for his striking force that on August 27th, three days before the battle, he told Kesselring that success depended on his getting the 6000 tons of fuel promised ten days earlier. Instead he got 1800 tons and had to shorten the radius of his turning movement. And Rommel himself was enfeebled by sickness and defeat. Rommel's doctor said that he 'can command the battle under constant medical attention . . . essential to have a replacement on the spot'. In fact 'he was so ill with an infection of the nose and a swollen liver, that he could not get out of his truck'. Gause, his chief of staff, was also sick.

In the words of Dorman-Smith's Appreciation of July 27th the Axis were 'hardly strong enough to attempt the conquest of the Delta except as a gamble and under very strong air cover'. And there was no German air cover.

Montgomery made much at the time and afterwards of his

cancellation of all provisional orders for the conduct of a retreat from Alamein. In the face of Rommel's offensive, Eighth Army would stay at Alamein, he dramatically proclaimed, alive or dead. He sought in his *Memoirs* to convince posterity that before his arrival,

> The men of the Eighth Army were looking back over their shoulders, wondering where they were going to withdraw to next. All available troops back in the Nile Delta were digging defensive positions, and the area of the Pyramids was being prepared for defence.

He claimed that he stopped all this.

Yet Winston Churchill, writing of his second visit to Cairo from August 17th to 23rd, describes in detail how he, the CIGS and General Alexander set on foot 'a series of extreme measures for the defence of Cairo and the waterlines running northwards to the sea'. The 51st Highland Division was posted in these defences. General Maitland Wilson (C-in-C Iraq–Persia Command) was to take command of the Delta troops 'from the moment when General Alexander told him Cairo was in danger'.

Gott, while commanding 13th Corps, had been ordered by Auchinleck to prepare detailed plans for the expected German attack on the southern flank. Before his death these plans had been largely completed and were adopted by Montgomery and by Horrocks, the new corps commander. In particular two alternative areas of ground had been selected, one north and one south of the Alam Halfa Ridge, where the British armour could wait defensively in hull-down positions and behind an anti-tank screen for Rommel's attack. Depending on the direction of the German main blow, the British armour would move from its assembly area to one of these selected battle stations. There was the question of who should give the order to move, when, and to which place. Montgomery rightly decided that he would do so personally. He has described an argument with the commander of 7th Armoured Division as to whether the armour should be 'loosed at the enemy'. He took the credit for preventing a possible mad charge and for introducing the conception of a defensive armoured battle.

> Monty's handling of armour [said General Leese later, speaking generally] was very different from the old British

tactics—there was no swanning, but proper co-operation of armour and artillery, and close-in with infantry in attacks on fixed positions. We never, never advanced with our armour—always slowly, supported by our guns. We tried to get the Germans to attack us.

But according to General Renton, GOC 7th Armoured Division, neither he nor Gott had any offensive move in mind for Alam Halfa; they knew too well the need to husband the armour and especially the Grants; it was only the matter of a move to one of the selected defensive battle stations that was in question. Gott had of course, like Montgomery himself, considered striking Rommel in his flank with armour and guns if the *Panzerarmee* should move far to the east.

For Montgomery, Alam Halfa, as his first, was a crucial battle. Although he likes to say he never worried, never lost sleep, the days that wound up to August 31st, 1942, made him taut and edgy. A few days before the battle he remarked to a subordinate:

"Couldn't sleep last night—couldn't sleep last night. Supposing he attacks in the north?"

He was especially worried about the possibility of Rommel 'attacking on either side of the New Zealand Division, crushing it and throwing it away'.

But the battle went as long anticipated. The sick Rommel put himself at the head of his three veteran German divisions, with the Italian 20th Corps on his left, and after dark on August 30th, the *Panzerarmee Afrika* began to work its way through the British minefields. These were thicker than expected; by dawn on August 31st, the German armour, instead of striking fast and deep towards the coast, had only just cleared their eastern edge. There was therefore neither strategical nor tactical surprise. As the German armour made its way eastwards, 7th Armoured Division slowly gave ground. From a British sky, an avalanche of fire swept ceaselessly over the German forces, whose progress on the ground was marked, like pins on a battle map, by tall columns of black smoke from burning trucks and tanks. Soft sand burned up the precious fuel.

By eleven in the morning of August 31st the British command knew that all of Rommel's German divisions were committed in the south; as they moved slowly on through the haze, they were watched through binoculars on the Alam Halfa Ridge. About one o'clock the Germans halted to refuel and then they came on again. For the British command there had been the uncertainty as to whether Rommel would swing far out for the centre and east of the Alam Halfa Ridge, where 44th Division was posted, or close in to attack the Ridge's western end, where there was 10th Armoured Division. Now Rommel was seen to turn sharply north, a move forced on him not by a planted 'false-going' map, but by the delays in the minefields and by shortage of petrol.

A sandstorm rose; and beneath the cover it gave from air attack the German armour attacked 22nd Armoured Brigade in its prepared and mined battle station just south of the tip of the Alam Halfa Ridge. Under raging field and anti-tank gunfire, the German attacks broke down. But they were not pressed with the old skill and resolution: unlucky casualties had unhinged the German structure of command. General von Bismarck, of 21st Panzer Division, had been killed; Nehring, commanding the Afrika Korps, wounded. In the subsequent reorganization, the Afrika Korps and both its armoured divisions found themselves in the middle of the battle with new commanders.

At nightfall, the German armour fell back to the south. The Ragil Depression was filled with German tanks and trucks, and all night green and orange tracer lit them up, as the British artillery and aircraft bombarded them. Montgomery now redeployed 10th Armoured Division to cover the gap between Alam Halfa and the main Alamein defences. He took Rommel's attack seriously: a South African brigade was taken out of the Alamein front and brought down to the Ruweisat Ridge, while a fresh brigade was brought up from the Delta to occupy the area east of the main battle vacated by 10th Armoured Division.

All through September 1st the panzers strove to break through the British defences and were each time thrown back into the soft sand of the Ragil Depression. That night 15th Panzer Division reported that it was completely paralyzed by want of fuel; the rest of the *Panzerarmee* was hardly better off. On September 2nd Rommel issued orders for a retreat.

He was in a situation of the greatest peril. He lay with three

265

MEDITERRANEAN
SEA

EL ALAMEIN

AUS DIV

S.A DIV

26 AUS BRIG.

161 IND. BRIG

9 IND. BRIG

RUWEISAT

5 IND BRIG

ALAM HALFA RIDGE

31. BRIG.

N.Z. DIV.

23 ARM BRIG.

133 BRIG.

22 ARM BRIG

8 ARM BRIG

MOBILE SCREEN

QARET EL HIMEIMET

⬭ MONTGOMERY'S DISPOSITIONS.
   COMPARE MAP OF DEFENCES AND PLAN
   PREPARED BY AUCHINLECK

---> INTENDED GERMAN THRUST

→ ACTUAL.

Map 21. Battle of Alam Halfa
August 31st–September 3rd, 1942

divisions in a shallow depression between the powerful British
forces at Alam Halfa and the Quattara Depression, far behind
the main axis of the British front. He was disorganized by
defeat, constantly bombed and seriously short of petrol. This

was the moment for an annihilating counter-stroke in the grand style, driving across Rommel's communications to the Quattara Depression, sealing his armour in a cauldron of bombardment, and achieving a complete and historic victory by Rommel's surrender *en rase campagne*. On September 2nd and 3rd, as Rommel edged awkwardly to the west, there was a chance that the sanguinary Second Battle of Alamein need never be fought. But there was no annihilating counter-stroke. After all, the Second Battle of Alamein had been scheduled; and to Montgomery's methodical and tidy mind unexpected opportunities, however great, were, in his desert days, embarrassing. As Rommel went back, Montgomery carefully regrouped and gingerly followed.

He later explained his failure to turn Alam Halfa into a historic victory by reference to the capabilities of his troops:

> The standard of training of the Eighth Army formations was such that I was not prepared to loose them headlong into the enemy.

This begged the question. A counter-stroke across Rommel's communications would have involved neither loosing his troops nor advancing headlong into the enemy. Curiously enough, he was later to miss another opportunity of an annihilating counter-stroke—after the German repulse in the Ardennes in 1944. Once again, he preferred to keep to his schedule and fight a set-piece battle later.

The moment passed, and the Germans, with their aptitude for swift recovery on a stricken battlefield, began a well-conducted retreat behind the familiar, skilful rearguards and anti-tank screen. Not until the night of September 3rd/4th had Montgomery succeeded in regrouping his forces for an attempt to interfere with this retreat. It was a half-hearted attempt, carried out by the New Zealand Division alone, and it was too late. There were two days of bitter fighting in which the New Zealanders became badly disorganized and even Montgomery had to admit that this methodical attack 'did not succeed in cutting (Rommel) off'.

By September 6th Rommel had brought his troops safely out of danger and into a bridgehead, bristling with anti-tank guns, on the eastern side of the British minefields. There was no attempt to turn him out. According to General Horrocks and to Montgomery himself in his *Memoirs*, Rommel was left in possession of this bridgehead, including the hill of Himeimat, in order that he might observe British decoy preparations before Second Alamein. Elsewhere, however, Montgomery wrote that he called off his pursuit because Rommel was evidently prepared to fight for his bridgehead.

Though a great opportunity had been ignored, Alam Halfa was a model defensive battle and which reflected credit on all concerned in it: the planners Dorman-Smith, Auchinleck and Gott, and the commanders Montgomery and Horrocks. It had no strategic consequences, but it was, in Montgomery's words, 'very important for the Eighth Army, and particularly for me. I said what Rommel would do, and he'd been beaten . . . and it produced faith in me, in my methods. . . .' By an irony, many authorities consider Alam Halfa, with its uncharacteristic features of indirectness, deception and manoeuvre, to be Montgomery's cleverest battle. General Sir Oliver Leese, who commanded 30th Corps at Second Alamein, said of it: 'I always thought Alam Halfa was Monty's finest battle—I know he based Medenine on it.'

Thus, in a secondhand coat of glory, Montgomery set out for the top.

CHAPTER TWO

ALAM HALFA delayed Montgomery's preparations for his own offensive by a fortnight. But he had already done much to make over the army in his image. There was the question of morale, to which he rightly attached very great importance. Here he was an innovator. He was the first British general to project himself to his public (the troops) like a politician or a crooner. Wellington and Marlborough would have found a calculated personal appeal to the army inconsistent with their professional rank. So would Montgomery's predecessors in the Middle East. Yet Marlborough and Wellington enjoyed the complete confidence and loyalty of their men, as had O'Connor, Auchinleck and Wavell, one of whom was very self-effacing and another taciturn. On the enemy side, Rommel was a most simple and unaffected man; but between him and his men existed a loyalty and a strength that recalls Nelson and his fleet. Nevertheless, Montgomery felt that to command successfully, to gain loyalty, he must embark on a publicity campaign.

The hats were the beginning, and certainly his black beret made him recognizable. Press men and photographers, kept at bay by Auchinleck, now flourished in the wartime desert as at a peacetime première. The army public relations staff burned with creative endeavour. The earliest of three years of spontaneous wayside encounters with the troops were arranged. All this would have been profoundly distasteful, even had it been necessary, to any man not abnormally vain. Montgomery actually liked all this contrived lionizing.

'I readily admit,' he confided to seven million people, 'that the decision to become the focus of their attention was personally enjoyable to me. . . .'

He would himself go to considerable trouble to draw a few salutes, especially in distinguished company. General Gatehouse was conducting Montgomery and Wendell Wilkie round the Alam Halfa battlefield to see wrecked German tanks. There were one or two scattered British tank units doing maintenance work. Montgomery told Gatehouse to go over to the nearest group. Gatehouse, who thought the Army Commander wanted to show his American guest tank crews cleaning sprockets and repairing tracks, stopped some distance away in order not to disturb the men. But Montgomery had the car driven right up to them. The soldiers dropped what they were doing, clambered up and saluted; Montgomery gave them a tremendous salute in return.

Montgomery launched himself into the work of training and reorganizing the battleworn army with an icy fire, a relentless energy. He wanted an efficient army, a professional army, above all a *tidy* army. He toured endlessly through his command, his bleak eyes seizing on the idle, the slack and the incompetent, his metallic voice questioning, ordering, denouncing and dismissing. He was like Florence Nightingale putting a hospital in order. All this was admirable.

Yet in purging the army he could be devious. After the Battle of Alam Halfa, the commander of 30th Corps, General

Ramsden, asked for four days' leave in Alexandria, while remaining on constant call in case of emergency. Montgomery was genial:

"Certainly, Ramsden. Come back refreshed for the battle."

Thirty-six hours later Ramsden received an urgent call to report to the Army Commander. Arriving at Eighth Army, Ramsden asked de Guingand, the Chief of Staff, if there was a battle imminent. But de Guingand would only answer:

"General Montgomery wants to see you."

Ramsden entered Montgomery's caravan. Montgomery told him that he had been in the desert nine months and that he had decided to replace him by Sir Oliver Leese. Ramsden, dumbfounded, referred to Montgomery's remark made only thirty-six hours before; Montgomery brushed this aside by snapping irrelevantly:

"This is war—this is war."

Ramsden was an able officer who had distinguished himself in the First Battle of Alamein; he could not see why he was to go, and he said so. In justifying his dismissal Montgomery now made an odd but profoundly self-revealing remark. He said:

"You're not exactly on the crest of a wave, Ramsden."

Montgomery later claimed he made two innovations for his battle of Alamein. One was the formation of a *corps de chasse*, 'mobile and strong in armour'.

> Because of the lack of such a corps we had never done any lasting good in our past offensives. The formation of this corps, three or four divisions, must be a priority task, and it would be to us what the Afrika Korps was to Rommel.

He described in his *Memoirs* how he put his ideas to Alexander, who approved them, and to Major-General Harding, Deputy Chief of the General Staff, who said he could organize such a corps. But this was no innovation at all; as long ago as O'Connor's campaign there had been a mobile and armoured *corps de chasse*—7th Armoured Division, which had won the victory of Beda Fomm. In *Crusader*, 30th Corps under Norrie had formed a mobile wing and had fought an armoured battle with the Afrika Korps, its German equivalent. The innovation under Montgomery lay in that the arrival of two additional armoured divisions, as well as fresh infantry divisions, allowed the formation of a third corps in the Army—10th Corps, to which was allotted the bulk of the armour (1st, 8th and 10th Armoured Divisions) and the New Zealand Division. The old *corps de chasse* now became a static infantry corps.

The second claim of innovation made by Montgomery is equally ill-founded. It relates to the placing of the main offensive effort at the Second Battle of Alamein.

> Now, in traditional desert tactics [said Montgomery on the television] it had always been to attack on the southern flank, the inland flank, and having broken in on the inland flank to swing northwards to the sea, where the only main supply route on this tarmac road hugged the coast. That had always been done, we'd always done it, and so had Rommel . . . it therefore seemed to me quite a good thing to do something else . . . *I* decided to put in our attack somewhere just north of centre.

That is, as the map facing p 116 of his *Memoirs* shows, just south of the Tel el Eisa salient. However, by a coincidence, Ramsden had been working on just such a plan for a fortnight before Montgomery arrived in Egypt—by Auchinleck's orders.

> I ordered [wrote Auchinleck in his dispatch] General Ramsden commanding 30th Corps to begin planning intensively for a deliberate attack south of the Tel el Eisa salient with a view to making a rapid advance along the coast road. I considered this operation offered the greatest chance of success . . .

It is understandable that in 1942 Montgomery would not wish to advertise the part played in his success by other generals—especially by generals not on the crest of a wave, such as Auchinleck, Dorman-Smith and Ramsden. But sixteen years later, in the security of his unrivalled fame, it would have been generous and graceful to have shared the credit with these men, all of whom had remained unjustly in the shadows since 1942. There of course remains the possibility that Montgomery over the years came genuinely to believe his own legend; this would be understandable in view of the volume of support it has received from well-known writers.

From Auchinleck's general conception of a breakthrough on the left centre of the Axis field-fortifications, Montgomery evolved his own organization and tactics for the battle. The whole action was to be fought according to a Master Plan. It would be a methodical, tightly controlled operation, because despite the current retraining of the army he concluded that the skill of the army would not justify more ambitious manoeuvres. Rommel and his officers, like Nelson and his, were so experienced, so imbued with common doctrine, so understanding of each other, that the Afrika Korps could fight a battle with an easy flexibility and local initiative. The Germans were like champion dancers—they had graduated from the set pattern of steps; all was instinctive. Under Montgomery, the British learned to lumber round the battlefield performing rigid beginners' evolutions beneath the sharp eye of the instructor.

But because of this want of faith in the abilities of his army, Montgomery had even to alter his own original tactical conception. Instead of a breakthrough, followed by a tank battle, and by the mopping-up of the enemy infantry, he now preferred an even tighter, more methodical scheme, by which the British armour would, from bridgeheads beyond the German minefields, hold off the enemy armour until the Axis infantry had been crumbled away. It was a realistic decision; it also brought the plan closer to the pattern of his own military temperament.

The four infantry divisions of 30th Corps were to smash two corridors through the German minefields, the northern towards Kidney Ridge, the southern over the Miteiriya Ridge. By an innovation of Montgomery, upon the 30th Corps front and axis of advance was superimposed a second corps, 10th, with three armoured divisions. When 30th Corps had cleared the corridors (or even if it failed to do so) 10th Corps was to pass or fight its way out and post itself defensively on open ground to the west. This cumbersome piling of three armoured and four infantry divisions on the same narrow front, but under different corps commands, took the chronic split between armour and infantry in the Eighth Army to the extreme. It was to have unfortunate results in the battle. After the Axis fixed defences had been crumbled, and the armour defeated, 10th Corps, the *corps de chasse*, would pursue and cut off the wreckage of the *Panzerarmee*. There was some dispute as to the main axis of this pursuit. Montgomery chose the one eventually followed. The old desert hands suggested a line five to ten miles farther south, where there was hard-gravel going above the Fuka Escarpment. But Montgomery, with the reluctance to stray far from the coast that most newcomers to the desert displayed, scouted these suggestions:

'No more manoeuvre—fight a battle.'

This decision also had unfortunate results.

There was an elaborate plan of deception to mislead the German command into thinking that the main attack was coming from the south. Thirteenth Corps, with 7th Armoured Division, was to make dummy attacks in the early days of the battle to sustain the deception.

The date of the Second Battle of Alamein was fixed with some skill. Both Montgomery and Alexander knew of course that the *Torch* landings were to take place in French North Africa in November and could conclude that the presence of a large new Allied army considerably nearer Rommel's unprotected base at Tripoli than Rommel himself at Alamein, would force Rommel to fall back on Tripoli before he was cut off and crushed between two armies each superior to his own. Now Montgomery calculated that his battle would take ten or twelve days. If therefore the opening of the second Battle of Alamein was fixed for *Torch* minus thirteen, he would be insured against defeat. Whatever happened in the battle, Rommel would have to start retreating on the thirteenth day. At first the Prime Minister urged that *Lightfoot* (an ironical code name for Second Alamein) should be launched independently of *Torch* in September or early October 'on the ground that this would impress Spain and protect the flank of *Torch*'. Alexander had other ideas:

> I have carefully considered the timing in relation to *Torch* and have come to the conclusion that the best date for us to start would be minus thirteen of *Torch*

which was then fixed for November 4th. October 23rd was full moon. But on September 22nd Eisenhower finally fixed the date of Torch as November 8th, which threw out all the delicate temporal calculations in Egypt.

But the really interesting question in the relation of *Torch* to Second Alamein is why this bitter battle, with its heavy losses, was fought at all. Of the *Torch* landings Rommel commented: 'This spelt the end of the army in Africa.' From that moment onward all his generalship was employed in getting his army safely back to join the German forces in Tunisia. It was the Allied forces in his rear that made him evacuate his strong defences at El Agheila. They would equally—even more so—have made him evacuate his defences at El Alamein, fourteen hundred miles away from his threatened base. Thus, it follows that, even if Montgomery had not fought his battle, Rommel would have been out of Egypt within a month and in Tunisia within three.

The famous Second Battle of Alamein may therefore go down in history as an unnecessary battle. Had Eighth Army held its attack until the moment Rommel had left the shelter of his fixed defences and begun to retreat, it could have completely destroyed the *Panzerarmee* at small cost. For Rommel would have been helpless, with 90,000 unmotorized infantry to cover with only 200 German tanks in the face of British command of the air, 1100 tanks and a completely mechanized army of 220,000 men.

Why therefore was Second Alamein fought before Rommel was forced to retreat by the *Torch* landings? It was the last purely British victory in the war against Germany; it was the swansong of Britain as a great independent power. After *Torch* the British war effort from Churchill and Montgomery downwards became subordinate to the American. Second Alamein was the last chance to restore British prestige, shaken after a year of defeat, with banner headlines, with the ringing of church bells, and with any other means that might make the victory as famous as Blenheim or Waterloo. If the battle had followed the Anglo-American landings, victory would have been ascribed partly to them. Was this why the offensive could not take place at the obvious moment when *Torch* had forced Rommel to abandon the Alamein defences? The ultimate judgement of history may well be to record it as a political victory.

As fought, Second Alamein has its curious features. In view of the immense disparity of strength between the opposing armies, it is surprising not that we won the battle, but that we almost lost it. In none of the well-known British accounts of the action is given a fair picture of British and Axis strength. In round terms, the British had 220,000 men to the enemy's 108,000; of the Axis strength, only 53,000 were German. But it

Map 22. Second Battle of Alamein: Dispositions on October 23rd, 1942

was in quantity and quality of equipment that the British superiority was crushing—in tanks, guns and aircraft. Montgomery had 1100 tanks fit for action, including about 270 of the superb Shermans and 210 Grants. Two hundred more tanks were brought up during the battle. Against this tremendous array the Axis could put into the field only 200 gun-armed German tanks, mostly Mark III's, and 300 Italian 'self-propelled coffins'. Only the Mark IV, with its long 75-mm gun, was a match for the Sherman; and of these the Germans had but thirty. The Eighth Army's assault was supported by 1000 field and medium guns amply supplied with ammunition. Infantry and armoured divisions were equipped with 800 of the new powerful 6-pounder anti-tank guns. There were 100 105-mm self-propelled guns. The Axis artillery consisted of old-fashioned short-range (five miles) Italian field guns. Of the anti-tank guns, only twenty-four were 88s. The British enjoyed total control of the air and their bombers could range freely over Axis concentrations and supply lines.

It is thus surprising that the *Panzerarmee* managed to slog it out for twelve long days with such a gigantically superior force. It is true that the Axis forces were cleverly dug in behind minefields, and British writers have made the most of these defences. Montgomery told his television audience: 'His (Rommel's) position was strongly organized in depth . . . the problem was to break right through these strong positions . . .' In his *Memoirs* he called it 'an immense undertaking'. General Horrocks has referred to 'the heavily defended minefields'. Churchill wrote that 'the enemy's front consisted not only of successive lines of strongpoints and machine-gun posts, but of a whole deep area of such a defensive system'. Simple facts and calculations demonstrate that these accounts grossly exaggerate. The Axis command deployed the equivalent of six infantry divisions, or 89,000 men, along a forty-five mile front: 2000 men to a mile. On the Dyle in 1940, the 45,000 men of three British divisions had held a front of seventeen miles, or 2650 men to a mile, with another six divisions in reserve. Yet no one considered that to be a strongly held front.

The entire Axis defence system (including minefields) was only five miles deep. It compares with depths of ten to twenty miles for defensive systems (German and Russian) in Russia.

There was no buffer, or delaying zone. Far from being a position of immense depth, the entire Axis defences could be smothered in fire from artillery behind the British start-lines. Montgomery himself expected to drive two corridors clean through it in fewer than twelve hours, according to the final orders to 10th and 30th Corps.

The Axis command did not have a free choice in placing their armour. Acute shortage of fuel made the swift, distant concentrations of other days impossible; the armour had to be stationed where it was hoped it would fight. Therefore, instead of a loose concentration held well back, perhaps near Daba, the Axis armour was placed close behind the front; and because there was not even enough fuel to move all of it from one flank to another according to British pressure, it was split—21st Panzer Division and Ariete in the south and 15th Panzer Division, 90th Light and Littorio in the north.

Last and perhaps greatest of the Axis weaknesses was the absence of Rommel, lying sick in a hospital bed in Semmering; the *Panzerarmee* was commanded now by General Stumme.

As October wore on, Montgomery grew understandably more confident and more cocksure. No desert commander had enjoyed such freedom from nagging by the Prime Minister; no desert commander had so received accession to his every material request. Behind him in the delta, his titular superior, Alexander, bereft of wide strategic cares, fulfilled loyally the role of housekeeper assigned to him by Montgomery, who neatly said of him: 'He was the perfect Commander-in-Chief to have in the Middle East, so far as I was concerned.' Montgomery had now achieved a personal grip of steel on his army through his training methods and inspections and through the trusted and able friends he had appointed to high posts on the staff and in the command. Only Lumsden, of 10th Corps, was not a 'Monty' man. But on the eve of battle, Montgomery tightened further his grip on his troops by a series of addresses on the coming battle down to the level of lieutenant-colonels. These were enormously effective, for in Sir Oliver Leese's words, 'he was completely convinced he was going to win the battle. He made everything crystal-clear.' With Montgomery's staccato lecture ringing in their ears, the colonels returned to their battalions with the feeling that they were personally in the

Army Commander's confidence and trust. These sentiments they passed on to their men. It was a brilliant exercise in calculated leadership.

During the night of October 22nd/23rd the assault troops moved into their forward concentration areas, and all through the following day, they lay, like O'Connor's men before Sidi Barrani, in trenches beyond the British front line. But there was no chance of discovery by German air reconnaissance; the Royal Air Force had such domination in the air that it was able to maintain standing patrols over the forward Axis airfields. At last night came to the 330,000 men poised in the quiet desert; they waited for the moon to rise and the battle to begin. Even history was given its task in the master plan. In a personal message to his army Montgomery wrote:

> The battle which is now about to begin will be one of the decisive battles of history. It will be the turning point of the war.

To command the battle, Montgomery left his main headquarters at Burg el Arab and moved into a tactical headquarters on the coast behind El Alamein. That evening, as the moon of battles rose, he went to bed early; and when the fire of a thousand guns lashed out at 9.40 pm, he says he was asleep. From the Mediterranean to the Quattara Depression, the British artillery poured high explosive over the Axis line; the Axis guns were silent, for Stumme had ordered them to conserve scanty stocks of shells. After twenty minutes the barrage lifted and over 70,000 men and 600 tanks advanced against the 12,000 Italians and Germans of the Trento and 164th Infantry Divisions on the Axis left centre: odds of six to one, not counting the armour. It seemed that the German line could hardly withstand such a blow longer than had the perimeter of Tobruk in June.

But, by morning on October 24th, and despite all the planning and method, the attack had already crumpled into a shambles. Because of the size of the assault force packed on so narrow a front, it had, like a swordsman in a close crowd, no room to fight. The infantry did not penetrate to the western edge of the German defence zone; the engineers did not clear through-lines for the armour; and the armour remained therefore jammed behind the infantry in the cul-de-sacs opened in

Map 23. Second Battle of Alamein: Breakdown of Master Plan
October 23rd–26th, 1942

the minefields. Upon this immobile mass, the Axis guns, both field and anti-tank, directed a heavy and accurate fire.

All that day the grand assault floundered in its narrow alleys in the Axis defences. And in the south, Horrocks's diversionary attack with 13th Corps had gone hopelessly astray. Seventh Armoured Division and 44th Division did not succeed in penetrating the two belts of German minefields, but were gravelled on mines which the Germans had scattered between the belts; and they remained marooned there throughout October 24th.

Chance however brought Montgomery compensation for the failure of his attack to reach its objectives; General Stumme, his opponent, died of heart failure on the battlefield and was replaced by von Thoma, with a consequent dislocation of the Axis command. But to balance this good luck, Rommel, though still sick, was flying out to take command of the *Panzerarmee*.

Montgomery had made it clear in his orders that if the infantry and engineers failed to clear lanes through the minefields, the armour of 10th Corps was to fight its own way out. There were three lanes to an armoured division, each wide enough for one tank. Therefore the British armoured Divisions were asked to debouch through a five-mile defile six tanks wide. If the leading tanks should be knocked out by German anti-tank fire, the defile would become a bottleneck.

During the afternoon and night of October 24th, the British assault force attempted this operation on both the main axes of the break-in. The northern attempt, towards Kidney Ridge, partly succeeded when some tanks of 2nd Armoured Brigade got clear of the western edge of a minebelt, but not of the Axis defence system. But the southern attempt, over the fireswept Miteiriya Ridge, stopped enmeshed in minefields at four o'clock in the morning of October 25th. Thus, after another twenty-four hours' fighting, Montgomery's assault had not reached the objective assigned for dawn, October 24th. It was not to reach those objectives for another nine days. This was the first crisis in the battle.

Lumsden of 10th Corps believed that it was impossible for his armour to fight its own way out in accordance with Montgomery's orders: it was a wrong use of tanks and would result in a massacre. He wished to pull his tanks out of the corridors, regroup them behind the Miteiriya Ridge and send them back into the battle when the infantry and engineers of 30th Corps had cleared a way through the Axis defences.

Therefore Leese and de Guingand, the Chief of Staff, decided that Montgomery must personally intervene. About two in the morning, when the exhausted men of 10th and 30th Corps were still floundering forward on the Miteiriya Ridge, de Guingand roused Montgomery and in his caravan one of the most tense conferences in the history of war took place.

The dull electric light shone bleakly on Montgomery's fox-like face, with its prominent cheekbones and the nose, moustache and mouth forming a muzzle that moved, almost twitched, as he talked; on Leese, huge, bland, red-faced, a roast-beef Englishman; on Herbert Lumsden, veteran armoured commander, cavalryman, gay, charming, handsome, theatrical, highly-strung. As in Norrie's headquarters on the Ruweisat Ridge in the July battles, Lumsden argued almost frantically that the armour must be pulled back because of its appalling casualties in an operation not suited to tanks. He quoted General Gatehouse, 10th Armoured Division, as saying that even if he succeeded in debouching beyond the minefields on to the southern face of the Miteiriyi Ridge, he would be shot to pieces by German anti-tank fire.

There now followed an episode, crucially important in the history of the battle, about which there are conflicting accounts. Acording to Montgomery, Lumsden asked Montgomery to speak himself to Gatehouse by telephone.

> I did so at once and discovered to my horror that he himself was some 16,000 yards (nearly ten miles) behind his leading armoured brigades (sic). I spoke to him at once in no uncertain voice, and ordered him to go forward at once and take charge of his battle . . .

Then, acording to Montgomery, he told Lumsden and Leese that his orders were unchanged, and that the armour *would* fight its way out. He kept Lumsden back a moment and 'I spoke very plainly to him'; he warned that he would replace both him and Gatehouse if there were more hesitations.

General Leese confirms that he and Montgomery measured the distance on the map from Gatehouse's headquarters to the front line, but Gatehouse, in fact, was not at his HQ, but up at the front. He has a very different version of this telephone conversation. Gatehouse was the most experienced tank commander in the British service; he had made his whole career in armour, for his own regiment was the Royal Tank Regiment. He had won four decorations for personal bravery. According to him, Lumsden returned from the conference in Montgomery's caravan and told him that his attack must continue. Gatehouse replied that he was refusing the order: it would destroy that armour which Montgomery was supposed to have formed as a *corps de chasse*. Lumsden warned him of the consequences of such a refusal. Gatehouse therefore went back and telephoned Montgomery himself, with Lumsden's agreement, from a field telephone line far behind the forward troops. There were sharp words along the field telephone wire; Gatehouse began by saying:

"What the hell's going on?"

His manner thereafter was far from deferential. Montgomery listened while Gatehouse told him the armour was expected to advance over the crest of the Miteiriya Ridge, through uncharted and uncleared minefields, covered by strong batteries of anti-tank guns, and be eight hundred yards down the forward slope by dawn. Because of the noise of tank tracks, surprise was impossible. Then Montgomery modified the scope of the attack from six armoured regiments to one: the Staffordshire Yeomanry. It lost all but fifteen of its tanks and the operation ended where it had started, behind the Miteiriya Ridge.

Yet Montgomery later told a television audience: 'The necessary part of the armoured division got established beyond the minefields.'

The real significance of the events of the small hours of October 25th, 1942, lies not in this controversy, but in that the offensive had staggered to the verge of defeat after just forty-eight hours' fighting—an amazing event, in view of the forces engaged, and one clearly, prima facie, calling Montgomery's generalship in question. However, Montgomery in both his books and during his television appearances rarely admits to major errors in generalship, although he does criticize others. The near-failure of his offensive on October 24th and 25th, 1942, Montgomery firmly blamed on alleged cowardice and want of energy on the part of the armour of 10th Corps and its senior officer. But it was illogical to blame the armour of 10th Corps rather than the infantry of 30th Corps, for 30th Corps had failed in its own allotted task.

In fact, the breakdown occurred because of the cumbersome two-tier organization of infantry and armour on the same narrow, mine-strewn front, and because the armour was given a role completely unsuited to it.

The basic problem in planning Second Alamein lay in the right tactical and organizational combination of armour, infantry and artillery in order to penetrate a continuous fortified line without flanks. For the armour, it presented, in General Leese's words, 'the novel task of close co-operation with infantry against fixed defences', and at Alamein was seen for the first time 'this game of fighting armour and infantry on a master plan'.

Clearly the armour and infantry in the corridors, dependent as they were on each other's success, must work intimately together and in perfect harmony as to timing and movement. In the German army, where all arms were trained and organized on the same system, this co-operation was natural. In the British army, despite Auchinleck's radical reorganization of the armour after *Crusader*, armour and infantry remained two separate services, trained and organized in different ways and split asunder by sectional pride. After the Gazala defeats, this gulf was widened by a profound suspicion on the part of the infantry of the armour's professional ability. Now, by a paradox, these two services had to be made to carry out a tightly dovetailed joint operation in minefields and under heavy fire. It was like asking an estranged man and his wife to make love.

Just before his dismissal, Auchinleck had set on foot his own revolutionary solution of this chronic separatism. He ordered that all distinction between armour and infantry division should be abolished; and the army reorganized into 'Mobile Divisions', mainly motorized infantry but each with an armoured brigade under command. Trained together, all arms commanded by common divisional commanders, these divisions would have been the mobile mixed combinations similar to those Rommel had in his German troops—the entire Eighth Army, and not just 10th Corps, would have formed the equivalent of Afrika Korps, but six times as large. Auchinleck's proposals aroused enormous opposition; every conservative instinct, regimental and separatist, was against it. McCreery, the Major-General, Armoured Fighting Vehicles in the Middle East, was a cavalryman; he objected strongly to Auchinleck's suggestions and was instantly dismissed. Auchinleck intended to replace him with Gatehouse. Had this come to fruition the training and organization of the British armour would have been for the first time directed by a tank officer. When Auchinleck went, the proposals were thankfully torn up and McCreery made Chief of the General Staff to Alexander. However the New Zealand Division for the rest of the North African campaign had an armoured brigade under command, and mobile infantry and tank co-operation was so good that Montgomery used the division more and more as the spearhead of his attacks.

It was then Montgomery's turn to think of an answer.

His solution was in every way opposite to Auchinleck's and in every way wrong, for it carried the existing dangerous separatism still further. He formed 10th Corps, containing the armour, and ordered it to fight a joint battle with 30th Corps, containing infantry. Whereas before in the desert armour and infantry in combined attacks had been at least co-ordinated by a common corps commander, and whereas Auchinleck intended they should be intimately co-ordinated by common *divisional* commanders, now the Army Commander himself formed the only command link. And thus in the crammed defiles in the minefields on October 24th/25th, two corps under separate commanders made separate efforts over the same ground.

Now, in the middle of the battle, Montgomery's resolution as a battlefield commander redeemed his clumsiness as a planner. In General Leese's opinion Montgomery 'was the greatest field commander since Cromwell. Only Napoleon was as good'. Remembering his enormous resources, Montgomery decided to drive the attack forward, come what may.

This was the moment, with the British attack stalled and in confusion, for a crushing German counter-blow, but Rommel had not yet arrived in Africa, and the inexperienced von Thoma only put in a piecemeal attack with 15th Panzer Division against Montgomery's northern corridor; it achieved nothing, and lost many tanks.

October 25th was another bad day for Montgomery. The

New Zealand Division's efforts at 'crumbling' had failed; now the Australians nearer the coast were to crumble. First Armoured Division was to advance westward from Kidney Ridge and if possible pass a brigade into the open desert and occupy Sidi Rahman, the nodal point of German communications. The division was unable to move at all. Sidi Rahman was not occupied until November 4th. In the far south, after 4th Light Armoured Brigade had run into mines and heavy anti-tank fire, Horrocks and 13th Corps were turned over to the defensive. But Montgomery did not bring 7th Armoured Division up to reinforce the main battle: 'as long as 21st Panzer Division was in the south, I required an armoured division in 13th Corps.' This contradicted his favourite principle of balance, where a 'balanced' commander 'need not react to the enemy move but can continue relentlessly with his own plan'.

On October 26th, the South Africans and New Zealanders made some ground on the Miteiriya Ridge; otherwise the great offensive remained stuck. Though the Master Plan had so completely foundered, Montgomery appeared unmoved.

> He was always calm; nothing disturbed him. It never struck him that anybody else could win. If things went wrong, we always had something else to put in—we were always in balance.

His orders were all personal, never written. His corps commanders saw him every morning and every evening of the battle. Some of the tired staff officers were shocked by the way his cold, glittering eyes stared out of a drawn face; by the fanatical expression; by the 'surgical callousness' over the mounting casualties. All day long on October 26th he stayed in his headquarters, thinking, and the army hardly stirred. It was almost as if he had run out of ideas.

He had in fact the task of cobbling together a fresh battle. For his existing bridgeheads had been sealed by powerful anti-tank screens; his infantry—in the Australian, Highland and South African Divisions especially—had been decimated to the point where replacements were an anxiety; he had already lost 200 tanks, equal to the German total strength; and 30th Corps was so disorganized that it needed a pause for recuperation. Axis resistance had been unexpectedly tough, for, despite deception measures 'probably unequalled in military

285

history', the Axis Command, in Montgomery's words, 'had withdrawn troops and guns from his forward positions in anticipation of our offensive, and we had therefore found him in greater depth than had been expected'.

At the end of the day Montgomery decided to regroup his troops and start again in a fresh direction—towards the coast in the Australian sector. The New Zealanders went into reserve, and their sector, which had formed one of the two main corridors of breakthrough in his master plan, was turned over to 13th Corps and became purely defensive. The whole of the following day, October 27th, found the Eighth Army still stuck fast, carrying out its reorganization. All this hardly squared with Montgomery's doctrine of balance, nor with the comment in a letter to Brooke on November 1st that 'I have managed to keep the initiative throughout, and so far Rommel has had to dance entirely to my tune'.

Rommel had now arrived on the battlefield. He immediately brought 21st Panzer Division northwards (it took less than a day) and thus left 7th Armoured Division sadly out of balance. Twenty-four hours after leaving his hospital bed he led his concentrated armour in a counter-stroke against the British armour at Kidney Ridge, coming in with the setting sun behind him. He had fewer than 150 tanks. Savagely bombed as he assembled and advanced, he was beaten off by the new 6-pounder anti-tank guns and by the heavy British armour with the loss of a third of his tanks. News reached Rommel at that moment that his army was almost out of fuel. Next day, October 28th, he attempted to attack again; Royal Air Force bombing broke the attack up before it reached Eighth Army.

Rommel now expected Montgomery to end the battle by launching immediately a decisive attack with massed forces. But Eighth Army was still being sorted out.

Since 21st Panzer had gone from the south, Montgomery now reacted by bringing 7th Armoured Division northwards. First Armoured Division and 24th Armoured Brigade went into the peace of reserve. Montgomery now abandoned hope of a breakthrough in the northern of the two original corridors as well as the southern; the master plan was defunct. The next attack would be on the coast. The battle had now lasted five days, and Eighth Army had been motionless for three.

'You always had a sense of time to spare,' said General Leese later of Montgomery's battles. 'We never went into battle unless we had enough of everything.'

Now the second phase of the battle began; and henceforth the sheer weight of British resources made up for all blunders. On October 29th the grand offensive got modestly under way again with a divisional attack by the Australians along the coast that cut behind part of the 164th German Infantry Division. It is to be remarked that Montgomery's attacks in this battle were generally piecemeal, one division at a time. But Montgomery learned that 90th Light was behind the coastal front, and although of course a balanced army did not have to react to enemy moves, but ruthlessly pursued its own plans, Montgomery now changed the point of his main attack south again to the New Zealand sector.

The impending blow on the New Zealand sector was intended as the finishing stroke of the battle. It would take nearly two days to organize. In Alexander's significant words: 'It was to be an operation very similar to that of October 23rd.' Thirtieth Corps was to open a gap right through the remaining Axis defences; 10th Corps would pass into open country. Montgomery fixed the objectives of the operation as the destruction of the enemy armour and the disintegration of the enemy army. He christened it *Supercharge*. It was scheduled for the night of October 31st/November 1st; and armoured cars were to be passing on to Rommel's communications by dawn on the 1st. On October 31st Montgomery had to postpone the attack twenty-four hours because 'the stage management problems . . . were such that if launched on this night it might fail'. It was a measure of the disorganization of 10th and 30th Corps.

On the night of October 30th/31st, a preliminary and diversionary attack by the Australians reached the coast and trapped part of 164th Division against the sea. In a violent counter-attack, 90th Light and a battlegroup of 21st Panzer Division rescued their comrades and destroyed eighteen British tanks.

When Montgomery first reached Egypt in August he had told his staff officers that 'the policy of fighting the enemy in brigade groups, jock-columns ,and with divisions split up into

287

bits and pieces all over the desert was to cease. In future divisions would fight *as* divisions'. Yet it is interesting to note that the 30th Corps force for *Supercharge* contained as many as three brigade groups: one from 50th Division, one from 44th Division, and the Greek Brigade. These were the last available reserves in the army.

Now came the last act of an exhausting, muddled and prolonged action. The Axis forces, heavily outnumbered at the beginning and without reinforcements or rest for seven days, had now fought almost to the limit of their strength.

At one o'clock in the morning *Supercharge* began; nearly 800 tanks, covered by 360 guns. But once again there was furious fighting and heavy losses among the attackers; 9th Armoured Brigade lost 87 tanks. Not until dawn on November 2nd did the British stagger at last out of that defensive system, into which they had broken with, in Montgomery's words, 'wild enthusiasm' ten days before.

And even now the battle had still more than a sixth of its course to run; for in front of the British armour of 10th Corps was Rommel and his two panzer divisions, 90 tanks against 700. At Tel el Aqqaqir was now fought the last great tank battle of the desert war, in which the odds were too grossly uneven to leave the issue in doubt. But Rommel fought one of the best actions of his career in order to gain time for the organization of the retreat that must soon begin. His counter-attacks almost broke through the British salient: and at the end of the day,, Montgomery's *corps de chasse* was still milling about impatiently in front of Rommel's guns. Though Montgomery had in his orders written that *Supercharge* 'will therefore be successful', it too had been a failure—it did not achieve any of the objectives assigned to it for November 1st by Montgomery's handwritten order. The British armour did *not* occupy the Tel el Aqqaqir area by first light, did *not* develop operations from that area 'as the sun rises' to destroy the enemy armour and bring about the disintegration of the enemy rear areas. As the news of failure came in, it seemed that the stubborn enemy would never break. All next day (November 3rd) the 10th and 30th Corps pursuit remained largely corralled by the German armour and anti-tank guns; and behind that skilful rearguard, the Panzer Army began to slip away from Montgomery's eager fingers.

For Rommel it was perhaps the trickiest moment of his career. He had to disengage a hopelessly outnumbered and partly immobile army in country that gave no natural protection against attack by huge masses of armour and lorried infantry. This operation must be carried through under ceaseless air bombardment and in the shackles imposed by shortage of fuel. Its success must rank as a prodigious feat of arms and leadership. Rommel held his tiny army together by force of character, by the loyalty of his veterans. In trances of exhaustion these men, the same who had taken Tobruk and Gazala, unreinforced, unrelieved, served their guns with instinctive skill, taking heart from the sight of the stocky figure of the Field-Marshal as he toured the battlefield fighting his thin line of battle in person like Wellington.

Rommel even hoped he might get the bulk of the infantry away 'since the enemy was operating with such astonishing hesitancy and caution'.

Now however Montgomery found an unlooked for ally in Adolf Hitler. On November 3rd, the Fuehrer sent Rommel a telegram ordering him to stand and die at Alamein. It was a typical piece of politicians' interference; it carried echoes of a similar British order. Rommel obeyed. His orders for retreat were cancelled; the flow of troops ceased along the precarious road to safety; and by order of the Fuehrer, the *Panzerarmee* waited patiently for annihilation. A personal emissary was sent to Hitler to point out that retreat was the only way of saving the army. On the evening of November 4th Hitler replied that in view of the situation, Rommel might act as he saw fit. Thus at the critical moment when the battle was about to become a pursuit, Montgomery was handed a bonus of thirty-six hours' start.

During November 3rd and November 4th, in obedience to Hitler's order, Rommel tried to hold on to his front; 90th Light were deployed in front of his 22 remaining tanks; massing in stately pursuit to the east and south were 650 British tanks of 10th Corps and 7th Armoured Division, supported by lorried infantry. Montgomery put in two more attacks on the flanks of the German corral and at last broke clean through into open desert; the Fuehrer's permission to retreat followed; and the Second Battle of Alamein had ended.

It ended so unspectacularly that the British Command could not make up its mind if the battle was over or not.

CHAPTER THREE

B RITISH LOSSES in the battle totalled 13,500 men (killed, wounded and missing) and 600 tanks. German losses were 180 tanks, 1000 dead and 8000 prisoners. Italian losses were 1000 dead and 16,000 prisoners.

On November 5th, as oil and blood leaked slowly into the sand of the battlefield that carried so many British dead, Montgomery held a press conference. He was in great form, bouncing with victory, and lightheartedly swapping banalities with the journalists. Then he told them, and through them the British public:

"Gentlemen, this is complete and absolute victory."

His titular superior, Alexander, signalled the Prime Minister to 'ring out the bells'.

As Clausewitz points out, the fruits of victory are gathered in the pursuit, but no fruits were gathered in the pursuit from Alamein. It was not therefore a 'complete and absolute victory'.

In order to gather these fruits, as Clausewitz also points out, the pursuit must be vigorous; Montgomery's pursuit after Second Alamein showed all the bustling confidence of an archdeacon entering a *maison clos* and its slow start throws a bleak light on the state to which the Eighth Army had been reduced by twelve days of murderous attacking.

Montgomery said that the good commander always thinks and plans two moves ahead. Montgomery had formed 10th Corps specially as a *corps de chasse*. His battles always went, he gave the world to understand, as planned. Yet after the British broke into open country on November 2nd it took Montgomery three days to organize a full-scale pursuit, which did not begin until November 5th, when Rommel, despite the thirty-six hours delay imposed by the Fuehrer, had already got a day's start. Why was not Montgomery's long-cherished pursuit force ready and poised for an immediate chase on November 2nd? It was because 10th Corps, which was supposed never to be involved in a static front, had been largely consumed in the 'dogfight' and what was left of it and of 30th Corps was too disorganized and exhausted to pursue anyone. A new *corps de chasse*, under command of 10th Corps headquarters, had to be hastily cobbled together on the battlefield; and when it got under way, it included 7th Armoured Division and the New Zealand Division, which had never been part of 10th Corps. In fact this *corps de chasse* seemed to embody the 'policy of fighting the enemy in brigade groups . . . and bits and pieces of divisions' that Montgomery had denounced on arrival in Egypt, for 1st and 10th Armoured Divisions had each borrowed a motor brigade from 44th Division. Here is the real proof of how badly the battle had gone, how utterly the master plan had failed, and how lucky Montgomery had been to have such immense resources that he escaped the fate of Cunningham and Ritchie.

On November 3rd, the New Zealand Division with 4th and 9th Armoured Brigades (the brigade group again) were ordered to go for Fuka. But now occurred the last mishap to be caused by the clumsy superimposing of 10th Corps on 30th Corps front; this scratch pursuit force got hopelessly tangled with the 10th Corps supply convoys; nightfall found it only halfway to Fuka. Meanwhile routeing and traffic control were chaotic.

On the morrow of its victory Eighth Army thus lay at a standstill, paralyzed by confusion as great as any seen under the predecessors Montgomery so despised. 'No more manoeuvre—fight a battle'—but the battle had been fought, and now there must be manoeuvre. It seemed as though Montgomery's vision and will had ended with the breakout.

At last on November 5th the full-scale pursuit under 10th Corps got under way. It was directed by Montgomery in short, tight turns to the coast, though all the experienced desert commanders advised a long march through the desert, parallel to the enemy, as far even as Tobruk. First Armoured Division cut into Daba and found Rommel gone. Tenth Armoured Division made only eleven miles towards the Fuka escarpment. The New Zealanders were held up most of the day by a wire fence, thought to bound a minefield, with German rearguards behind it. The minefield turned out to be a British dummy laid in the summer. Harding, a veteran of the desert, took 7th Armoured Division well south along the Fuka escarpment, but got tangled with the New Zealanders' supply trucks, and was delayed in a dummy minefield. The pursuit was thus highly dispersed, the mistake of which Montgomery was to accuse Eisenhower after the Battle of Normandy in 1944; Montgomery argued that the pursuit in 1944 would have succeeded if all administrative resources had been put behind one axis of advance; ironically the argument applies equally to his own advance after Second

Map 24. Failure of Broad Front Pursuit After Second Battle of Alamein

Alamein. During November 6th, Montgomery closed his principal trap at Baggush, just east of Matruh; it was empty. The sole catch of the day was a remnant of 21st Panzer Division, which, immobilized for want of fuel, was brought to action by 22nd Armoured Brigade. It held off the British until nightfall, received some fuel, and slipped away.

On the German side, the retreat was orderly and controlled. In General Leese's words:

The German is very, very quick about sorting himself out—forming new battlegroups. This is helped by his training, which is uniform throughout all divisions.

Now, with his further escape on November 6th, Rommel's acute danger was over. For there is a law of diminishing returns in the efforts of a pursuer to cut off an enemy, who is marching away in a straight line.

On the night of November 6th, as the disappointed pursuit headed once more inland, heavy rains fell and turned the soft sand south of Mersa Matruh into a quagmire. Now the *corps de chasse* became stuck fast. This circumstance, which took place therefore *after* Montgomery had cut into the coastal road four times and found it empty, and *after* Rommel had irrevocably increased his lead, Montgomery ingeniously used as an excuse for his total failure to catch Rommel after Second Alamein. This excuse was started on its rounds as soon as November 10th in a letter to General Brooke: '. . . what saved him was the rain; I had nearly reached Matruh and was getting in behind all his transport when torrential rain turned the desert into a bog . . .' It turns up in Churchill's *War Memoirs*:

> By nightfall on the 6th they (the pursuit) were nearing their objective, while the enemy was still trying to escape from the closing trap. But then rain came . . . The twenty-four-hour respite prevented complete encirclement.

It has been repeated in other accounts. But Montgomery's account does not even on its own premises make sense. The rain fell impartially on Briton and German; and the *Rommel Papers* make clear that the Axis retreat was as greatly hampered by it as the British pursuit.

*　　　*　　　*

With the failure of the immediate pursuit from Alamein, both armies settled down to a long march of fifteen hundred miles. Here, in mobility and manoeuvre, Montgomery was as lost as a dray horse on a polo field. The Maréchal de Saxe wrote that the pursuer 'must attack, push, and pursue without cease. . . . All manoeuvres are good then: it is only precautions that are worthless.' Montgomery disagreed. His experienced desert commanders pleaded to be allowed to race hard through the desert, in order to force Rommel to battle and destroy him. Gatehouse of 10th Armoured Division asked if he could take his division ('the strongest in Egypt and with a complete B echelon') immediately on to Sollum and Tobruk. But Montgomery said there was to be no mad rush which might expose him to a riposte. He repeated this over and over again to different audiences; that he was not going to risk at all coming back again 'like the others'. No initiative was allowed even to corps commanders: Montgomery kept the army tightly under his own rigid control, and Rommel was delighted and astonished that his retreat was being so little pressed. "I wonder," he said to Bayerlein, "why he doesn't hurry? But it's lucky for us."

Montgomery's caution in this long pursuit illustrates his obsession with tidiness and method. It also shows a curious limit to one of his most publicized characteristics: the belief in his own ability.

For this was not entirely a rational caution. Rommel now had only ten tanks. His tiny force was known to be intermittently paralyzed by want of fuel.

Eighth Army was now traversing Rommel's old ground—El Adem, Knightsbridge, Sidi Rezegh—and the memories of thunderbolt attacks out of the setting sun, of manoeuvres of astonishing speed and skill were evoked by the rusted wrecks of these ancient battlefields. Rommel! His stocky figure, with the pugnacious face under the goggled cap, was still held in awe and admiration by both armies. There was magic there; who knew what he might still do, despite his ten tanks and want of petrol? Better not go out there in the desert—*his* country—and mix it in a fluid battle of manoeuvre, not even with two armoured divisions at your back. He might do something unorthodox; something not covered by the master plan. He might be twice as quick on his feet. He might be the better general. And thus Montgomery, who had seen himself on arrival in Egypt as the 'anti-Rommel', also fell under his spell; and the *Panzerarmee*'s shield during that epic retreat was its commander's reputation. And this interpretation is corroborated by a senior officer close to Montgomery at the time, who agrees that 'Rommel's reputation did make an impression on Monty's mind'.

So through Sollum and Tobruk and Gazala Eighth Army trailed after Rommel, while its commanders chafed and grumbled and Montgomery remained, in Pope's line, 'willing to wound, yet afraid to strike'. Rommel went without haste, falling back from petrol dump to petrol dump with his ten tanks and 10,000 men, leaving behind extensive mining and booby-traps. Some days one or both his panzer divisions lay stalled helplessly in the open desert for want of fuel. No fresh forces reached him from Germany and Italy; none were likely to; and there was no hope of fighting any kind of general action. 'Rommel was not the same as he had been against the Auk,' General Leese was to say later. 'He could have been very formidable had he not been made to dance to our tune.' All Rommel could do was make faces at Montgomery in order to keep him to a slow pace. In General Leese's words:

> In the retreat I never saw Rommel fight a real action; there was no battle crisis until Mareth. But there was a lot of fighting—a battle every day, because you couldn't take chances with German rearguards. Rommel fought every day with something.

Montgomery took Tobruk on November 13th; his eleven days for the distance from Alamein compares with Rommel's nine in the reverse direction, when he deployed for, fought and won a battle on the way. Amid the rocks of Gazala Rommel halted his men, fought a short action, and then faded into the west behind mines, blowing the road at every escarpment, booby-trapping abandoned trucks and houses; even the palm trees under which his pursuers might rest. He was receiving half his essential quantity of petrol; for a time he had no shells for the army artillery. His men had been fighting non-stop since October 23rd. It was an amazing display of military virtuosity.

Now Montgomery stood at the gates of the Jebel Achdar, where O'Connor had stood two years before. Those with him who had served with O'Connor pressed him to throw a powerful force through Msus to the coast road and there repeat the total victory of Beda Fomm. He refused, saying that he was determined he would not repeat the mistakes of the past (Beda Fomm?) and place himself in a weak position which might give Rommel a chance to launch a counter-stroke. Yet it was well-known that at this moment Rommel had not more than thirty-odd tanks—a trickle of replacements had arrived—and that he was desperately crippled by want of fuel; Montgomery was in no way exposed to the same risks as O'Connor, who had flung his tiny mobile force across the then unreconnoitred desert into the path of an immensely stronger army. But siege, not manoeuvre, was the *forte* of Montgomery's exact talents: though he agreed to let a light force make the journey through Msus, the main body of the army plodded on behind Rommel's rearguards. The light force got bogged by rain and caught nothing.

Benghazi fell on November 20th after a delay that enabled the Germans to wreck the port and destroy stores, and on November 24th, Rommel halted in his old defences at El Agheila. Here he bravely deployed. There were the two divisions of the Afrika Korps, in the total strength of a brigade; 90th Light (one and a half battalions); 164th Infantry Division (3000 men with no weapons heavier than machine guns); a battalion of parachutists; the Italian 20th Corps in the strength of a brigade; and eight batteries of guns. Rommel had thirty tanks, twenty armoured cars, forty-six anti-tank guns and forty 88s. With this scarecrow force he prepared to defend a line a hundred and seventy kilometres long; more than twice the length of his front at Alamein. It was outrageous bluff.

It succeeded. Montgomery came up with the 120 tanks of the 7th Armoured Division, and the infantry of 51st Highland Division; looked at El Agheila; and settled down for three weeks to prepare for a set-piece attack on this formidable obstacle. This process he describes in his *Memoirs* as 'hustling' Rommel and getting possession of El Agheila by 'bluff and manoeuvre'. In a television performance he said of Rommel and the El Agheila defences: 'Well, we soon turned him out of there.' Yet elsewhere he wrote: 'I decided that bluff would not remove him', and 'I would be unable to start my operations against the Agheila position until mid-December'.

At the back of Montgomery's mind—and of his troops' minds—was the fear of Rommel suddenly debouching in surprising strength as in 1941 and 1942. Yet the situation was utterly different: on November 8th the Anglo-American forces had invaded French North Africa, and by November 24th were nearing Bizerta and Tunis. An American airborne force was in southern Tunisia, dangerously near Tripolitania. There was thus no possible question of Rommel staging a counterstroke from El Agheila that would take him further away from his endangered base and from the German forces now being built up in Tunisia. From November 8th, Rommel's one intention had been to effect a junction with von Arnim before Allied forces could get between them. And the fresh troops and equipment which might in other circumstances have come to Rommel were being fed into Tunisia. By an irony, those forces for which Rommel had asked before Second Alamein, which very probably would have enabled him to win that battle and which the Fuehrer had refused him, were to provide as prisoners early in 1943 the Allies' greatest triumph so far in the war.

So Rommel therefore stopped at Agheila only to rest his troops, reorganize them and gain a little time before slipping away again. With a particle of Marlborough's strategic imagination Montgomery could have divined all this; called Rommel's bluff, and brought him to battle immediately with more than 120 tanks against 35.

While the three-weeks'-long preparations for a set-piece attack on the Agheila position were going on, Montgomery went back to Cairo on leave. He was a full general now: and Second Alamein had already turned on the tap of public adulation. He bathed gratefully in the resulting gush. He showed his flair for timely public appearances by reading the lesson at the Sunday Evening Service at St George's Cathedral and recorded archly that 'it caused quite a stir'. Success and renown inflated his ego; he had already demonstrated, as he was increasingly so to do in the next few years, an unwillingness to hear suggestions or advice. But, with tact, ideas could still be got over to him. General Leese, who was to succeed him in Italy as Eighth Army Commander, recalls how he and de Guingand would consider how tactfully to approach him with a suggestion.

> One of them would go to his caravan in the evening, and put their case. Monty would shake his head and say:
> 'Can't do that, can't do that.'
> Then in the morning he might say: 'I've been thinking, and had an idea . . .' He would then explain the idea which would be the one put to him the night before.

The legend was beginning to be established: the caravan set apart, never to be disturbed except by an inner acolyte; the withdrawing from the society of men of his own age into the society of admiring young disciples; the sandwiches eaten in the desert during visits to lower formations so that he should not have to mix socially in the messes. There was not now a senior officer left with Eighth Army who had shown himself unmoved by his spell and critical of his genius, for both Lumsden and Gatehouse had gone.

Yet, like the right and wrong side of a mirror, all this bright glorification of self seemed to be backed by a profound and sombre self-doubt. Did Montgomery feel that his authority, his hold on the loyalty of the army, might be weakened by mixing freely in the messes of its various formations? Why did he progressively withdraw to his Tactical HQ and the society of young men who must always agree with him? The answer to these questions can perhaps be found in his desire for overwhelming material superiority, in his love of exact tidiness, in the artificial predestination of the master plan.

Meanwhile Rommel was now experiencing, like Auchinleck and Wavell, the benefit of advice from home. Berlin and Rome demanded a fight to the last on the El Agheila line; Rommel demanded the troops, tanks and air cover. The critics thus silenced, Rommel prepared to slip away. Montgomery's offensive was due to open on December 15th. On the night of December 7th/8th, the Italians drove out of Agheila with headlights blazing and amid stupendous uproar. The oasis of Marada was also evacuated; and Rommel and his handful of Germans were left in the vast freezing winter spaces of Agheila. Not surprisingly, Montgomery was aware that the Italians had gone and he therefore advanced the date of his attack to December 13th. By a coincidence Rommel had fixed the time of his retirement for the night of December 12th/13th. On the 12th, as a German account puts it, 'Montgomery gave signs of life', by reconnaissances in force.

The winter rains fell across the bleak scene of mud, gravel and camel thorn. As the day wore on, the usual preliminary bombardment by air and artillery began to wax in weight and fury. It went on all through the night; then the set-piece mass-attack rolled majestically forward and by late afternoon was through the Agheila line. But all this dread preparation and careful onslaught was wasted; Rommel had slipped away in the night without losing a man. Only elaborate mining and booby-traps received the British. Montgomery had shouldered down an open door. In his *Memoirs* he said of Agheila: 'Everything went well.'

While 7th Armoured Division and 51st Division pushed cautiously along the coast road (the main blow had been, as usual, frontal), the New Zealand Division felt for Rommel's desert flank. General Leese said later:

> We did not have enough tanks for a flanking movement in addition to those we had to maintain on the battlefront as a firm base.

According to official returns, 7th Armoured Division and 4th Light Armoured Brigade had 163 tanks fit for action, plus a squadron in reserve.

Now Montgomery was blessed by double luck. The 54 tanks of the Afrika Korps had reached Mugta on the coast road when the pursuing tanks of the 7th Armoured Division caught up with them. Harding (7th Armoured Division) put in an immediate attack with sixty of the heavy Shermans. But the German armour had no fuel for manoeuvre; only enough for a direct march. At the same time, the New Zealanders (with a brigade of tanks under command) reached the coast at Merduma, on the German line of retreat. Because of the German want of fuel, therefore, Montgomery had at last trapped the Afrika Korps, and could fight a battle against his immobile opponents with about 200 tanks to 54. By a further stroke of luck, Rommel was not in command that day; General Fehn was new from Russia and had no experience of the desert. Total victory seemed imminent. Cairo Radio, who must have got it from the Eighth Army, and the BBC proclaimed that Rommel was in a bottle that Monty was about to cork. But the Afrika Korps was too potent a brew for a teetotaller to hold; next morning, December 16th, both panzer divisions, fighting in battle groups, smashed through the New Zealanders and disappeared. British light forces kept a distant contact while Eighth Army halted to reorganize.

For Rommel this was a time of bitterness; he chafed under the frustration of facing an opponent for whom he had scant respect, but whom he was unable to fight because Berlin and Rome refused all reinforcements and supplies. Now he was foolishly ordered to make a last stand at Buerat, which though a naturally strong position, was not properly fortified, was easily turned, and was far too long a front to be held by a small force such as his.

On December 21st Montgomery began to advance again. It was not easy: as General Leese said:

> Clearing the two to three hundred miles of the road between Agheila and Syrte of mines cost heavy casualties among the engineers and had a strong moral effect.

Fifteenth Panzer Division and 90th Light fell back slowly from Syrte, fighting for four days a skilled, dangerous and cunning rearguard action. On December 29th, all was quiet again; the Panzer Army deployed at Buerat; and Montgomery began to organize his long and tenuous communications so that they might support another set-piece attack. Montgomery wanted the port of Tripoli urgently, before the Germans could wreck it as they had Benghazi. He wished to attack before the Germans could anticipate him by withdrawal; and because of the need for speed he only gave himself three weeks to get ready. In his own words, 'I decided to plan for the Buerat battle on the basis of ten days' fighting using four divisions.' Rommel had only 38 tanks, twenty per cent of his establishment in anti-tank guns, 10,000 Germans and 30,000 Italians without transport!

Throughout the advance from Egypt Montgomery had been moving all the time a second corps one stage behind the forward troops to 'preserve balance'. It was 10th Corps, the *corps de chasse*.

By January 15th, Montgomery was ready to attack Buerat. On the 12th, he issued another of those personal messages to the troops: 'ON TO TRIPOLI!' These messages seem closely modelled on Napoleon's orders of the day to the Army of Italy, as in fact Montgomery's *Memoirs* closely resemble in style the memoirs of the Emperor: unconscious revelation of high personal valuation.

Rommel had managed to persuade Mussolini to let him send back from Buerat those troops without transport; and once again his small force of Germans prepared to match skill against numbers.

After elaborate air and artillery bombardment, 51st Infantry Division, under Montgomery's personal command, attacked astride the coast road, while 7th Armoured Division and the 2nd New Zealand Division, under Leese, cut round Rommel's desert flank to deliver the main blow. Another armoured brigade was in reserve. For once, the need for speed determined Montgomery's plans and leadership; yet even now he was held back by his own character. His final orders for the troops making the decisive swing round the German flank 'provided for a

Map 25. Buerat to Tripoli
January 15th–23rd, 1943

due measure of caution to be exercised . . . as I wished to avoid heavy casualties to our tanks'.

Of the issue of a battle between 450 tanks and 50 there is no doubt. Fifteenth Panzer Division, on the German right wing, fell slowly back on Tarhuna before Leese's attack, destroying 52 British tanks; and the rest of Rommel's command fell back in step. Montgomery's advance, which started later, made good progress; 90th Light had already withdrawn.

Now occurred an astonishing thing. This imposing offensive, whose essence was speed; which required, in Montgomery's words, 'tremendous drive and energy'; which was Montgomery's one and only attempt at war in Rommel's style, moved so slowly that it lost all contact with the enemy, who was retiring in no haste. It began to seem even possible that Tripoli would not fall in time to serve as a new base port; that Eighth Army might have to retreat to secure its supplies. Doubt, nagging uncertainty, now blew coldly into the cosy world of balance and master plans; and with nearly 500 tanks under command against 50, Montgomery began seriously to wonder if he would succeed. He blamed the slowness on his men, and dispensed to at least one subordinate what he called an 'imperial rocket'.

His march failed in its original object. He never 'crashed' (his word) through the steady, controlled retreat of the *Panzer-armee*, which held him at its own pace, and which gave up Tripoli only when the port had been completely wrecked. On January 23rd, 1943, Eighth Army entered the town and paused to regroup. The prize which might so easily have been O'Connor's; the prize to capture which Wavell and Auchinleck had built a great base out of the empty sand and rock of Egypt; the prize for which the troops of Cunningham and Ritchie had fought so gamely, was now Montgomery's. For the soldiers, however, Tripoli did not signify laurel wreaths, but cafés, boulevards, trees and gardens. To them, beer spoke louder than posterity.

The capture of Tripoli was, of course, the occasion of another personal message to the troops:

> Today, January 23rd, exactly three months after we began the battle of Egypt, the Eighth Army has captured Tripoli . . . By skilful withdrawal tactics the enemy has eluded us . . . The defeat of the enemy in the Battle of Alamein, the pursuit of his beaten army and the final capture of Tripoli, a distance of some fourteen hundred miles from Alamein, has all been accomplished in three months. This achievement is probably without parallel in history . . .

Four days after the capture of Tripoli, in pouring rain, was fought the last action of the desert war. At Zuara, a force of 7th Armoured Division met rearguards of 90th Light; there was a four-day struggle for the place, and then 90th Light, who had fought with as much élan in their last engagement in defence of infamy as in their first, fell back along the dismal road of retreat. On February 4th Churchill and General Brooke visited Tripoli, and Montgomery arranged a spectacular victory parade. On February 12th, second anniversary of Rommel's arrival in Africa, the last rearguards of the *Panzerarmee Afrika* retreated across the Tunisian frontier.

The desert war was over.

NOTES ON THE SOURCES

PART I

CHAPTER ONE

With the exception of that on p 34, all quotations from General O'Connor are from personal communications to the author. General O'Connor's comment on p 34 on his seniors' conception of the scope of the attack is from *Against Great Odds*, by Brigadier C. N. Barclay, p 19.

All Brigadier Caunter's comments and recollections are communications to the author, as are those from Major-General E. Dorman O'Gowan (Dorman-Smith) and General Sir Alexander Galloway. The extract on p 36 from the letter of November 28th, 1940 from Wavell to Wilson is taken from *The Mediterranean and The Middle East*, by I. S. O. Playfair, Vol I, p 265.

The account of the trial attack and evolution of the final tactical plan for attacking the Italian camps (pp 34 and 35) is based on information supplied by Major-General Dorman O'Gowan (Dorman-Smith) and Major-General A. H. Gatehouse.

CHAPTER TWO

All quotations from General O'Connor are from personal communications to the author, as are those from Brigadier Caunter. The figures of the result of the Battle of Sidi Barrani are taken from *The Mediterranean and The Middle East*, by Playfair. The quotation on p 42 from a telegram from Churchill to Wavell is taken from Churchill's *Second World War*, Vol II, p 483, as is the interchange of messages between Mussolini and Bergonzoli on p 43. The figures of the result of the capture of Tobruk are from Playfair, *op cit*, as are those of remaining Italian strength in Libya. The messages from Churchill to Wavell and to the Chiefs of Staff on p 48 are taken from Playfair, Vol I, pp 227 and 338; that on p 49 to Wavell from Playfair, Vol I, p 339. The figures of results of the capture of Tobruk are also from Playfair. The account of the tent incident at Sandhurst on p 52 was given to the author by General Sir Alfred Godwin-Austen.

All quotations from General O'Connor are communications to the author, except for that on p 66 about the possibilities of success of an advance on Tripoli, which is taken from Barclay, *op cit*, p 74. All quotations from General Sir Michael Creagh, Brigadier Caunter, General O'Gowan (Dorman-Smith) and General J. M. L. Renton are from personal communications to the author. The account of the sending of the victory message to Wavell on p 60, and of O'Connor's manner after victory, was given to the author by General O'Gowan. General O'Gowan also gave the author the account of O'Connor's visit to the captured Italian officers, and of his own visit to Wavell's headquarters (p 62). The quotation from Churchill's message of congratulation to Wavell over Beda Fomm is from Churchill, Vol III, p 58. The quotation on p 63 from General Kennedy's minute of December 13th, 1940, on Salonika is taken from *The Business of War*, p 69. Churchill's remark about firing squads is taken from the same source, p 75. The quotation from a general staff minute of February 16th, 1941 on p 64 is also from *The Business of War* (pp 83 and 85). Field-Marshal Lord Alanbrooke's judgment on Greek intervention on p 64 is from *The Turn of the Tide*, p 248. Churchill's apologia for the Greek intervention is from Churchill, *op cit*, Vol III, p 27. Wavell's telegram of February 10th, 1941 to London on p 66 is quoted from *The Business of War*, p 75. Rommel's opinion of O'Connor's chances in an advance on Tripoli (pp 66–7) is taken from *The Rommel Papers*, p 94.

PART II

All quotations from Field-Marshal Sir Claude Auchinleck, General Sir Frank Messervy, General Sir Michael Creagh and Major-General O'Gowan (Dorman-Smith) are from communications to the author. The quotation from Churchill about destroying Rommel's army (p 72) is from Churchill, *op cit*, Vol III, p 197. The quotation from his signal of May 12th, 1941 to Wavell about using the 300 new tanks and the need for victory in the Desert is from Churchill, *op cit*, p 264. Wavell's signal of the same day is from the same source, Vol III, p 277. Mrs Churchill's reference to the Premier's state of mind on p 73 is also from Churchill, *op cit*, p 276. The account of the state of

7th Armoured Division before *Battleaxe* was given in a communication from General Creagh to the author. The account on p 75 of General Beresford-Peirse's confusion of 'forward rally' with 'rally forward' was given to the author by General A. H. Gatehouse. Churchill's comments on p 77 on Wavell's responsibilities are taken from Churchill, *op cit*, Vol III, p 217. The exchange of signals on p 79 between Churchill and Auchinleck about an early offensive is taken from Churchill, *op cit*, Vol III, p 324. Churchill's comment on p 79 on Auchinleck's visit to London is from Churchill, *op cit*, p 326. Auchinleck's reaction to this visit was given to the author by the Field-Marshal.

PART III

CHAPTER ONE

With the exception of that on p 91 at the press conference before *Crusader*, which is taken from *They Sought Out Rommel*, p 4, all quotations from General Sir Alan Cunningham are personal communications to the author. Auchinleck's reasons for choosing Cunningham as 8th Army Commander on p 83 are in a communication to the author. Quotations from General Godwin-Austen and General Gatehouse are, unless otherwise noted, communications to the author. The contemporary public relations booklet quoted on p 87 is *They Sought Out Rommel*. For the summary of British armour organization for *Crusader*, the author is indebted to Playfair, *op cit*, *The Sidi Rezegh Battles*, by Agar-Hamilton and Turner, *The Tanks*, by Captain B. H. Liddell Hart, and conversations with General Cunningham, General Gatehouse and General Galloway. The quotation from Cunningham on p 90 on British action depending on German reaction is from Agar-Hamilton, *op cit*, p 69. Churchill's comment about generals' comforts is from Churchill, *op cit*, Vol IV, p 321; his signal to Auchinleck about the inactivity of Middle East armies on p 92 is from the same volume, p 425. Auchinleck's reference to the unreadiness of the South African Division on p 92 is from his *Despatch*, p 311; the quotation about the tight margins in supply is from a communication to the author. The reference to the chances of success is likewise a communication to the author. Churchill's message to the army quoted on p 94 is from Churchill, *op cit*, Vol IV. p 434. The account of Cunningham's state of mind before *Crusader* is derived from eye-witness impressions given to the author by General Godwin-Austen, General Sir Arthur Smith and others. See also Kennedy, *The Business of War*, p 181.

CHAPTER TWO

Unless otherwise noted, all quotations from Field-Marshal Auchinleck, General Cunningham, General Godwin-Austen, General Creagh and General Gatehouse are from communications to the author. Sources for Cunningham's state of health are similar to those for the close of Chapter One, although in personal communications to the author General Cunningham has denied that he was at all unwell. In the author's opinion, the balance of evidence lies the other way. The figures for the losses incurred by 22nd Armoured Brigade in their attack on Bir Gubi (p 97) is taken from the Account of the Operations of 7th Armoured Division, November 18th–27th December, 1941, Secret, January 31st, 1942. All orders, movements and casualty figures for the British armour are based on this document. The general account of the *Crusader* battle is based on Agar-Hamilton, *op cit*; Playfair, Vol. II; Auchinleck's *Despatch*; Liddell Hart, *op cit*; the Account of the Operations of 7th Armoured Division; *Panzer Battles*, by F. W. von Mellenthin; *The Rommel Papers*, *Rommel et l'Afrika-korps* by H. G. von Esebeck. Cruewell's orders on p 98 are from von Mellenthin, *op cit*, p 62. Cunningham's orders to his corps on p 102 are quoted from Agar-Hamilton, *op cit*, p 201. The references to the resistance of British artillery at Sidi Rezegh on p 102 are from the *R.A. Commemoration Book*, p 189. The meteorological description on p 104 is from *Those Against Rommel* by Alexander Clifford, p 142. The quotation from General Gott on p 110 about a tank commander's role is taken from *The Seventh and Three Enemies*, by G. M. O. Davy, p 144. The German comment on p 111 on British and German panzer organization is from von Mellenthin, pp 52–3; the British comment on p 111 from the Account of the operations of 7th Armoured Division, p 102 (issued under the name of the divisional commander, General Gott). The extract from a letter from Godwin-Austen to Freyberg on p 114 is taken from Agar-Hamilton, p 286. The quotation on p 115 from Auchinleck about Cunningham's reaction to the setback in *Crusader* is from a communication to the author, as is Auchinleck's own reaction (p 115). The German opinion of Auchinleck's decision to continue the offensive is from von Mellenthin, p 75; Churchill's from Churchill, Vol IV, p 445. Bayerlein's description of the

battlefield on p 116 is from *The Rommel Papers*, p 162. The
quotation from General Norrie on p 117 is from a letter written
to the South African War Histories, quoted in Agar-Hamilton,
p 291, footnote. The extract from Auchinleck's directive on p
118 is also from Agar-Hamilton, p 308; and the quotation on
p 118 of Auchinleck's account of Cunningham's reaction to
Rommel's counter-stroke is from his *Despatch*, p 339. The extract about the conversation in Air Marshal Coningham's
caravan is from Eve Curie's *Journey Among Warriors*, p 52.
Major Stirling's description of Cunningham on p 120 is taken
from Virginia Cowles' *The Phantom Major*. Sir Arthur Smith's
impressions of Cunningham at the time of his relief are quoted
from a communication to the author.

PART IV

CHAPTER ONE

Unless otherwise noted, all quotations from Field-Marshal
Auchinleck, General Godwin-Austen, General Messervy,
General Galloway and General Smith are from communications to the author. The quotation from a public relations officer
on p 126 is from *They Sought Out Rommel*, p 33. The reference
on p 127 to the inevitability of German retreat is from von
Mellenthin, p 81. Churchill's tribute on p 127 to Auchinleck's
will-power is taken from his *War Speeches*, Vol II, p 136. The
German description on p 128 of the state of the battle is
from von Mellenthin, p 80. The description of British rout on
p 135 is from Pitt-Rivers, *Royal Dragoons History*, p 34; and the
German description from von Mellenthin, p 87. Auchinleck's
approval of Ritchie's change of plan (pp 136–7 is quoted from
his *Despatch*, p 317. Auchinleck's reference to Godwin-Austen's
request for relief is from his *Despatch*, p 317. The account of
General Dorman-Smith's visit to Eighth Army's headquarters
at Auchinleck's request, and the subsequent picnic at Fayoum,
were given to the author by General Dorman O'Gowan (Dorman-
Smith).

CHAPTER TWO

Unless otherwise noted, quotations from Field-Marshal Auchinleck, General Messervy, General Renton, General Ramsden and
General Dorman-Smith (O'Gowan) are from communications
to the author. General Gott's reference to future organization of

armour on p 139 is taken from the Account of the Operations of 7th Armoured Division, p 106. Auchinleck's reference on p 140 to the rigidity of pre-war British organization is taken from his *Despatch*, p 368. Auchinleck's notification to London (p 141) that Tobruk would not again be held in isolation is from his *Despatch*, p 318. De Guingand's reference to the strain on Auchinleck of Churchill's requests is from his book *Operation Victory*, p 108. The extract from Auchinleck to Ritchie on p 145 on the necessity of using divisions as divisions is from a letter of May 20th, 1942, quoted in his *Despatch*, p 391. The German reference to what actually happened is from von Mellenthin, p 94. Figures of British and Axis strengths on p 148 and relative effectiveness of equipment is taken from Liddell Hart, *op cit* and Playfair, Vol III. The account of the relaying back by armoured cars of information of Rommel's advance, and the inertia of Eighth Army formations in passing it on, was given to the author by General Renton (then commanding 7th Motor Brigade). The account of Rommel's appearance before Retma on p 150 was given to the author by Colonel R. N. Bruce. What Renton found at Bir Gubi (p 150) is as recounted to the author by the general himself. The belief of Lumsden quoted on p 155 was a communication to the author from General Messervy. The extract from Ritchie's letter to Auchinleck on p 155 is quoted from Agar-Hamilton and Turner, *Crisis in the Desert*, p 39; that concerning the attack in the Cauldron (p 155) is from a letter of June 3rd, 1942, given in Auchinleck's *Despatch*, p 392. The Eighth Army signal to Auchinleck on the results of the first day of *Aberdeen* (p 156) is quoted in *Crisis in the Desert*, p 46; and Ritchie's comments on the action in a signal to Auchinleck (p 156) from the same work, p 48. Gott's comments are from p 51.

CHAPTER THREE

Quotations from General Messervy and General Ramsden are communications to the author. Auchinleck's estimate of the atmosphere at HQ, Eighth Army (p 161), is quoted in *Crisis in the Desert*, p 68. The extract from Churchill's signal to Auchinleck about holding Tobruk (p 163) is from Churchill, *op cit*, Vol IV, p 303. Auchinleck's letter to Ritchie instructing him to hold the line Acroma-El Adem and defend Tobruk (p 164) is given in *Crisis in the Desert*, p 78. Ritchie's signal of June 14th, 1942 (p 164) is given in same work, same page. Ritchie's summary of his policy in regard to Tobruk (p 165) is also given in *Crisis*, p 79. Account of conference of June 14th, 1942 given to the author by General Dorman O'Gowan. Account of meeting between Ritchie and Corbett given to author by General Corbett. Churchill's signal giving War Cabinet's expectation that Tobruk would be held for certain is taken from Churchill, *op cit*, Vol IV, p 305. Auchinleck's reply of June 16th is given in same work, same page. Churchill's claim that Auchinleck should have fortified Tobruk is quoted from Churchill, *op cit*, Vol IV, p 306. His claim that London had no inkling that evacuation was contemplated is quoted from the same work, p 340. Auchinleck's Operation Instruction No 110 is given in his *Despatch*, p 378. The comment from Kennedy and the fact that the Instruction was passed to Alanbrooke is from Kennedy, *op cit*, p 243. The account of Auchinleck's visit to HQ Eighth Army at Sollum (p 168) was given to the author by General O'Gowan, who accompanied the C-in-C. The pithy 'garden roller' comment on Tobruk's anti-tank defences (p 169) is from Sir Compton Mackenzie's *Eastern Epic*, Vol I, p 563. The extract from Auchinleck's signal to Ritchie about the need for urgency and all exchanges of signals between General Klopper (Tobruk fortress commander) and Ritchie are from *Crisis in the Desert*. Account of Auchinleck's visit to Ritchie on June 22nd, (p 174) given to author by O'Gowan, an eye-witness. Description of Matruh defences on pp 175–6 is quoted from Kippenberger, *Infantry Brigadier*, p 126.

PART V

CHAPTER ONE

All quotations from Field-Marshal Sir Claude Auchinleck are, unless otherwise noted, personal communications to the author, as are those from General Galloway, General Corbett and General O'Gowan (Dorman-Smith). The letter from Auchinleck to Brooke on pp 182–3 is quoted in *Auchinleck*, by John Connell, pp 608–9. The letter from Auchinleck to Churchill is quoted from Churchill *op cit*, Vol IV, p 320. The account of the flight from Cairo to Matruh was given to the author by O'Gowan and confirmed by Auchinleck. The account of the interview between Auchinleck and Ritchie was given to the author by Field-Marshal Auchinleck. Auchinleck's instructions before the Battle of Mersa Matruh (p 189) are quoted from Eighth Army Operation Instruction, June 25th, 1942. The description of the C-in-C's journey back from Matruh on p 193 was given to the author by Field-Marshal Auchinleck. Freyberg's 'Balaclava' (p 194) is quoted from *Crisis in the Desert*, p 258. The reference to the Royal Navy's precipitate evacuation on p 197 is based on Lampton Burns, *Down Ramps*, p 57.

CHAPTER TWO

All quotations from Field-Marshal Auchinleck, General Dorman-Smith (O'Gowan), and General Ramsden are communications to the author unless otherwise noted. Impressions of corps commanders' conference on pp 207–8 were given to the author by O'Gowan. Impression of Gott at the time p 210 given to the author by Field-Marshal Auchinleck. Rommel's estimate of Auchinleck's generalship on p 210 is from *The Rommel Papers*, p 248, as are Rommel's exhortations to his troops on p 211. Auchinleck's signal to his men on July 3rd, 1942 (p 212) is quoted from *The Battle for Egypt*, J. I. Scoullar, p 175. Brooke's account of Churchill's impatience on p 212 is taken from *The Turn of the Tide*, p 419. The story about the 'ladies' of Alexandria was recounted to the author by O'Gowan. The quotations of the opinions of a NZ brigadier on the feasibility of Eighth Army plans (p 216) are from Kippenberger, *op cit*, pp 149–50. The quotation from Rommel on p 218 is from *The Rommel Papers*, p 252, and those on p 219 from p 254. The quotation from Rommel about the possibility of his front breaking on p 221 is from his *Papers*, p 257, as is the extract about Auchinleck's blows on the Italians.

CHAPTER THREE

The fact that the army's morale was by no means depressed by nearness to its base was noted by General Renton, who mentioned it to the author. All quotations from Field-Marshal Auchinleck, General Ramsden and General Dorman-Smith (O'Gowan) are communications to the author unless otherwise noted. The 'unpleasant' telegram (p 223) is mentioned in *The Turn of the Tide*, p 420. The extract from Churchill's telegram on July 12th, 1942 (p 223) is quoted in Mackenzie, *op cit*, p 584–5. The quotation on p 224 about Auchinleck's plans for July 21st is from the *Despatch*, p 366. The extract from Gott's orders on p 224 are taken from *The Battle for Egypt*, p 327. Impressions of Auchinleck's appearance at this time (p 225) are based on eyewitness impressions and contemporary photographs. Quotations from Rommel on p 227 are from *The Rommel Papers*. Description of Churchill's impatience on p 227 is taken from *The Turn of the Tide*, p 433. The account of the Morshead crisis (pp 227–8) is derived from communications to the author by Generals Ramsden and O'Gowan, and additions and amendments by Field-Marshal Auchinleck. Access to Auchinleck's letter of 1943 to General Ramsden given to the author by General Ramsden. Churchill's impatience of July 30th (p 230) is described by Brooke on p 433 of *The Turn of the Tide*. The extract from Auchinleck describing his shortage of men is from his *Despatch*, p 367. Rommel's opinion of Auchinleck's success at First Alamein is from *The Rommel Papers*. Bayerlein's is quoted from an interview of January 2nd, 1960. Horrocks' opinion of Auchinleck's First Battle of Alamein is on p 111 of *A Full Life*. See pp 108–12 of Horrocks for a full tribute. The description of Auchinleck's corps commanders' conference of July 30th is based on communications to the author by Generals Ramsden and O'Gowan. The quotation from Auchinleck about the need for mobility and maximum use of artillery (pp 234) is from the *Despatch*, p 367. Description of Auchinleck's leisure activities after July 30th was given to the author by the Field-Marshal.

CHAPTER FOUR

The quotation from Churchill about the year's defeats is from Churchill, *op cit*, Vol IV, p 322. That on p 236 about his political weakness in July from the same work, p 356, and the question on p 237 is from p 374 of that work. Dorman-Smith's advice to Auchinleck and his rejection of it is based on a communication from O'Gowan (Dorman-Smith). The account of the events leading up to the 'Cairo Purge' are based on Churchill, *op cit*, Vol IV, *The Turn of the Tide*, *Operation Victory*, and material supplied to the author by Field-Marshal Auchinleck and Generals Corbett and O'Gowan. The interpretive use of this material is the author's. Access to the letter quoted on p 237 was given to the author by General Corbett. The reference to Churchill's offer of the Middle East Command to Brooke on August 4th (p 238) is based on Churchill, *op cit*, Vol IV, pp 375–6. But Brooke, in *The Turn of the Tide*, pp 439–44, says Churchill offered him Eighth Army on August 4th and the Middle East Command on August 6th, 1942. Description of Churchill's arrival in desert based on photographs and O'Gowan. Churchill's appreciation of RAF hospitality on p 238 is taken from Churchill, *op cit*, p 377. The contemporary account of Churchill's reception by men of Eighth Army on p 238 is from Denis Johnston's *Nine Rivers to Jordan*. The quotation about pudgy fingers is from O'Gowan. The Prime Minister's letter to the

Deputy Prime Minister on pp 239–40 is quoted from Churchill *op cit*, Vol IV, p 328. The further quotation from a letter of August 21st, 1942 (p 240) is from Churchill, *op cit*, Vol IV, p 421. Jacob's account of Auchinleck's reception of the letter of dismissal is quoted from *The Turn of the Tide*, p 451.

The letter itself is given in Churchill, *op cit*, Vol IV, pp 382–3. Auchinleck's manner at dinner that night and subsequent remark to de Guingand are from *Operation Victory*, p 134. The quotation from Churchill on p 244 about want of plan in Eighth Army is from a letter to the Deputy Prime Minister written on August 21st, 1942, after an overnight stay with Montgomery at Eighth Army, and given in Churchill, *op cit*, Vol IV, p 421. Alexander's description of Auchinleck's plans on p 245 is taken from his *Despatch*, p 841. Auchinleck's last order of the day to his men is quoted from his *Despatch*, pp 367–8. Access to General Corbett's letter to the Deputy C-in-C in India, quoted on p 246, was given to the author by General Corbett. The description of Auchinleck and Dorman-Smith's dinner together is based on an account to the author by O'Gowan (Dorman-Smith). The contemporary opinion of the higher war leadership on p 246 is taken from Denis Johnston, *op cit*, p 43. The enemy opinion is Bayerlein's, from an interview of January 2nd, 1960. Churchill's belated recognition of Auchinleck's burden (p 247) is taken from Churchill, *op cit*, Vol IV, p 379; Churchill's solicitude for Alexander's peace of mind (p 247) is taken from the same source, same page. Churchill's directive to Alexander on p 247 is taken from Churchill, *op cit*, Vol IV, p 385.

PART VI

CHAPTER ONE

The quotation from Kesselring is from his *Memoirs*, p 111, and from Mussolini from *Mussolini's Memoirs*, p 219. Rommel's opinion of the effects of the Anglo-American invasion of French North Africa is from *The Rommel Papers*, p 345.

Quotations from Generals Messervy, Godwin-Austen, Galloway, Leese and Ramsden are communictions to the author, unless otherwise noted. Montgomery's mature reflections on setting light to fellow cadets are to be found on p 24 of his *Memoirs*. The account of Montgomery's little play on p 252 is quoted from *Montgomery* by Alan Moorehead. The account of Montgomery's encounter with Abdul Karim was given to the

author by General Godwin-Austen; Montgomery's action over
the 'civil officer' was given to the author by General Ramsden,
who also described Montgomery's departure from his brigade in
Palestine. The description of Montgomery's last conference in
Belgium in 1940 on p 256 was given to the author also by General
Ramsden. The account of planning and mounting the Dieppe
raid is based on Stacey, *The Canadian Army* (Official History
Summary), and the quotation on p 257 is taken from this work,
p 56. The quotation from Montgomery on training in England
in 1940–42 (p 258) is from his *Memoirs*, pp 70 and 72. Description of Montgomery's taking over from Ramsden was given to
the author by General Ramsden.

The quotation from the Official History on the state of the
army's morale on Montgomery's appointment is to be found in
Playfair, Vol III, p 376. The History also denies that the army
was in any way 'dispirited'. The quotation from Montgomery
on p 259 about his insubordination in seizing command of
Eighth Army is from the *Memoirs*, p 103, and of his instant
retreat from the scene from p 100. The fact that Auchinleck
never received this signal was confirmed to the author by Field-
Marshal Auchinleck. The account of Montgomery's first conference, with air cover, was given to the author by Brigadier
E. T. Williams. The account of Montgomery's visit to Eighth
Army units and collecting hats and badges was given to the
author by General Ramsden, who was present. The relevant
part of the *Memoirs* is p 111. The effects of Montgomery's
personality on General Horrocks were recounted to the author
by General Ramsden. The quotations illustrating the similarity
between Auchinleck's plans and Montgomery's plans are as
follows: First Montgomery quotation is from the *Memoirs*, p 108.
Quotation from Alexander's *Despatch* is from p 841. Next quotation of Montgomery's is from the *Memoirs*, p 108. The quotation from Dorman-Smith's Appreciation is from p 398 of
Auchinleck's *Despatch*. Brooke's comment on p 261 on Montgomery's lecture is from *The Turn of the Tide*, p 478; Churchill's
from Churchill, *op cit*, Vol IV, p 418. Figures of relative strengths
for the Battle of Alam Halfa are taken from Liddell Hart, *The
Tanks*. Rommel's state of health is taken from the *Rommel
Papers*, p 270, and footnote, p 271. The quotation about his
inability to leave his truck is from Desmond Young, *Rommel*,
p 169. The quotation on p 263 from Montgomery about the
preparation of defences in the Delta is from the script of his
television performance on December 12th, 1958. Churchill's

reference to similar measures set on foot by himself and others is from Churchill, *op cit*, Vol IV, p 468, and the reference to Wilson's taking command in the Delta from p 424. The account of Gott's plans was given to the author by General Renton (7th Armoured Division), Gott's immediate subordinate. General Renton denies there was any idea of 'loosing the armour'. The account of Montgomery's state of mind, and comments before Alam Halfa, were given to the author by General Renton. The disorganization of command in the *Panzerarmee* (p 265) is detailed in von Esebeck, *op cit*. Montgomery's reference to the quality of his men in the matter of a pursuit after Alam Halfa (p 267) is from his book *El Alamein to the Sangro*, p 8. The quotation on p 267 on the failure of the New Zealand attack is from the same work, p 9. General Horrocks gave the explanation referred to on p 268 in *The Sunday Times* of October 20th, 1957. Montgomery's second explanation is in *El Alamein to the Sangro*, p 9. Montgomery's estimate of the value to him of Alam Halfa on p 268 is from a television performance, December 12th, 1958.

CHAPTER TWO

Montgomery's admission of vanity is taken from the script of a television performance, December 12th, 1958. The incident with Wendell Wilkie was recounted to the author by General A. H. Gatehouse. The account of General Ramsden's dismissal was given to the author by General Ramsden. The quotation from Montgomery on p 270 about the formation of a *corps de chasse* is from the television performance on December 12th, 1958; that about the placing of the main assault at Second Alamein from the script of the same performance. The relevant quotation from Auchinleck's *Despatch* is to be found on p 367. General Renton, General Gatehouse and others communicated to the author Montgomery's insistence on his line of pursuit. The quotation was made in the presence of Renton. The quotation from Churchill on p 273 on the date of *Lightfoot* is from Churchill, *op cit*, Vol IV, p 474; Alexander's view is quoted from the same source, same page. Figures for Axis and British strengths at Second Alamein are from Liddell Hart, *op cit*, Vol II, and official records. The quotation of Montgomery's about Rommel's defences on p 276 is from the performance of December 12th, 1958, and on the task of attack from the *Memoirs*, p 116. Horrocks' comment is from *The Sunday Times*, October 27th, 1957. Churchill's is from Churchill, *op cit*, Vol IV, p 487. The figures for the British front in Flanders in 1940 is from the

Official History of the Campaign in Flanders, p 38. The quotation on p 277 of Montgomery on Alexander is from the *Memoirs*, p 118. All quotations from General Sir Oliver Leese and General A. H. Gatehouse are communications to the author, unless otherwise noted. The extract from Montgomery's personal message to his troops on p 278 is taken from the *Memoirs*, p 127. The reason for the absence of Axis counter-fire is given in von Esebeck, p 137. Account of the Second Battle of Alamein is based on Alexander's dispatch [particularly interesting], on Montgomery's version in *El Alamein to the Sangro*, his versions in the *Memoirs* and on the television, on versions by Liddell Hart, *op cit*, by General Horrocks in *The Sunday Times*, de Guingand in *Operation Victory*, Rommel in *The Rommel Papers*, account by von Esebeck, *op cit*, on divisional and regimental histories and on unpublished material, some of it from a confidential source. Description of the difficulties of 10th Corps and its bottlenecks on p 280 given to the author by General Gatehouse. Description of conference in Montgomery's caravan on pp 281–2 based on de Guingand, *op cit*, amplified by General Leese. Montgomery's version of his conversation with Gatehouse and Lumsden is quoted from the *Memoirs*, p 130. Gatehouse's version is a personal communication to the author. The eyewitness account of the opening of Gatehouse's call to Montgomery is from a letter by T. Cadogan in the *Daily Express* of November 6th, 1958. Montgomery's account of the results of the attack over the Miteiriya Ridge is quoted from the television performance of December 12th, 1958. The quotation about not moving 7th Armoured Division on p 285 is from *El Alamein to the Sangro*, pp 18–19, and the next quotation is from the *Memoirs*, p 88. The phrase 'surgical callousness' is used by Moorehead, *op cit*, on p 137. The complimentary reference (p 285) to his deception measures is from the script of his television performance on December 12th, 1958. The next quotation, about Stumme's preventive withdrawal, is from *El Alamein to the Sangro*, p 20. The letter from Brooke is given on p 515 in *The Turn of the Tide*. The quotation about postponement of *Supercharge* on p 287 is from p 136 of the *Memoirs*. Montgomery's references to 'jock' columns is also from the *Memoirs*, p 101. 'Wild enthusiasm' (p 288) is to be found on p 88 of the *Memoirs*, and the reference to the success of *Supercharge* from the same source, p 135. Rommel's comment on Montgomery's caution (p 289) is from *The Rommel Papers*. Figures of Axis losses for Second Alamein are taken from von Esebeck, *op cit*, p 162.

The description of Montgomery's post-battle press conference is based on Moorehead, *op cit*, p 128. It may be compared with impressions of Wellington at a similar hour. The quotation about brigade groups and bits and pieces is from the *Memoirs*, p 101. The letter to Brooke quoted on p 293 is to be found on p 518 of *The Turn of the Tide*. The relevant quotation in Churchill, *op cit*, is in Vol IV, p 484. The account of the pursuit from Alamein is based on British and German sources already mentioned, and on unpublished material supplied by General Gatehouse and others. The author has also discussed this episode with General Leese, General de Guingand, Brigadier E. T. Williams and others. All quotations from General Leese are communications to the author, unless otherwise noted. The quotation from Rommel on p 294 is from Bayerlein in an interview of January 2nd, 1960. Figures of Axis strength during the retirement on Tunisia are taken from von Esebeck, *op cit*. Montgomery's reference to bluff and manoeuvre on p 296 is taken from the *Memoirs*, p 146. The television performance is that of December 19th, 1958. The other quotations on El Agheila are from *El Alamein to the Sangro*, p 30 and p 29. Montgomery's visit to evening service (p 297) is to be found on p 147 of the *Memoirs*. The German reference to Montgomery showing signs of life (p 298) is from von Esebeck, p 169. Montgomery's summary of the attack on El Agheila on p 299 is from p 147 of the *Memoirs*. The quotation about plans and quantities for attacking Buerat on p 300 is from *El Alamein to the Sangro*, p 32. The same work, p 35, supplies the quotation about not risking the tanks (p 299). The figure for British tanks at Buerat is from *El Alamein to the Sangro*, p 34; for German from von Esebeck, *op cit*, p 176. The 'tremendous drive' comes from *El Alamein to the Sangro*, p 35. The personal message to the troops on the capture of Tripoli is to be found in full in *7th Bn., Argyll and Sutherland Highlanders*, by Ian C. Cameron, pp 70–71.

APPENDIX 'A'

Note by William Collins, publishers of Lord Montgomery's *Memoirs*, to appear in the front of future editions of the book with the full agreement of the author:

Since the publication of this book, the author, in a broadcast in the BBC Home Service, stated that he was grateful to General (now Field-Marshal) Sir Claude Auchinleck and the Eighth Army under his command for stabilizing the British front on the Alamein position, thereby enabling the author to conduct his successful offensive, known to the world as the Battle of Alamein, in October 1942.

The publishers think that readers of this book, who neither heard the broadcast nor read the accounts of it in the Press, might reasonably assume that, immediately before the author took over command of the Eighth Army, General Auchinleck was preparing to withdraw into the Nile Delta, or even beyond, in the event of a determined attack by the enemy.

They wish it to be known that a number of other writers, and notably General Alexander (now Field-Marshal Earl Alexander of Tunis) in a despatch published as a supplement to the *London Gazette* of February 3rd, 1948, make it clear that after General Auchinleck, commanding the Eighth Army, had successfully halted the enemy's attack in July 1942, it was his intention to launch an offensive from the Alamein position when his Army was rested and had been regrouped.

APPENDIX 'B'

APPRECIATION OF THE SITUATION
IN THE
WESTERN DESERT
El Alamein, 1445 hours,
July 27th, 1942.

Object

1. The defence of Egypt by the defeat of the enemy forces in the Western Desert.

Factors

2. *Comparison of Strength.* Table A¹ shows a rough comparison on a brigade group basis, based on what we now know of the enemy's present strength and his reinforcement schedule. From this it seems that the enemy will hardly be able to secure a decisive superiority over us in the first half of August, provided we fight united, since the Germans would begin any offensive with an inferiority of about three infantry brigade groups and possibly forty per cent superiority in armour. The enemy may also be inferior in artillery. It would seem that, though the Axis forces are strong enough for defensive action, they are hardly strong enough to attempt the conquest of the Delta except as a gamble and under very strong air cover. There remains for the Axis to use one German Air Landing Division, but this is taking over IS duties in Greece and Crete and seems unlikely to be an asset. It might, however, be used to redress the balance at a decisive moment. Throughout August the anticipated balance of strength hardly justifies a German offensive, unless we make a serious mistake and leave an opening. He may, however, be reinforced in the second part of August, though nothing is known to be scheduled. On the other hand the Axis may make great efforts to strengthen *Panzerarmee* in the shortest time.

3. *Land Forces—Numbers and Morale.* Broadly speaking, though all our forces have been through hard times, their morale is high. German morale is probably a little lower and Italian morale not more than fifty per cent. In view of the known in-

¹ Not reproduced.

efficiency of the Italian forces, any offensive action taken by the Axis forces in August would have to be eighty per cent German.

4. *Material*. The Eighth Army has some sixty Grant tanks now and will receive another sixty Grant tanks early in August, but there will be no more coming until September. The deduction is that it is necessary to husband our armour carefully in view of the fact that during August the enemy may build up to between 150 and 200 German tanks.

Eighth Army's deficiencies in transport are mounting. A summary of the present state of equipment of the major formations of Eighth Army is attached as Appendix X[1]. It is also necessary to husband our ammunition resources. These stand at present as shown in Appendix B[1] attached. The enemy has, however, similar deficiencies and his reinforcing division is notably deficient in anti-tank weapons and transport.

5. *Training*. None of the formations in Eighth Army is now sufficiently well trained for offensive operations. The Army badly needs either a reinforcement of well-trained formations or a quiet period in which to train.

6. *Fighting value with reference to air forces*. At present we have such air superiority that, while our troops are relatively free from molestation, the enemy is continually attacked by night and day. Our land forces are considerably heartened by this, and a large measure of tactical freedom and security accrues from it. Unless the enemy is strongly reinforced and our air forces are correspondingly reduced, this superiority will assist our offensive or defensive and gravely impede the enemy. Our air superiority is a very considerable, if somewhat indefinable, asset.

7. *Vulnerable Points*. To us the two vulnerable points are Cairo and Alexandria. Occupation of the Cairo area by the enemy would eventually dry up the Sweet Water Canal besides securing an important area for air and land maintenance. Alexandria is useful as a naval base and port of ingress for supplies. The present position of Eighth Army at El Alamein denies direct access to either place by road and flanks any attempt to by-pass. The defences of Alexandria—Cairo—the Delta proper, east of the Nubariya canal and the Wadi Natrun area will be well forward by August 14th and should be complete in so far as defences are ever complete by the end of August. Bottlenecks exposed to air action are the Nile crossings at Cairo and northwards; these are being supplemented by two floating bridges south of Cairo and by improving the routes from these bridges eastwards. All

_____
[1] Not reproduced.

arrangements for demolitions in the Delta are being made. The enemy has few really vulnerable points. There are bottlenecks at Sollum and about Matruh and Baggush, and his long L of C is vulnerable to attack by raids from the air or inland or from the sea. But otherwise the enemy is not physically vulnerable, except to direct assault. Morally his Italians are always vulnerable. The soft-sand areas of the country east of El Alamein, notably the 'Barrel Track' axis, the Wadi Natrun, the sand area to its north, are all added difficulties for the enemy's movement, particularly as they cannot be widely known to him.

8. *Ground*. The armies are now in close contact over a forty-mile front between the sea and the Quattara Depression. Most of the area is open and can be largely controlled by artillery fire. The front divides into three main sectors:

A. From Tel Eisa to exclusive the Ruweisat Ridge. This area is held by two divisions (five infantry brigade groups). The Tel Eisa salient has considerable offensive value, but is not essential to its defence, unless the Miteiriya Ridge is also held by us. Most of the area is difficult for wheeled movement. It is on our side strongly defended by the fortified locality of El Alamein and the mined positions to the south. This area is well supported by strong prepared localities to a depth of twenty-five miles. The enemy lies in open flat country. His positions lack any well-defined features and are covered by extensive minefields. At El Daba he has dumps.

B. From inclusive the El Mreir depression to inclusive the Bab el Qattara Depression. This area is held by two divisions (four brigade groups) supported by the equivalent of one armoured brigade. We hold the high ground in this area at Pt 63 on the Ruweisat Ridge. This position is naturally strong and has been fortified to considerable depth. The enemy holds strongly a series of depressions which give good cover. His front has been well mined and has some wire.

In sectors A and B both the enemy and ourselves have attacked in turn without success.

C. From exclusive the fortified locality in the Bab el Qattara depression to inclusive the complete obstacle of the great Qattara Depression. The enemy is well posted on strong ground at Kelat and Taqa in positions which he has prepared for defence. The object of these positions is to protect his southern flank from being turned by our mobile troops. We have no defences in depth opposite this sector, which is lightly covered by mobile troops.

9. *Time and Space.* Had the enemy the available resources, Italy and Germany are far nearer to El Alamein than is anywhere in the United Nations. The enemy should therefore be able to reinforce quicker than we. On the other hand, apart from distant Benghazi, he has only two serviceable sea ports, Tobruk and, much less useful, Matruh. He may also make use of the railway to a limited extent. He is faced with long road hauls and a sea passage vulnerable to air and submarine attack. This affects the building up of reserves for an offensive. We are nearer our bases. Our limitation is the rate that men and material can reach Egypt from overseas. His limitation is the rate at which it can reach his troops when it arrives. This indicates the necessity of blocking Tobruk and Matruh and attacking his road and rail transport and his shipping.

10. *Political Factors.* Hardly enter into this appreciation, except inasmuch as pressure may be put on the Axis command to press on to Egypt before their army is ready or has sufficient margin of force. Our danger lies in a politically unstable Egypt in our rear. So far this danger has not developed.

11. *The Russian Front.* The operations of Eighth Army are linked to the fate of Russia. Should the Axis penetrate the Caucasus, Eighth Army might be reduced to the lowest margin to provide reinforcements for the new front. Moreover a considerable Axis success in Russia would release air and land forces and equipment for the reinforcement of the Western Desert.

12. *Maintenance.* The enemy is experiencing great difficulty in maintaining his present forces at El Alamein. This condition may improve gradually when more heavy transport vehicles come from Italy. It is not likely to improve so much that he can maintain an appreciably larger force than that envisaged in Appendix A.[1] Our maintenance presents no real difficulties, except that our stocks of 25-pounder shells are not inexhaustible, and we could certainly maintain forces of double the present size of Eighth Army in this area if they existed.

Courses open to ourselves and the enemy.

13. *Ourselves.*

A. To continue to attack the enemy in the hope that he will crack before his army is reinforced by fresh troops. The pros and cons of attacking are:

[1] Not reproduced.

In the northern and central sectors we have made two attempts to break the enemy's front without success. Failure has been due to lack of trained troops, rigidity of organization and limited resources in armour and infantry and it seems that the enemy's positions are now too strongly held to be attacked with success with the resources available.

We have also attacked in the southern sector, but weakly and largely as a diversion. Our attack failed, but the enemy though strongly posted is not numerous here, and this front might go if suddenly attacked. If it did go, it offers access for our mobile troops to the enemy's flanks and rear.

The problems of attack on this front are, firstly, how to find the supporting fire without unduly weakening the northern and central sectors. Secondly, how to find the troops. The only formation which might be used is the weak NZ Division supported by its own artillery, the artillery of 7th Armoured Division and some of 5th Indian Division's artillery. This would have to be deployed in secret and developed as a complete surprise. Failure would probably make the NZ Division unfit for further operations for a considerable time. Having in mind the weakness in numbers and training of this division the chances of success can only be rated as 60–40. Failure would seriously deplete our present resources. On the whole this attack hardly seems advisable at present.

B. To adopt the tactical defensive until we are strong enough to attack, which, unless the enemy's position deteriorates, will not be till mid-September at the earliest. The obvious objection is that we give the initiative to the enemy if he is able to use it. It is very doubtful if he will be able to take the initiative till late in August with any hope of success. In fact if he attacks before, provided we have a reserve in hand including up to one hundred Grant tanks, we have a good chance of defeating him seriously in the area El Alamein–Hammam. Moreover the critical period for the preparation and manning of the Delta and Cairo defences is now over. There is little danger of the enemy getting any value out of by-passing the Eighth Army on its present ground. There may be a critical period late in August before the new divisions (two of armour, two of infantry) are ready, but this might be tided over by preparing their artillery battle groups in advance of the rest of the divisions and so reinforcing Eighth Army. (This project requires further examination.) This defensive could also be mitigated by enterprises against Siwa and the southern section of his front and by seaborne attacks.

14. *Courses open to the enemy.* The enemy must resume the offensive without delay, but he is unlikely to be able to do so before mid-August and even then no real margin of superiority except in AFVs, is apparent. He will certainly try to attack before the end of August and as Eighth Army defences gain in strength and depth he will be more than ever tempted to avoid them and seek success in manoeuvre. This may well land him into serious difficulties in the soft desert.

Alternatively, he may have to adopt the strategical defensive because our forces are too strong and too well placed for attack. If he does, he may either stand his ground or withdraw to an intermediate position covering Matruh, which will eventually be to our advantage for he will still be in striking distance when we are again fit to attack. If he goes back to the Egyptian frontier, it is questionable whether he should not be left undisturbed.

15. *Course recommended.* Seeing that we are hardly fit at present to do any more attacks, our best course is the defensive combined with offensive gestures from time to time, including raiding. The cover plan should be such as would induce the enemy to strike prematurely, i.e., mid-August, say, between August 10th and 20th. Meanwhile the Army front should be strengthened, and so held that at least one formation could come into reserve and train. At the same time the command of Eighth Army should be put on a permanent footing.

16. *Plan recommended.*

Intention. Eighth Army will defeat any attempt of the enemy to pass through or round it.

17. *Method.*
   (a) *Forward troops*—
      30 Corps: 1 South African Division, 9 Australian Division.
      13 Corps: 1 New Zealand Division, 7 Armoured Division.
   (b) *Reserve*—
      5 Indian Division (4 Indian Division eventually): 1 Armoured Division.
   (c) *General line of* FDLs. El Alamein defences—
      Pt 63 (eastern) on Ruweisat Ridge—vicinity of Alam Nayal. South of Alam Nayal the flank will be covered by 7 Armoured Division.
   (d) *General line of reserve positions*—
      For forward bodies, the most western line of the new rearward position.

Should it be desired to avoid the full effect of an enemy attack in great strength the above FDLs can become the outpost line and the main front can be withdrawn accordingly.

(e) *Matruh*. Should be blocked by the Navy without delay.

Tactical Technique and Future Organization

18. In the light of the course recommended it will be necessary to adjust our tactical technique. This should be based on three facts:

A. We have to be prepared to fight a modern defensive battle in the area El Alamein–Hammam. The troops detailed for this must be trained and exercised so as to get the maximum value from the ground and the prepared positions.

B. Eighth Army may have to meet an enemy's sortie developing into manoeuvre by the southern flank from his firm front on the general line Bab el Qattara–Taqa Plateau. We must therefore organize and train a strong mobile wing, based on 7th Armoured Division, comprising a divisional artillery, 7th Motor Brigade, 4th Light Armoured Brigade, and possibly extra Crusader units. This mobile wing must be well trained in harassing defensive technique.

C. Eventually we will have to renew the offensive and this will probably mean a breakthrough the enemy positions about El Alamein. The newly-arrived infantry divisions and the armoured divisions must be trained for this and for pursuit.

19. From the point of view of GHQ, the organization of our available forces in August and September might take the form, as shown on following page.

This goes further than the present appreciation, but can hardly be separated from it because, should this idea be adopted, it means that the formations now in Eighth Army will not be relieved and the new formations will be built up and reorganized irrespective of the immediate needs of Eighth Army.

20. *Summary*. The enemy now holds in sufficient strength for his purpose a front from which he cannot be dislodged by manoeuvre or any attack Eighth Army can at present deliver. We are strongly posted for a defensive battle. The enemy is attempting to build up his strength and renew his attack on Egypt. Eighth Army requires re-equipment and training before it will be fit for offensive operations. During August it is unlikely that either ourselves or the enemy will be strongly reinforced on land; a successful offensive by either side is therefore unlikely.

GHQ

Eighth Army.	Delta Force.	BTE	The General Reserve.
Function: to hold the El Alamein defended area and to prevent its being by-passed. Also to hold the Natrun area.	To defend Alexandria and the Delta.	To defend the Cairo area.	

HQ General Reserve.

HQ

30th Corps 13 Corps Reserve (13 Corps also commands Mobile Wing).	Inf Divs (two)	Armd Divs (two) *NB* This force may be reorganized into Mobile Divisions.

Provided the land and air situation does not change, Eighth Army can be reinforced about mid-September by two armoured divisions and two infantry divisions. This may give us a superiority sufficient to justify a direct attack on what may be by then a strongly organized front. Alternatively, we may develop a threat to the enemy's rear via Siwa. The immediate need is to reorganize present forces with Eighth Army and to rearrange the front so as to provide an army reserve. The longer-term policy is to train the newly-arrived divisions for the counter-offensive which it is hoped might begin in the latter part of September.

E. Dorman-Smith, Major-General.

[Accepted by General Auchinleck, C-in-C, ME]

APPENDIX 'C'

MAJOR-GENERAL E. DORMAN-SMITH

'I hope you are teaching your students that a little unortho-doxy is a dangerous thing—but without it one seldom wins battles.' *Wavell to Dorman-Smith*, 1940.

In the course of this book, General Dorman-Smith's name appears at various moments of great significance, either when he has supplied military ideas of originality and success (as in the First Battle of Alamein) or when like Cassandra he has foretold woe to come (as before *Battleaxe* and the Gazala battles). His is a strange story: up to 1942 regarded as among the most brilliant and erudite staff officers in the British Army, he sank after the Cairo Purge into professional obscurity. Yet even today his name comes up early in conversations about the Desert Campaigns as a subject for praise or obloquy. His career is a fascinating ex-ample of the deserts accorded to intellectuals in British life—especially brilliant ones who forget to conceal their brilliance, who forget to tolerate the mediocrity around them.

As a subaltern in the First World War, he served with the Northumberland Fusiliers in Flanders and Italy. He temporarily commanded a battalion at Passchendaele. He received three wounds and the Military Cross before he was twenty. After the war, he returned to his regiment, was adjutant for three years, and between 1922 and 1926 instructor at Sandhurst. During the next two years he was a student at the Staff College, Camberley (passing in at his first attempt and in his second year being placed in the top four of the college). Afterwards he was In-structor in Tactics at the School of Military Engineering, a new post. In 1931 he was appointed Brigade Major to the 6th Experi-mental Brigade at Blackdown, under Brigadier Archibald Wavell. This was a plum appointment: it marked the general very high opinion of his capacity. In 1934 and 1935 he was in SD2, the department of the War Office concerned with the preparation of the army for modern war. This was another key post, wherein Dorman-Smith played an important part in the steps taken to motorize completely the British Army, as had been urged by Fuller, Liddell Hart and others since 1918. At that time a British expeditionary force in a future European war was visualized as a mass infantry body like that of the First World War. Some (like the future Field-Marshal Montgomery) even doubted whether we should send an expeditionary force at all. Dorman-Smith at a private dinner with Duff Cooper, Minister for War, produced maps on which he had plotted a German advance through the Low Countries, proving that by concentrating highly mobile forces at narrow points of attack the Germans could break any front designed on current French or British theory. He proved conclusively that Britain was bound to be involved in major ground fighting in the next war, and added that this war was coming certainly and soon. Dorman-Smith went on to list deficiencies in organization and equipment in the British army and plead for mechanization. But Duff Cooper, who had had similar ideas pressed on him by other radicals, was too lazy or too much a member of the Establishment to upset the military *status quo*.

Dorman-Smith, after serving as an instructor at the Staff College in 1936 and commanding an infantry battalion in Egypt in 1937–8 (and converting it into a mobile unit), became Director of Military Training in India. This was a prospective step towards the highest posts of the Army: Gort, CIGS, had occupied this post. In India Dorman-Smith worked closely with General Auchinleck, Deputy Chief of the General Staff. Despite severe shortages of equipment, radical reforms were carried out in the backward and hidebound Indian service; upon such fine units as 4th and 5th Indian Divisions was to depend desert victory in 1940–43. Between 1932 and 1938, Dorman-Smith obtained all possible brevet promotions—from Captain to Brigadier in peacetime in ten years. In 1940, a Middle East Staff College was opened at Haifa. Teaching here could have a decisive influence on the future armies of this important theatre. At his own request, Dorman-Smith was appointed Commandant, although the transfer from India involved demotion and loss of pay. Wavell, now C-in-C Middle East, had a very high opinion of Dorman-Smith's professional knowledge and inventive brain. He sent him to O'Connor's headquarters to observe the rehearsal of the tactical plan of attack at Sidi Barrani and to advise upon it. Seizing on Gatehouse's suggestion of a tank-attack on the unmined north-west corner of Nibeiwa, Dorman-Smith evolved the unorthodox and successful plan of attacking from the west with tanks and lorried infantry after an unregistered barrage ('Firing for Demoralization', he called it) from the east. He incorporated his ideas into a paper, 'Attack on a

329

Desert Camp', reprinted as an appendix to Wavell's dispatch. During the end of O'Connor's campaign Wavell sent him up again to observe and write a full report on it. As an old friend of Harding and O'Connor, Dorman-Smith took part in the discussions that led to the great march to Beda Fomm.

From April to June 1941, Dorman-Smith held temporarily the post of Director of Military Operations in Cairo. While in Cairo, Harding discussed with him the plan for *Battleaxe*. Dorman-Smith criticized it strongly, pointing out that if the flank guards supplied by the weak 7th Armoured Division were beaten by German armour, the infantry attack on the Axis frontier defences would be caught in the flank. In his view the plan was a slavish and inapt copy of the Sidi Barrani plan. His own suggestion was to establish an artillery, anti-tank and 'I'-tank screen on the plateau west of Capuzzo, behind which the infantry would besiege the Axis frontier defences. Seventh Armoured Division would draw the German armour on to the screen. Rommel would in any case be forced to attack to relieve his frontier troops. The plan thus combined, as did all Rommel's, offensive strategy with defensive tactics. It was not adopted.

While there was no question about Dorman-Smith's able mind and profound military knowledge, there was a darker side to his career, adumbrating professional extinction should he ever once fall from grace. He had had an astonishing run of quick promotion. He wore his brilliance openly on his sleeve. He was a theoretician and a perfectionist; he did not always understand how to handle the common clay of mankind. He could not and would not compromise in the comfortable British way. In his career he created much admiration, many special friendships, but also a general fund of ill-will among the hidebound, the slow and the 'Establishment'. The British prefer practical, 'liveable' men to purist brains; Dorman-Smith would have done better in the German Army. Those who bore him ill-will seized and enlarged on the fact that some of Dorman-Smith's tactical and strategic inventions were not practicable; and attempted to write him down as a military dreamer. This, too, is a characteristic British attitude to original thinkers. Both Auchinleck and Wavell were wiser: they used those of Dorman-Smith's inventions which their own practical sense told them would work, and rejected the rest. In Auchinleck's words: 'To a particular problem, Dorman-Smith might produce ten solutions. Out of the ten, you could pick perhaps four that were practicable, and one that was a winner.'

In February 1941, Auchinleck sent Dorman-Smith to report on the state of Eighth Army (as fully recounted in the text of this book). In mid-May 1942, he became acting Deputy Chief of the General Staff in Cairo, an appointment confirmed on June 16th. It was at his suggestion that Auchinleck wrote to Ritchie to advise him to hold all his armour concentrated well north astride the Trigh Capuzzo before Rommel's offensive of May 26th. Dorman-Smith had equally valuable advice to give after the fall of Bir Hacheim, when Ritchie was standing with his back to Tobruk and his communications. There was the question whether to fight on this line, or retire to the frontier, abandoning Tobruk, or fight on a third position, covering Tobruk, but giving up the exposed Gazala salient. Dorman-Smith strongly recommended the third course, which formed the basis of Auchinleck's orders to Ritchie of June 14th–15th, 1942. On June 25th, Dorman-Smith accompanied Auchinleck when the C-in-C took over command of Eighth Army at Mersa Matruh in the face of imminent final catastrophe caused by the failure of the 'practical' men. The full story of their professional collaboration and decisive success has been told in this book. Auchinleck freely gives Dorman-Smith credit for the tactical and organizational ideas that saved Egypt at First Alamein: the fluid, mobile defence, the avoidance of 'boxes', the concentration of the armour, the centralized army-control of artillery, the directing of British attacks on the Italians, the establishment of a defended and refused left-flank at Alam Halfa. Without the quick-thinking, imaginative and unorthodox Dorman-Smith at his side, it is possible that Auchinleck, for all his supreme qualities of resolution and leadership, might not have been able to outgeneral Rommel in the swaying First Battle of Alamein. This period was the summit of Dorman-Smith's professional career —and, it may be thought, not an unworthy height to reach. His testament as a military thinker is the Appreciation of the military situation in the Middle East submitted to Auchinleck on July 27th, 1942, and reproduced as Appendix B to this book. On August 8th he was relieved of his post (as has been recounted).

This fall was final. There was no recovery. All those in the army who bore him ill-will, who had never forgiven him his brilliance and unorthodoxy, saw to that. On reaching London he was reduced to colonel's rank, later to be appointed brigadier commanding a Welsh infantry brigade in Kent. Dorman-Smith (who of course did not know why he had been dismissed in Cairo) settled down to make a success of his new, if junior appointment. He disproved his earlier reputation of being a theorist unfit for direct command by handling his brigade in a big exercise, *Spartan*, in spring 1943, with outstanding ability. But in October General Neil Ritchie became commander of 12th Corps, of which Dorman-Smith's brigade formed a part. It was thought that the presence of the man who had helped save Egypt might be embarrassing to the man who had lost the Gazala battles. Dorman-Smith was immediately removed and spent several months in idleness. In March 1944, his repeated requests for an appointment were granted: he went to Italy to command an infantry brigade in the Anzio beachhead. This brigade delivered a model attack on the Aquabona ridge (vide *The Tanks*, Vol II, p 278), after which the division was in reserve until August 1944. Dorman-Smith had now been broken twice; yet his abilities were once again beginning to rebuild his career. However, in August 1944, as the brigade moved into the front at Florence, Dorman-Smith was suddenly and unexpectedly removed from its command by the divisional commander on the grounds that he was unfit for brigade command. No explanation was given. He was sent back to England, once more without employment and under a cloud of mystery. No explanation or justification for this third breaking of his career was ever given, despite Dorman-Smith's efforts to obtain one from the authorities. On November 1st, 1944, he was removed from the active list of the army, so ending his military career. In view of Dorman-Smith's general army record and his conspicuous success as a brigade commander both in England and at Anzio, this unexplained relief from his last command, following two earlier (and utterly unjust) reliefs, leaves the strong impression that after the Cairo Purge the word quietly filtered through the military 'Establishment' that Dorman-Smith was not to be given a chance to rebuild his career.

Most British defeats have been caused by stupidity. This continuing British military fashion, this melancholy sequence from Yorktown through the Duke of York's campaigns, through the Crimea, the Zulu and Boer wars, the two great wars to the Suez operation of 1956 is starkly illuminated by the treatment accorded to Dorman-Smith.

INDEX